THE WOMAN WHO WOULD BE QUEEN

A biography of the Duchess of Windsor

BY GEOFFREY BOCCA

THE
WOMAN
WHO
WOULD BE
QUEEN

A biography

of the Duchess of Windsor

RINEHART & COMPANY, INC. • NEW YORK • TORONTO

Contents

THE WOMAN WHO WOULD BE QUEEN

A biography of the Duchess of Windsor

Introduction

It is not unusual for a man or woman to emerge in a particular moment of history, to dominate that moment, stir the passions of the world, and then die in obscurity. Fame tends to evaporate quickly, and obscurity has a way of embracing even those who try most fiercely to resist it.

When death comes to a person who has once known great fame, the public receives a slight shock of surprise. It is a shocking thing to realize that a person already dead in the public consciousness, has in fact continued to live.

Logically the Duchess of Windsor should today be an obscure woman, or at best an occasional curiosity. Her place in history was set solely by the tumultuous events of a fortnight in December, 1936, culminating in the Abdication of King Edward VIII. Historically speaking she has accomplished nothing since. She wanders from resort to resort, aloof and silent. She occupies various rungs in the lists of best-dressed women. The disasters which have consumed the world in which she once flourished have passed her by. She lives in a kind of prewar bubble.

Yet she has never ceased to fascinate. An aura of immortality illuminates her. She has never left the center of the world stage, and if she died tomorrow she would die as she has lived since her marriage, as one of the most persistently controversial, complex and absorbing personalities of our day.

There are many answers to this paradox, and one of the aims of any biography of the Duchess of Windsor must be to trace them. One of the most immediate, present-day reasons for interest in the Duchess, however, lies in the fact that she has aged so little. Had she become less handsome with the years, had the hair turned white, the back become less straight, the figure less slender, she might have passed from the spotlight, and time would have softened and dimmed her memory.

But she has broken the rules of time. She remains one of the world's elegant and unchanging women. She glows with an inner fire which turns the past into the present and makes the Abdication seem like yesterday. Her face in the papers is still the face of Mrs. Ernest Simpson; the same prim hair style, the intelligent, watchful eyes, the tight smile. While other characters involved in the Abdication grow older, become senile, and one by one die, the Duchess is the victim of her own appearance, and to look on her is to feel oneself back in 1936, in the cold, anxious nights of waiting; back with an exhausted Prime Minister, Stanley Baldwin, his head in his hands in his rooms at the House of Commons; a distraught King crying out alone in Fort Belvedere; the winter mists rising from the River Thames to hide the dreamy turreted Fort and all its unbelievable secrets.

This is the face of a woman whose strange life might have taken a strangely different course. Had the Abdication crisis ended differently, Edward would still be King. The Duchess of Windsor would be Queen, performing all the functions which Queen Elizabeth II is performing now. Would it, or could it ever, have been a good thing? Who can tell?

The men who wrought the downfall of her husband are nearly all dead now, but no one has tried to undo the work they did. The popular, courageous reign of King George VI, the Duke's brother, came and went. Queen Elizabeth came to the throne where she now sits, a radiant figure commanding vociferous loyalties. Winston Churchill, champion of Edward VIII's cause in 1936, has been Prime Minister twice. But the Windsors are left where they were in 1937, and recognition of the Duchess by the British Court seems to be as far away as ever.

The biography of any living person is at best provisional. But love is a great quickener as well as a preserver of history. Love is the reason why Lord Nelson's life is so much richer than the Duke of Wellington's; and Browning's than Tennyson's. A great love story never dies, and Edward VIII will be a hero to future centuries when abler kings are mere names and numerals. Mrs. Simpson will certainly live as one of the great romantic figures of history.

The contrast between the dream and the reality was seen in all its irony on the night of January 5, 1953, when the present way of life of the Windsors was celebrated in festivities that lasted until dawn.

It was one of those winter evenings unique to New York when sub-freezing, forty-mile-an-hour winds meet from four different directions at the corner of every city block, sending hats flying and numbing the cheekbones.

Weather so wild made it a suitable night for great indoor occasions. Winston Churchill was in town, sitting before the fire in the home of his old friend, Bernard Baruch. And at the Waldorf-Astoria the "Duchess of Windsor Ball" organized by Elsa Maxwell, patronized by the Duchess of Windsor in aid of wounded ex-servicemen, was held amid trappings that were breathtaking even by New York standards.

The grand ballroom at the Waldorf was hung with draperies of coral pink. The tableclothes were also pink and held in place by huge pink satin bows. Silver candelabra held pink candles and there were center-pieces of pink carnations. Suspended from the ceiling in a three-tiered perch, birds of paradise fought gallantly for life against the fumes of perfume, cigar and cigarette smoke rising in warm, exotic waves from the floor. The décor was by Cecil Beaton, the British Court photographer and designer, and the whole thing was conceived to set off a special ball gown which the Duchess of Windsor was to wear later in the evening.

The guests were there to pay thirty dollars a head for the benefit of wounded soldiers and at the same time to pay tribute one way or another to the two romantic exiles now apparently permanently in their midst.

The table of honor in the ballroom was set close to the dance floor and opposite the orchestra. The Duke and Duchess of Windsor sat side by side with half a dozen special guests. The Duchess was scintillating in a white ball gown—the first of three which she was to wear in the course of the evening. Her dark hair, as usual, was parted in the middle and pulled back with two small side bows of wine-colored velvet.

Slender as ever, the lines on her neck alone showed the mark of her fifty-seven years. But her light blue eyes shone. Her face was lively and dynamic. Her partner at the table was Jimmy Donahue, the boyish, balding playboy, heir to most of the Woolworth millions. Donahue has spent many of his thirty-seven years alternately amusing and horrifying American society, and he has been a great favorite in the past few years at the court of the Windsors, where his boisterous exuberance has fulfilled a definite need.

Court jesting on a large scale has been a Donahue stock-in-trade for years. As a boy he shocked his mother by dancing in the chorus of Broadway musicals. In 1935, he yelled "Viva Ethiopia" at a big Fascist rally in Rome, and was firmly escorted by the unamused carabinieri to the first ship scheduled to depart Italy's shores.

In recent years he has put his antic services extensively at the service of the Windsors, who appear to love it. Not long ago he horrified the exclusive Colony restaurant by bringing in three seedy violinists to serenade the Duchess and two other friends. Such a thing had never happened at the Colony before and the manager protested frantically to the laughing Duchess. Donahue airily waved away the protests, and the violinists, to the mingled delight and annoyance of the other guests, stood around the table and serenaded the Windsor party throughout lunch.

On the night of the ball, Donahue and the Duchess had their heads together and were buried deep in conversation that made now one and then the other gurgle with laughter. The Duchess chattered gaily, her hands moving in expressive gestures, confident even while the flash bulbs popped around her that however she looked the cameras could do her no disservice.

The Duke across the table, sitting next to Mrs. Lytle Hull, listened in desultory fashion to the gales of laughter, and seemed preoccupied. Now almost sixty, the Duke carried his years with grace in accordance with his age. He looked an elderly man, but the boyishness was still there; it is something which will probably never desert those antique-youthful features. Two bottles of pinch-bottle Haig were on the table, but he sipped only water and allowed his attention to wander. Sometimes he looked abstractedly at the dancers, whistled a bar or two of the music or clapped his hands once or twice in time to the beat. He had little to say to Mrs. Lytle Hull or indeed to anyone else.

"Say," hailed one acquaintance, "I'm glad to see someone else here in a white tie."

"Have to wear it once in a while," the Duke said briefly, which seemed to close the conversation.

The Duchess flashed him an understanding smile and together they rose to join the packed mass of dancers. Cecil Beaton, who was dancing energetically with Mrs. Winston Guest, a blonde beauty, saw the royal couple, and, smiling charmingly, cut in. Beaton should have known better. The Duke hates the American cutting-in practice. For a few bars the Duchess danced politely with Beaton, and the Duke with Mrs. Guest, then the Duke and Duchess reclaimed each other and danced back to the table.

At the far end of the table of honor, Elsa Maxwell, the professional party-giver and hostess originator of the ball, kept an unblinking, guardian eye on the couple. But she was not in time to stop a middle-aged woman press agent in extravagant décolleté from flopping down on a vacant chair next to the Duke. The corners of the ex-King's mouth drooped apprehensively, but he managed the semblance of a smile, and said, obviously repeating a well-tried defensive formula, "What is your name and whom do you represent?"

"My name is babble. I represent babble babble. I think you are wonderful. I think the Duchess looks just beautiful. The American people adore you both. Would you sponsor our product which is babbling . . . ?"

Elsa Maxwell stamped and fumed and finally hauled away the interloper, hissing in her ear, "The Duke does not like talking to publicity people." But the woman was on her way talking eagerly to an envious acquaintance. "Did you see me? I sat with him. And I didn't call him Your Highness or anything because we Americans don't do that sort of thing! And he asked me what my name was! Oh, he was so cute!"

Little contretemps like this are not unusual in the present existence of the Duke of Windsor. The Duchess does not inspire the same emotions. Her personality is something too positive and diamantine for such familiarities, so the sensation-seekers and bobby-soxers always aim for the easier target.

Throughout the dinner of *vol-au-vent, filet mignon* and ice cream, the Duke was as silent as the Duchess was voluble. First of the high spots of the evening came with the coffee, and it was provided by the well-known society band leader Meyer Davis, whose son, Garry, once started a "One World" movement in Paris, renouncing his American citizenship.

Davis had specially composed for the occasion a number called "The Windsor Waltz" which went like this:

> *Beautiful ladies,*
> *Dance to the Windsor Waltz*
> *As you whirl and glide*
> *Let your eyes confide*
> *The secret dreams of your heart.*
> *If you wish for love warm and shining*
> *The one who's just for you,*
> *Surrender your hearts when the Windsor Waltz starts*
> *And make your wish come true.*

A press agent had earlier asked the Windsors to dance it solo, and the Duke had said hastily he didn't think it was the thing to do.

The official climax to the evening came with a fashion parade. Society celebrities acted as models, draping themselves in coy clusters at each end of the ballroom stage. Then Meyer Davis sounded a dramatic roll of drums, and Colonel Serge Obolensky, the suave, monocled, Russian-born, Oxford-educated socialite (once married to an Astor and now a New York hotel director) walked slowly across the empty dance floor on to the stage ("The Windsor Waltz" *rallentando*). The curtains parted and there was the Duchess of Windsor in a white taffeta gown heavily beaded in coral with coral panels. It was specially made for her in Paris. It cost $1200.

It was undeniably impressive. The Duchess would have made a great mannequin. She put her hand on Obolensky's arm and led the parade of society models onto the floor ("The Windsor Waltz" *allegro brillante*). She was completely poised, completely graceful, utterly confident. But her smile was strained.

The ball continued all night. The Duke and Duchess left comparatively early and returned to their suite on the twenty-ninth floor of the Waldorf Towers, but the party did not end until close to daybreak.

It was all very enjoyable, the kind of thing that kept the Duchess of Windsor in the news, but it did have repercussions. It led some people to wonder whether the Duchess was acting correctly in posing as a mannequin, and it led, for various personal reasons, to a widely publicized break in the long and famous friendship between the Duchess of Windsor and Elsa Maxwell. Still it could not be considered an occasion of international importance, and it would be quickly forgotten if the world could forget that the Duchess is the wife of the former King of England. But neither history nor the Windsors will allow the fact to be forgotten. Edward's reign of forty-six weeks is in the history books; his portrait appears in any schoolboy's collection of "Kings of England." The Duke's struggle to have the title of "Royal Highness" given the Duchess, the Duke's memoirs, his magazine articles and his conversation, which so often starts with the words, "When I was King," are a constant reminder of the past. To solve the many mysteries of the Windsor story, a few premises must be established. One is that none of the parties directly concerned in the Abdication ever foresaw that more than half a generation later nothing would be solved or settled as to the Windsors' status.

Another is that this form of existence need not have been, and that the Windsors, with the large fortunes they have had at their disposal at one time and another, could have made a very different life for themselves if they had wished to do so.

This book stems from these standpoints, and tries to tell why the

Windsors do not attend the Court which the Duke once commanded; why their exile continues; what are the might-have-beens in the Windsors' position in the world, and the part played by the Duchess of Windsor in bringing her husband to such a peculiar haven through the storms that have torn at them throughout this long and moving love story.

"THE WOMAN
I LOVE"

I

The Girl on
East Biddle Street

Wallis Warfield was the second Baltimore belle to marry a king. The first was Betsy Patterson who married Jerome Bonaparte, youngest brother of Napoleon. But Jerome, unlike Edward VIII, preferred the throne to the woman, and on Napoleon's order he abandoned his wife to become King of Westphalia.

A lot of people in Baltimore, Maryland, are convinced that only Baltimore girls can get away with this sort of thing. It may have something to do with the atmosphere of the place, and it has certainly been noticed before. Twenty-nine years before Wallis Warfield was born, Charles Dickens visited the city in the course of his reading tour of the United States and commented, ". . . the ladies are remarkably handsome with an Eastern look upon them, dress with a strong sense of colour, and make a brilliant audience." Possibly in Baltimore, America comes closest to England. North Charles Street, the city's smart shopping center, with its dignified antique shops, quiet couturiers and milliners, gives a sense of being nearer in spirit to Bond Street than to Fifth Avenue. Baltimore's suburbs with the neat houses sprouting Victorian bay windows are agreeably Bayswaterian, and even the new apartment buildings are smaller than comparable ones in New York and look more like some postwar British housing development.

Many educated Baltimoreans speak with an accent closer to the English accent than even educated Bostonians. This has misled some of the

Duchess of Windsor's critics into asserting that "she speaks with an English accent she sometimes forgets." The Duchess does nothing of the sort. She speaks Baltimorean with the overtones of her English influences.

Like many other mothers, Wallis Warfield's mother, who was born Alys Montague in Virginia, claimed ancestry back to William the Conqueror. Alys Montague Warfield had records which proved, to her own satisfaction at least, that her family was founded by Droge de Monteacuto Montecute who landed in 1066. There is no question that the Montague or Montagu family of Virginia has links to the English Montagus who today are one of the most thriving aristocratic families in England. This makes the Duchess of Windsor a very distant kinswoman to the Duke of Manchester (Alexander George Francis Drogo Montagu) and the Earl of Sandwich (George Charles Montagu).

The Duchess has never claimed for herself the family associations which her mother claimed for her, but some eager biographers have done it for her, so that there has grown up in some parts of the United States a myth about the Duchess's aristocratic heritage. This has had certain consequences. Several writers have written indignantly about the Royal Family's persistent aloofness towards "a fine American girl who comes from a better family than the Queen of England does."

One of the worst offenders was the novelist, Upton Sinclair, who was one of Wallis Warfield's cousins, and adored Wallis when she was a little girl. Sinclair asserted that Wallis had Indian blood in her veins and was a descendant of Pocahontas. The connection even with Sinclair's explanation was somewhat ephemeral. Wallis's great-uncle Powhatan Montague, whose brother, William Montague, was her maternal grandfather, had a family tree which sought to prove that he was a direct lineal descendant from the little seventeenth-century Indian heroine, Pocahontas, whose father's name was Chief Powhatan.

If this is a fact, it gives Wallis another unsuspected family link. Her old friend, Lady Louis Mountbatten, has also claimed to be a descendant of Pocahontas.

The record is at least plain on one point. Wallis came from sound, well-established American stock on both sides; on her mother's, the Montagues of Virginia and on her father's side, the respected Warfields of Maryland. There are several Warfields today well-known in Baltimore affairs, mostly in law and insurance, and one member of the family, Edwin Warfield, a distant uncle of Wallis's, was Governor of Maryland from 1904 to 1908.

Family connections are all very well, but Wallis was born with very little else. Her father was Teackle Wallis Warfield, a retiring, ailing boy who worked insignificantly as a clerk in Baltimore. In spite of ill health he was at times capable of positive thought and action. To demonstrate the first he declared he loathed the name of Teackle (wished on him to ingratiate an influential uncle of that name) and thereafter signed himself T. Wallis Warfield. He demonstrated the second by a whirlwind courtship of Alys Montague, a girl of seventeen with blue eyes and the prettiness of a doll. He married her when he was about twenty. Sometime later, in order to relieve the strain of Warfield's bad health and Alys's pregnancy, Warfield's mother, Mrs. Henry Mactier Warfield, suggested a holiday for both at her expense, and they went together to the lovely Blue Ridge Summit resort in Pennsylvania, taking a room at the Monterey Inn.

Both Warfield and his wife wished passionately for a boy. On June 19, 1896, Lewis Miles Allen, a twenty-two-year-old doctor just out of college, received an emergency summons to the Monterey Inn. Alys's regular doctor was away from the resort on another mission and Allen brought Bessie Wallis Warfield into the world in her mother's hotel bedroom.

Allen, who later became a wealthy obstetrician and died in 1949, did not know for forty years that he was responsible for one of the world's most sensational women. But he did see her several times as a child and later recalled her as "quite pretty, with long hair and an exceptionally magnetic personality." The word "magnetic" was to be used many times by others who described Wallis's childhood and youth.

The Warfield family returned to Baltimore with a depressing burden of financial problems. Three years later T. Wallis Warfield died and the problems became even tougher, so Alys, a child bride and child mother, now a widow, turned the house which she and her husband had taken on marriage into a boarding house. It was a hard beginning for Wallis.

Today, 212 East Biddle Street, as the childhood home of the Duchess of Windsor, is possibly the most famous address in Baltimore, and thousands come to stare at it every year. This has made it a very dubious piece of property to own. A few months after the Abdication of Edward VIII, a New York businessman bought the house and opened it as a Duchess of Windsor "museum." Several thousand people paid fifty cents each to go through it, but it was not a commercial success. One disadvantage was that it had been completely remade inside since Wallis's day, and the only surviving items that could be connected to Wallis were the bathtub she had used and an old gas cooker intriguingly labeled "Windsor."

The house did not hold enough interest to make it a paying proposition as a museum. At the same time it attracted too much interest among tourists and visitors to make it comfortable as a home. Consequently in the past fifteen years it has been occupied and vacated by a succession of discontented tenants, and has deteriorated into a battered, flaking building divided into four rather tawdry apartments.

In 1896 it was pleasant enough, in a district similar in tone to London's Chiswick or Brooklyn's Bay Ridge. At the front it had the three marble steps peculiar to Baltimore's style of architecture. The habit of marble steps continues pleasingly, in Baltimore, but not at 212 East Biddle Street. At some point along the past fifty years they disappeared and have been replaced by steps of a more doubtful geological origin.

Most of Alys's lodgers were relatives both near and remote. Baltimore at the time of Wallis's birth was still affected in unique ways by the Civil War, even though by then it had been over for more than thirty years. Although the State of Maryland fought on the side of the North, it had and still has today strong emotional and family ties to the South. Baltimore, said Dickens, was haunted by the ghost of slavery and wore "a look of sullen remembrance." Here it was "the ladies used to spit when they passed a Northern soldier." After the war when the South was prostrated by defeat, Baltimore became a place in which the dispossessed, impoverished Southerners could find refuge and escape from the miseries of the Reconstruction period.

Virginian families moved to Maryland in thousands. Alys herself was the daughter of one of these, and to others she let out rooms. It was not a very successful commercial proposition. Many other Southern women with Baltimore homes were doing the same thing with little better success. In time Alys gave up the house altogether and with her tiny income moved into an even more modest home in the Preston Apartments on Guildford Street. She is reported by one old friend to have made a little money here by inviting friends or "paying guests" to lunch. In this way, and by other feeble little ventures into the business of subletting apartments, Alys managed to keep going.

Life was both severe and sad for Southern women like Alys, and the children of these women, the girls especially, had a strong tendency to inherit the mood of sadness. Which made Wallis all the more noticeable as the outstanding exception to the rule.

From an early age she made up for her lack of conventional prettiness with vivacity, magnetism and a charm that is still remembered in Baltimore. Even before she became conscious of her own ambition and sense of self-preservation, this dynamic, dark-haired girl was beginning to interest people of influence and wealth.

This she did partly by her own nature, and partly by rather touching design. One of Wallis's Baltimore relatives believes that Wallis as a child was made very much aware of the insecurity of her position, and that Alys, probably without even noticing it, kept impressing on the child the fact that she would have to make her own way in life without money or assistance.

Whatever it was, Wallis quickly attracted guardians. Her rich uncle above all was enchanted by her. He was Solomon Davies Warfield, her father's brother, and a railroad magnate reputedly worth $3,000,000. Another friend was her grandmother, Mrs. Henry Mactier Warfield, who took little Wallis under her wing and regaled her with stories of the Civil War and with sage advice. "Never marry a Yankee," she told Wallis, "and never marry a man who kisses your hand." (Her husbands consisted of one Yankee, one half-Yankee, and one Englishman.) Her aunt, Mrs. D. Buchanan Merryman—later famous as "Aunt Bessie" of the Abdication period—also looked after the little girl fondly and became her lifelong friend and confidante. Another aunt, influential, persuasive Lelia Montague, daughter of Powhatan Montague, lavished on Wallis much worldly wisdom, and in one way became largely responsible for her present personality.

It was S. Davies Warfield, Wallis's "Uncle Sol," who decided that something practical had to be done about Wallis. Alys was too poor to educate her properly. Sol thereupon formally took over the responsibility of educating Wallis and introducing her to society.

This had a profound influence on Wallis's development. It is doubtful whether the gentle Alys could ever have been a restraining influence on Wallis, but now Wallis was effectively removed from any control that might be exercised by her mother, though mother and daughter continued to love each other genuinely.

Uncle Sol chose Arundel, a fashionable day school which no longer exists, as Wallis's first school. Relieved of the responsibility of bringing up her daughter, Alys promptly remarried. Her second husband was a local politician named John Freeman Raisin, but a jinx seemed to pursue her domestic life, and Raisin also died, only two years after their marriage.

After Arundel, Wallis went to Oldfield's, in Cockeysville, Maryland, a school of fifty-six girls so snobbish they did not even compete at games with other girls, preferring to play among themselves. The school motto was "Gentleness and Courtesy" which was also the name of the two school netball teams. Wallis played for "Gentleness."

Wallis made friends quickly and the friends she made she kept. This was no small achievement. The girls she met at school were all the children of people of means. With Wallis's mother making do as best she could, Wallis could not even begin to reciprocate the hospitality she received from others. Her friends realized this and because Wallis was so gay and such a good sport they accepted the situation frankly without condescension.

The seal of approval was bestowed on Wallis in her middle teens not so much by her circle of friends as by the Maître d'Hôtel of the Belvedere Hotel (today the Sheraton Belvedere).

In the unhurried days before World War I the smart thing to do in Baltimore was to stroll on sunny days from the Washington Monument on Mount Vernon Place past the North Charles Street mansions to the Belvedere where one paused for tea. The tearoom at the Belvedere had fine china and a huge fireplace. It also had a maître d'hôtel so expert in the shadings of Baltimore society that he knew at a glance whether people approaching the tearoom should be obsequiously admitted or smoothly diverted elsewhere.

Possibly he had heard that Mr. S. Davies Warfield was extremely interested in his niece's welfare. Probably he, like most other people, was swept away by Wallis's gaiety. At any rate he decided she was a girl to be admitted and always escorted her with unction to the choice tables. Wallis made the place her headquarters for gay luncheons and teas with her girl friends.

The young ladies of Oldfield's school went to bed early, rose shortly after dawn, and were forbidden to have boy friends. Summers were a relief, for then Wallis went to the freer and easier community of Miss Charlotte Noland's Summer Camp for Girls, a mile and a half from Middleburg, Virginia. Little as Wallis liked athletics, she loved her summers at camp with picnics and lazy romantic days in the open air, reading aloud volumes of poems by Kipling and Robert Service. She loved also the "Indian Love Lyrics" of Laurence Hope and the adventurous stories of Bret Harte.

Burrland Camp was started in 1907 and Wallis first went there in the summer of 1909. It was there that she learned to swim after her own fashion, developing a style which impresses her friends to this day. One friend describing Wallis's swimming, said, "She lowers herself gently into the water, then sort of cruises around like a rather dignified octopus. It is a very pretty sight really."

Wallis at this time was also described as "fun-loving but free from girlish horseplay." The girls at camp went on hay rides, blackberry-picking expeditions and rides in coaches-and-four. Once they went on a coon hunt which ended in maidenly terror when the coon turned out to be a skunk.

The older girls slept on screened porches in the "big" house. Younger girls and boys were segregated in tents with wooden floors.

In Baltimore, after these expeditions, Alys was beginning to notice a difference in Wallis. Once, according to a New York writer, she threw a tantrum when her mother bought her a white dress for a party. "I want a red dress," she sobbed. When her mother, faintly, asked why, Wallis declared frankly, "Because in a white dress the boys won't notice me!"

There was little danger of that. However uncertainly Wallis learned country lore or how to play netball, she was learning with unerring precision just what was attractive to boys.

II

Baltimore Girls
and Baltimore Boys

Recollections of Wallis by the local young men are vivid, summed up by Basil Gordon, a cousin from a somewhat younger age group. "She was the brunette type," he said, recalling his childhood impressions. "Very witty and vivacious. She attracted men the way molasses attracts flies."

The names of two young men of the period were especially linked to Wallis's. One is Carter C. Osburn. The other is Lloyd Tabb. Both were gentlemen in the excellent Southern tradition. After many years of prosperous but obscure business life in Maryland, they suddenly found themselves famous in 1936 by their youthful association with the incredible Mrs. Simpson.

Both might have been embarrassed so many years afterwards by the spate of words which came out at the time describing the Duchess of Windsor's childhood. Instead they accepted their position with good humor and cheerfully admitted their old infatuation.

Osburn was the son of a well-to-do Baltimore banker, a tough, beefy young man. Present-day Baltimoreans who were in the circle of friends agree that Osburn was "Wallis's first." "He was so wildly in love with her he couldn't see straight," one of Osburn's friends chuckled recently. "I do believe," he added, "Carter never really got over her."

Even at the time of the Abdication, Osburn continued to have strong views on the subject of Wallis. "I resent this business," he was heard to say in 1936, by which time he had become a car dealer. "Why should the King abdicate just because Wallis is an American? She would have made a good queen." And friends assert Osburn has nursed a brooding Anglophobia ever since.

Tabb was so impressed by Wallis that he preserved some of her letters, as well as a keen memory of the times they had together. "We used to have close-harmony parties on the porch or down in the garden of our house at Glenora," he said. "Wallis, curiously enough, rarely joined the singing, though she obviously enjoyed the efforts of the others and was one of the best at thinking up new numbers. Having made suggestions she would lean back on her slender arms. Her head would be cocked appreciatively and by her earnest attention she made us feel we were really a rather gifted group of songsters."

When Wallis was sixteen she went on holiday to Maine, and Tabb invited her to stay at Glenora on her return.

"Well," she wrote happily in reply, "I must say I'm thrilled to death about coming to Glenora. It will certainly seem like old times. I am leaving here tomorrow, Monday, and will get to Baltimore on Tuesday, so if it is convenient and your mother really wants me, Saturday would be a good time for me. When your Mother writes to me don't forget to give her 212 East Biddle Street as the address. This certainly is one peach of a place. Thursday night there was a big dance given for me. It was some party towards the end of the morning. Hope to see you soon, as ever, Wallis." The date was 1912.

Tabb and Osburn were not alone. One of Wallis's ex-beaux took to drink and went seriously to seed after she went out of his life. Another, Tom Shryock, later a Colonel in the National Guard, became almost incoherent when he talked of her.

"Unless you know Wallis Warfield it is impossible to describe her," he said. "She is one of the nicest, one of the grandest people in the world. Words cannot express the high regard I have for that woman. Why, when she went to the theater she would turn to the usher, smile and thank him for showing her the seat. It didn't make any difference who it was who did anything for her, a policeman, a newsboy, anyone—she was immediately grateful and courteous." Shryock remained a close friend of the family.

In 1947 he and the Duke of Windsor met at a reception in Washington, D. C. The encounter between the husband and the old beau of the world's most romantic woman produced something noteworthy in the way of anticlimax.

"Bet you didn't buy those shoes in America," said the Duke.

"No, sir," said Shryock. "Imported English leather."

The only remembered occasion when Wallis was thought to be more interested in a certain boy than the boy was in her was with a young man named Harvey Rowland whose good looks were enhanced by his reputation as "the richest boy in Baltimore." Nothing came of this relationship, but generally speaking Wallis could have picked from a good selection of the city's males.

Her successes with the fashionable Baltimore boy market gave her a sense of gentle cynicism towards the sex. Normally careful with her books, she made one mark in her volume of Shakespeare at Oldfield's against a line of Benedick's in "Much Ado About Nothing."

"I do much wonder," the passage reads, "that one man seeing how much another man is a fool when he dedicates his behaviours to love, will, after he hath laughed at such shallow follies in others, become the argument of his own scorn by falling in love." Which of her conquests she had in mind at the time she has doubtless forgotten; there seemed to be a touch of irony in her relations with all her boy friends.

Young Tabb called on her one day after a debutantes' ball in which he had led the dances. Wallis was too young to join the season, but she heard all about it. "Ah!" she cried, "the leader of the younger set attends me with honors."

Tabb visited Wallis frequently at camp. She was one of the "Big Four" girls there, the others being Martha Valentine (later Mrs. John Cranley of Richmond), Eleanor Brady and Mary Kirk. They alone claimed the right to go into town and get the mail. Redheaded Mary Kirk was her closest friend, the daughter of Mrs. Henry Kirk Junior, one of Baltimore's most prominent hostesses. Mary, a girl with a reputation for being a bit on the wild side, and Wallis together were a formidable combination. Mary was to play an unusual part in Wallis's later life.

Wallis in her teens was a girl full of impish smiles, with dark, unplucked brows, a high intelligent forehead and a sort of old-fashioned radiance, like a mid-Victorian duchess. A friend, summing up her character, described her like this: Intelligence—above average. Conversation—enlightened without self-consciousness. Boy friends—never "acted silly" with them. Older people—always considerate to them.

Unlike other girls, however, Wallis could never take things for granted. Her mother's poverty made too much of a difference. Wallis all the time had to keep fighting, to rely on her charm when other girls were able to fall back on their money. Sometimes she appeared to fade momentarily into the background. "She was not considered one of the belles of Baltimore," one of the undisputed beaux of Baltimore recalled many years later, "nor was she acclaimed as an outstanding dancer, and Baltimore was famous for its dancers. She was attractive and popular and clever, but not one of the foremost girls of the period. She was always well groomed, but she was never a leader in style."

Wallis was not a leader in style because her small stock of clothes had to serve too many purposes, but as another friend said, "Wallis had so much poise that she could put on a black skirt and a shirtwaist and look more glamorous than a lot of other girls in evening dress."

Without detracting in any way from Wallis's achievement in being accepted by a society to which she could make little logical claim, it was probably her Uncle Sol who made the difference. He paid her school bills, promised to look after her during the impending ordeal of her debut, and cared for his bereaved sister-in-law until her remarriage. Uncle Sol was an imposing uncle to have around. He made a fortune from the Seaboard Air Line Railway which he directed. He was a bachelor, tall, dignified, puritanical, aristocratic.

He also had a stern awareness of the moral duties of citizenship. He received a political appointment, as Baltimore Postmaster, directly from Democratic President Grover Cleveland in 1894, and handled it so well that the appointment was renewed by Republican President William McKinley and Republican President Theodore Roosevelt.

Wallis's girl friends and boy friends knew that Wallis was very close to her uncle, but the fact that he was paying for her upbringing did not seep through to them until many years afterwards. They realized only that he was putting many facilities at her disposal, one being a car that in retrospect is recalled, probably inaccurately, as the largest car in Baltimore. Often he would send it with a uniformed chauffeur to the Belvedere to pick up Wallis. Trying desperately hard to look casual, Wallis, Mary Kirk and a few of their closest friends would climb, awed, into the yawning interior of the automobile while the chauffeur held the door open for them. Then, to the excited gasps of the less favored friends, the purring monster would sweep magnificently away through the undulating Baltimore streets.

Upton Sinclair said in later years that in Baltimore there were three topics of conversation. Number one: who married whom. Number two: clothes. Number three: good things to eat. None of these topics put much wear and tear on the intellect, and many young people found the company insufferable. For these people the solution was emigration to New York or even to London or Paris.

Wallis never found either Baltimore or Baltimore's topics of conversation dull. She reveled in them. She sharpened on them the epigrams for which she was later renowned. She never missed a girls' lunch and was always fun and full of smart small talk. "I don't know how Wallis did it," one of her contemporaries said not long ago. "I came out the same year Wallis did, and I think that girls' luncheons were the most boring functions of the social season. But Wallis never seemed to have enough of them."

An important aspect of Wallis's personality was that, although she was variously described by her friends as "imperious" and even "garrulous" and "dominating," her friends remained faithful. Her popularity in her youth was genuine, and she was liked as much by her girl friends as her boy friends.

Wallis had everything required for the kind of success which American town society knows and appreciates. One can make an unprovable guess that Wallis's historic rise in life was the result of accident rather than the relentless ambition with which she is often credited, and that in other circumstances she might have become a trim kind of Marquand heroine with one or more good marriages in Eastern society. She would have been an esteemed hostess and leader in society, well-read, well-traveled, prominent in women's work, popular with her friends, energetic at organizing lectures by visiting celebrities, intelligent and enlightened in local politics.

Wallis's social course was first set, however, while she was in her teens by her persuasive and determined aunt, Lelia Montague, a beautiful woman whose relationship to Wallis was more like that of a cousin. This has been revealed in some of the writings of Upton Sinclair. Lelia, when she was very young, married a wealthy Baltimorean, Basil Gordon, who died soon after their marriage. After that, Lelia, living between Baltimore and Washington, found herself wooed by two impressive suitors. One was Senator Alfred Beveridge of Ohio, and the other a distinguished Marine officer, George Barnett.

Lelia chose the Marine, and some years later she used her considerable influence in Washington to get her husband a major-generalship over the heads of others. Barnett, an erect, soldierly man, commanded the United States Marines in France with distinction.

Lelia's father and Wallis's maternal grandfather were brothers. Upton Sinclair was also related to the family in this line. He was Lelia's first cousin, his mother being the sister of Lelia's father. Lelia played a big part in Wallis's debut and in her life from then on. When the time came for Wallis to make her debut, one of her hands rested on the arm of Major-General George Barnett, the other on the arm of a cousin, Henry Warfield, Junior.

The year of a debut is a nerve-racking one for any girl in high society.

[24]

She worries about her clothes, her dates and whether she will be invited to the right parties. That is true all over the world, but in Baltimore it was a little bit worse. Before World War I there was a certain invitation that was absolutely vital to the success of a girl's debut, and many hearts have been ridiculously and unforgivably broken just because the invitation did not appear in the mailbox.

The Bachelors' Cotillon Club was the most fashionable and exclusive club in the city for the younger men. Twice a year on the Monday of Christmas week and the Monday of New Year the club gave balls or "germans" as they were called. They were the most spectacular affairs of the year in Baltimore. Gold damask hangings decorated the walls. Brocaded pillows were used as steps to the stage. The candelabra was silver and the footmen wore splendid maroon coats with brass buttons.

A popular girl would be invited to both the Monday germans, but it was to the first that a girl considered she positively had to go, or die. It was another illustration of Wallis's popularity that she was one of the forty-nine debutantes invited to the first Monday german in 1914. In this particular year it was marked by a feeling of strain that had never been known before. The war in Europe had begun and stirred an uncomfortable sense of unrest among the younger smart set. Already one or two of the more popular boys in the Baltimore set had drifted across the Atlantic into the British and the French armies.

The strain had its effect on the Baltimore season. One of the local newspapers wrote soberly: "Entertainments to be given this season for and by the debutantes are likely to be marked by a simplicity not known in Baltimore for a generation or more. Thirty-four of the forty-nine 'buds' who will make their bows this year have signed an agreement insuring the absence of rivalry and elegance in respective social functions and pledging the signers and their families to refrain from extravagance in entertaining."

Wallis was one of the "buds" who signed. Originally Uncle Sol had planned to give his niece a lavish debut but, like other prominent Baltimoreans, he was disturbed by the events in Europe and went to the extent of announcing publicly in the newspapers that he did not intend to give a big ball for Wallis, not he explained "while thousands are being slaughtered in Europe."

What Wallis lost through her Uncle Sol, however, she gained through her other relatives, General and Mrs. Barnett, who gave some large parties for her and her friends.

The Lyric Theatre, Baltimore, where the first Monday german was held, smelled rich with the perfume of green smilax, that strange aromatic flower which so peculiarly catches an atmosphere of sunshine and leisurely living. Wallis and the rest of the debutantes looked appropriately radiant in white satin and chiffon dresses which appeared so fetching at the time and seem so hideous today. The favorite dance was the one-step. The girls never missed a dance.

By the time the orchestra played the last waltz, "Millicent," everybody was ready to accept that it had been a fine evening and as good a deb party as could be expected under the circumstances.

For the next two years Wallis studied in between parties. She perfected her languages, learning to speak French and German extremely well. In later years her German slipped, but she maintained a reasonably good French.

In 1916, Lelia Barnett decided that for Wallis, now nineteen, it was time for a change. Mrs. Barnett was enjoying her marriage to an eminent military man and was inviting to dinner parties at Wakefield Manor, her Washington home, some prominent members of what was known as the "Army-Navy Set." Occasionally a politician or two would join the party, and the air after dinner would become electric with stimulating discussion. Wallis suffered a deep fit of depression when her grandmother died a year or so after her debut, so Lelia invited Wallis up from Baltimore, so that she could "meet some interesting people." Wallis came and was fascinated. She did not return immediately to Baltimore. With her studies over, Lelia decided that her exceptionally gifted and charming young cousin should look ahead. Obediently Wallis did.

III

"Win's" Wife

The social whirl which now began under the guidance of Lelia Montague Barnett led to Wallis's first marriage. It was an odd business, standing out in the life of this remarkable woman as one incident of pure mediocrity.

The excuse for the marriage was simple and universal. Thousands of other girls were making the same mistake for the same reason, and thousands more were to do the same thing twenty-five years later. But somehow one would have expected Wallis Warfield with her peculiar talents to rise above normal circumstances. In this case she didn't. The facts were that she was too young and there was a war on.

It began late in 1915 while Wallis was a guest at the Washington home of the Barnetts, and discovering, wide-eyed, that Washington society moved on different planes from Baltimore society. The old Baltimore passions for clothes and food did not apply in Washington where there were few good shops and still fewer good restaurants.

Talk, she found, was less about marriages than about politics and the European war. The fact that Wallis even in those days was uncommonly well dressed seemed to matter so much less in Washington than it had in Baltimore.

But Wallis was never prepared to take a back seat for very long, and soon she was arguing with the rest of the Barnetts' guests, arguing, clearly, positively and articulately though without much political wisdom.

Wallis began to enjoy the ways and thinking processes of the professional service officers invited home by General Barnett. Coming as she did from a strongly pro-British family and circle in Baltimore, and irritated at the arguments of people who would have liked the United States to stay out of the war, she was fascinated at the attitude of the Navy and Marine officers to whom such argument was academic. They obviously considered they were already in the war and simply waited for the signal to start firing. With General Barnett at the head of the table they sat over their liqueurs talking strategy, disputing the merits of Joffre and John French—Haig, Foch and Allenby not having yet arrived to give color to the Allied picture. They boasted how America would settle the whole thing swiftly and painlessly once war was declared, and most of them were impatient to begin. It was heady stuff for an intelligent, imaginative girl of nearly twenty.

Early in 1916, Lelia and Wallis, followed shortly afterwards by Wallis's mother, traveled to Pensacola, Florida. Lelia's younger sister Corinne had married a naval lieutenant, Henry Mustin, whose particular job sealed for Wallis the excitement of her new life. Mustin ran the new flying school opened by the Navy at Pensacola and instructed eager young lieutenants, ensigns and midshipmen in the ways of biplanes.

The impact of Wallis with her almost irresistible charm on the young naval officers was as powerful as it had been on Osburn, Tabb, Shryock and company of Baltimore. She was dated every night, and there was nothing unusual in the conversation she had with one especially attentive lieutenant in the Mustins' living room. The lieutenant respectfully asked Miss Warfield if he might see her the following evening and make a party of four with Lieutenant and Mrs. Mustin. Wallis regretfully said no, she had a date. The lieutenant respectfully suggested the night after. Wallis said no, she had another date. The night after that? No. Or after that? Why yes, she would be delighted. And Lieutenant Earl Winfield Spencer with the elation of a young man in love went back to his quarters to try and live out the next few days with what patience he could.

Spencer was a dark, laughing, quite wild, chunkily built young man of twenty-seven, the eldest in an affectionate, closely knit family of four brothers and two sisters. Spencer's mother was British, from Jersey in the Channel Islands. His father was a prosperous member of the Chicago stock exchange, and the family home was in Highland Park, Illinois.

Spencer was a promising naval officer who was learning to become a pilot. The Navy was his one passion and interest.

Once he managed to command Wallis's time in the evenings, Spencer did his best to keep it—not always with success. Wallis continued to have other dates while "Win" fretted alone in the evenings, but the Mustins quickly noticed that Wallis's enthusiasm for boys in general had dimmed.

With her various dates she continued, as always, to be entertaining and amusing, but she tended towards listlessness. Only with Spencer did she appear to recover her normal verve.

Their relationship began to look serious. Wallis undoubtedly saw Spencer not as he was but against the background of his hazardous existence. She was moved and agitated by the atmosphere of war that was everywhere in Pensacola, and trembled when she saw Spencer flying overhead in sputtering biplanes. The enthusiasm of the officers for the new weapon of war alarmed and at the same time intrigued her, and Corinne Mustin noticed that the Florida sun was giving her young guest no tan. In fact she was getting paler.

All at once it became too much for her. Wallis told her mother she was leaving and abruptly packed her bags. Together they returned by train to Baltimore. Not long afterwards Spencer managed to get himself leave and followed. They met at Lelia Barnett's house in Washington and a breathless courtship began. Three months after they first met, the paragraph that had become inevitable appeared in one of the Baltimore newspapers:

> An engagement just announced of unusual interest to society in Maryland as well as Virginia is that of Miss Wallis Warfield, daughter of Mrs. John Freeman Raisin and the late Teackle Wallis Warfield to Lieutenant E. Winfield Spencer, U.S.N., of the Aviation Corps, son of Mr. and Mrs. E. Winfield Spencer of Highland Park, Chicago.

The next few months for Wallis were spent in the exciting vacuum that comes to a popular girl between the moment of engagement and the fact of marriage. The Warfield relatives and Wallis's friends did her proud. There were parties for her in Washington and Baltimore, given by the Barnetts and Uncle Sol respectively. Mary Kirk's mother organized a large party at the Baltimore Country Club for her daughter's friend.

At the age of twenty, Wallis was married to Lieutenant Earl Winfield Spencer at the Christ Protestant Episcopal Church in Baltimore. The time was six thirty P.M., the date November 8, 1916, five months before America entered World War I, and twenty years, one month and two days before the King of England gave up his throne for her.

The wedding invitations were printed on the largest cards ever seen in Baltimore. Mary Kirk was among the bridesmaids and so were Mary Graham and Mercer Taliaferro, other friends of Wallis's. The wedding was well up to Baltimore standards. Contemporary reports describe tall white tapers burning before an altar banked high with Annunciation lilies. Candles and white chrysanthemums decorated the church, the candles flickering against the gray walls and stained-glass windows as the rain fell steadily outside.

The bridesmaids wore orchid-colored faille and blue velvet gowns, blue velvet hats, and they carried yellow snapdragons. Wallis, walking down the aisle on the arm of her tall unbending Uncle Sol, wore a gown of white panne velvet, its bodice embroidered with pearls, and a velvet court train, one of the first ever seen at a Baltimore wedding. Under the skirt was a petticoat trimmed with old family lace. Her headdress was a crown of orange blossoms with a veil of tulle, and her bouquet was of wild orchids and lilies of the valley.

As for Spencer, his good looks were to pass from him early and he later became thickset and jowly, but that night he looked as magnificent in his dress blues as one would expect of an adventurous young sailor.

He had selected his ushers from among his fellow officers; all young, all pink with health, and rounded off on top with a crew haircut which then, as now, was so popular among college boys. It was a wonderful evening for the Baltimore girls.

One of the bridesmaids was Win's sister Ethel, and the best man was his brother Dumaresque Spencer. Hindsight gives the excellent Spencer family an uneasy, almost an interloping place in the picture—like people invited to the wrong party. However this was the Spencers' evening as much as it was the evening of the assembled Warfields and Montagues; but having turned up from Illinois for the wedding they trooped immediately back again, never to reappear in the story.

Yet the Spencer story was also an eventful one, for if ever there was a family racked by tragedy it was the Spencers. Dumaresque went to France to join the Lafayette Escadrille, and was shot down and killed. Another brother, Egbert, was thrown from his horse, and died from the effects of the injury. A sister committed suicide, and the mother was killed in an automobile accident. Win Spencer, too, was heading for a personal tragedy of his own.

Uncle Sol gave a reception for the young couple at the Stafford Hotel, after which a car even larger than Uncle Sol's stopped at the door to take them to Union Station.

That night a handsome young man and his bride, the girl in a going-away dress, the man caped according to the winter uniform of the Navy, arrived at White Sulphur Springs, Virginia, which then as now was one of the most fashionable spots on this earth. It was an interesting selection for a Wallis Warfield honeymoon. As a little girl Wallis had spent holidays there with her grandmother, Mrs. Henry Mactier Warfield. Later on, as Duchess of Windsor, she was to return to White Sulphur Springs, and make it, along with Palm Beach and the Riviera resorts, one of her nomadic homes.

This period, the second decade of the twentieth century, found Britain's Prince of Wales also at White Sulphur Springs. In fact, in 1919 and 1920, his path crossed Wallis Warfield Spencer's more than once. It was a coincidence full, no doubt, of romantic symbolism, presaging the future. He turned up at the Springs three years after Wallis's honeymoon there, then actually bumped into her a year later in California.

For a honeymoon Wallis and her husband took one of the trim vacation cottages in the district. After a few days, they went north for a week to Atlantic City, which probably was a relief after the exclusive, conservative atmosphere of the Springs.

The war seemed closer than ever. The aviation training scheme had been intensified, and between flights the men moped restlessly and waited. After a few months of almost unbearable anticipation, it happened. On April 6, 1917, the United States declared war on Germany.

It was as an instructor flier that Win Spencer received his wartime orders, and to his fury was ordered not to Europe or to sea but to San Diego, California.

San Diego, with the shift of world forces from the Atlantic to the Pacific, sizzled with excitement, and it had a roaring time in World War II. In 1917, however, it was a complete backwater of the war. Spencer was in charge of the only up-to-date organization in the area, the North Island Aviation School. The only units of the United States Navy based there were an old cruiser, the *Oregon,* a veteran of the Spanish-American war, a few subchasers and a gunboat, the *Vicksburg.*

Spencer had a small private income which supplemented his lieutenant's pay, but it did not make the young couple in any way well off. Wallis had no income of her own at all. They found a small house in fashionable Coronado and began their first home, Wallis cooking and keeping the house with the assistance of one part-time maid, Spencer returning in the evening after instructing his student pilots.

There was plenty to keep them happy, however, and the atmosphere of California helped. It was warm, new and in many ways, strange. Years afterward Wallis was still talking about it. Once, in London, while she was Mrs. Simpson, she reportedly held up one of her celebrated collections of jewels to a friend. "See this," she said. "Someday, when I can't stand being away any longer, I'll sell it and go and live in California."

But even in California she had steady bouts of homesickness and kept up a fond and regular correspondence with her friends and relatives in the East. The letter which probably made her pine most for home was the one of incoherent delight she received from Mary Kirk, who was engaged to be married.

Mary's story was typical of several that were happening in Baltimore. The hearts of the city's belles were currently skipping whole series of beats. Into Maryland from Europe had come a large group of young French officers. Their job was liaison and intelligence work with the United States Army, and Baltimore became their headquarters. The Belvedere Hotel at teatime and Miller Brothers' Restaurant at dinnertime had become brighter as a result of the appearance of young Frenchmen in their powder-blue jackets, red riding breeches and top boots.

Mary had met and fallen head over heels in love with one of them, a captain named Jacques Raffray, who in private life was a prosperous insurance broker and jeweler. In 1918 they married. Wallis would have dearly loved to attend the wedding, but the distance was too great, and her husband seemed established in San Diego indefinitely.

Wallis and Spencer were still there in 1920 and at a ball at Coronado, Wallis saw the Prince of Wales for the first time. It was not in any way dramatic, and even long-standing friends have seldom heard the Windsors mention it, but the fact of its happening at all gives enough sense of fate and predestination to delight the storytellers.

Reports of the little incident vary, but it may have happened more or less like this. The Prince with Lord Louis Mountbatten was on his way on the battleship *Renown* to Australia and New Zealand via the Panama Canal. Six days steaming from Panama brought the *Renown* to San Diego where she stopped for forty-eight hours to refuel. The Prince of Wales was just beginning his fabulous decade of travel, romance and popularity, and as usual, as soon as the local authorities heard he was in town, he was immediately hauled ashore for some impromptu feting.

It was quite sudden and unannounced. Wallis and her husband, driving in evening dress down Ocean Beach to Coronado, had no idea that any distinguished guest was to be present and did not much care. When they arrived at the dance, the news was passed on to them by a friend, "The Prince of Wales is here." Wallis and Spencer murmured, "Really," and, absorbed in domestic troubles, thought little more about it. There was no earthquake, no flash of lightning, no chill down the spine, no meeting of souls.

It is almost impossible to believe that Wallis, for all her ambition and will of steel, could imagine that she would ever marry this idolized prince. At the moment she was penniless, miserably married to an honest dullard, stuck in one of the most isolated corners of America.

By that time Wallis and Spencer had been married for four years. Outside of flying and the Navy, Spencer had few interests. He liked to stay home and read a book or talk shop to other officers. He also liked to drink. Wallis was eager to be out and doing something different every night. While Spencer remained at home Wallis had acquired the habit of going out alone and making friends of her own. Her circle grew and grew until she became the center of a thriving social life all her own, a social life in which her husband played little part.

She made many friends. One was a pretty girl called Katherine Moore, who had served as a nurse in the French Red Cross during the war, and was later to become an important character in Wallis's life. Others were the Fullam sisters, Rhoda and Marianna, daughters of Admiral Fullam, commander of the San Diego base. The girls would meet at the smart Coronado Hotel or travel up to meet other friends who lived in Santa Barbara.

Spencer was transferred to Washington late in 1920. This brought Wallis closer to her home and friends, but it brought her no nearer to marital happiness. The break came when Spencer was posted to Shanghai, and Wallis and he agreed, amicably enough it seems, that this was the appropriate moment to part.

They were not divorced until 1927, and in 1926 Spencer was still regarded as one of the Navy's better pilots. But the divorce coincided with a strange and unhappy degeneration in Spencer's life. He never rose above the rank of lieutenant commander, and he married three more times. In 1936 he was executive officer of the aircraft carrier *Ranger,* but broke his leg on a shooting expedition in California and was relieved of his position. He was looked after by an old friend who, the following year, became his third wife. But, like the first and second, this marriage did not last.

In a particularly unsavory divorce action in 1940, by which time Spencer had been retired for two years through ill health, his wife alleged he went on "week-long sprees" and declared she feared for her life. She alleged in court that he was "a mental case," and her daughters said that when he got drunk he would speak in Chinese. Spencer denied the whole thing. The divorce was granted. This wife died of a stroke in 1944.

In 1941, Spencer married his fourth wife and finally found the happiness he had sought all his life. Even this was marred by a strange incident, never properly explained, when, in 1943, he was found on the floor of his home in Ventura, California, stabbed in the chest and bleeding profusely. Spencer said something to the effect that he had cut himself opening a tin, and the matter was dropped.

Both wars passed Spencer by. In the first he was an instructor, and by the second he was retired even though he was not yet fifty. In 1950, aged sixty-one, he died, leaving an estate of $25,000 to his wife, but making no reference to Wallis in his will. For all his moroseness and the unhappiness of his life, Winfield Spencer in his own way was a gentleman and never made an unworthy remark about his first wife. Usually he avoided the subject, but would say briefly, "She was a wonderful woman" to people who brought her name up. He was expansive only once, to a reporter at the time of the Abdication. "She was most attractive," he said. "She had one of the most powerful personalities I have ever known any person to possess. She was lovely, intelligent, witty, good company—stimulating I think is the word that best describes her. . . . I think Wallis was a wonderful woman. She will always command my admiration and respect."

In 1920, with Spencer on his way to China, Wallis found herself alone in Washington, free, and with her confidence in herself fully restored. By that time she was twenty-four and extremely attractive in a conventional way. She was small and quite plump, but her face with its high cheekbones, her dancing blue eyes and her ever-ready laughter, gave her an unforgettable allure. Her hands, which were large and strong, were her least beautiful feature.

One of Wallis's greatest assets was her voice. It was summarized best by Janet Flanner (Genet of *The New Yorker*) who once called it "two-toned, low and lower." It was a voice with the natural charm of the South.

The woman described above is no glamour girl. Nor was she rich. Her secret was her personality. The basic assumption in the life story of the Duchess of Windsor is that no other person could have toppled the King of England from his throne and that, if Wallis had never appeared, Edward VIII would still be reigning. Whether Wallis guessed it or not, her arrival in Washington was the turning point in her career. The interlude of mediocrity was over.

IV

Divorce and Remarriage

Washington, Europe, Shanghai, Peking, New York were all to see something of Wallis in the next few years as she progressed through the stages of divorce and remarriage towards her next and most important stop, which was London, England.

It would be unfair to assume that she was totally unmoved at the failure of her marriage. If she had been, it is inconceivable that Spencer would have spoken so warmly about her in the years that followed. But Wallis soon accepted the inevitable. The fact was that an extraordinary person had been briefly attracted to an ordinary person, and Wallis simply outgrew Spencer.

Left alone in Washington, Wallis met an old friend, Mrs. Luke McNamee, wife of a naval intelligence officer who was frequently away on lengthy missions. Together, they rented a small but tasteful house in Georgetown, and set up house as roommates, sharing the expenses.

Both knew some interesting people, and Wallis had had a fine training in the skills of entertaining from Lelia Barnett. She was given assistance socially by her aunt, Mrs. D. Buchanan Merryman. This amiable, forthright character—so well-known in Washington today that she can go into almost any shop, buy something, and say simply, "Charge it to Aunt Bessie"—had many friends in Washington society.

A whirl of parties began which beat anything Wallis could remember in Baltimore. This was the great party era, brought on by Prohibition when everybody drank far more than was good for them. Wallis, for her part, drank very little, sometimes nothing at all. Yet in spite of this, or because of it, she was usually the heart and center of the parties. The boarding house keeper's daughter was not doing as well as she was to do shortly, but she was still doing uncommonly well and Alys was proud of her.

Alys, now married for the third time, had taken a job as manager of the Chevy Chase Country Club, and was often there to greet her daughter when Wallis came in with friends.

Rhoda and Marianna Fullam had also moved to Washington from San Diego and joined the parties. Wallis made a new friend in Ethel Noyes, daughter of the president of the Associated Press and later the second wife of Sir Willmott Lewis, Washington correspondent of the *Times*. Through these and various other acquaintances left over from the prewar days when Lelia Barnett entertained at home, Wallis sailed steadily into a circle which consisted largely of soldiers, sailors and diplomats.

For nearly three years she lived a society life that was little different from that of her friends. She might have been forgotten today except for one thing which made her stand out, her friendship with a brilliant man. There are conflicting stories about how they met, but it may have happened in the way described by the author, Laura Lou Brookman.

In the early nineteen twenties there was a small, exclusive society of epicures who called themselves the "Soixante Gourmets." These were mostly foreign diplomats well-known in Washington for their good talk and good taste. Despairing of the cuisines of even the best Washington restaurants, they formed the society to enjoy a good private lunch every day at a Washington hotel.

Washington was not then the frenetic political center it is today. In the 'twenties it was a sleepy Southern town which closed down completely over week ends while politicians and diplomats escaped from the fiendish gusts of winter and the humid horrors of the capital's summer to their country places in Virginia and Maryland.

The lunches organized by the epicures lasted for several hours and were supplemented by fine wines rarely seen in those days. Wallis was invited and there met Don Felipe Alberto Espil, thirty years of age, an up-and-coming first secretary in the Argentine Embassy. Espil was suave, sophisticated, dark, powerfully built, possessed of a first-rate mind and a sense of unswerving integrity. He eventually justified all his blossoming promise. He was made Argentine Ambassador in Washington in 1931 and held the post until 1945. Later he was Argentine Ambassador in Madrid, and for a few months, in London. Today he lives in prosperous retirement in the Argentine.

When Wallis met Espil he had been in Washington only a year, but he was well-known in the city for an interesting variety of reasons: for his ability as a diplomat, for the impassiveness of his smile—"the Mona Lisa of the Pampas" he was called by a friend—for the quality of his Savile Row clothes, and for his hypnotizing artistry at the tango.

The friendship between Wallis and Espil was long and sincere, and it is possible that they might have married had Wallis been free. But in 1923 Wallis took off for her first trip to Europe, and Espil began a long courtship of a Chicago beauty named Courtney Letts. This courtship went on for ten years, Courtney selecting and shedding two millionaire husbands before she said "yes" to Espil. They were finally married in 1933, Senora Espil later appearing from time to time on the "ten-best-dressed" lists with the Duchess of Windsor.

After 1923 the relationship between Espil and Wallis became abruptly more casual. Quite suddenly Wallis resolved to leave Washington and go to Shanghai. Her decision was unexpected, and has never been explained. It is likely, however, that Wallis had hoped for marriage to Espil, and that when she saw his thoughts directed elsewhere, she elected to make a clean and complete break.

Wallis's decision, announced one evening, upset her mother. But Wallis's education and upbringing had for years been in the hands of less impoverished members of the family. Wallis was twenty-seven. She had a deep love for her mother, but she had seldom in her life looked to her for either guidance or authority. She brushed away Alys's weak remonstrances and set out.

Her choice for her new home was curious. Shanghai was where her estranged husband was stationed, yet Wallis appeared to have no intention of rejoining him. Her subsequent divorce action confirmed that there was no reunion between them. Spencer was assigned to the Yangtze Patrol which kept him away from his base for long periods, and it is possible that he never even knew that Wallis was in China. At any rate in later years, when he reviewed their life together, he talked about San Diego and Coronado and Washington but made no reference to seeing her in China. Few, if any, of the close friends Wallis was to make in China ever set eyes on him.

Almost as soon as she arrived, Wallis traveled to Peking to visit her old friend from Coronado days, Katherine Moore. It was one of the eventful journeys of her life. Katherine had married a wealthy young American sportsman named Herman Rogers, who was later to play a key role in Wallis's matrimonial adventures.

Rogers was a tall, athletic New Yorker, who had graduated from Yale in 1914 and from the Massachusetts Institute of Technology in 1917.

World War I frustrated his ambitions of becoming a successful engineer, and as he possessed a substantial inherited income he decided to go abroad to places where life was both fun and cheaper, always, however, asserting his loyalty to America by running up the Stars and Stripes above his house wherever he lived.

He took his bride to China where he intended to learn Chinese and write a book. He succeeded in doing both, but later forgot most of his Chinese, and found no publisher for the book. Sport and parties took up most of his time. He was an excellent polo player, tennis player, yachtsman and marksman. He gave some of the gayest parties in Peking.

Rogers and his wife befriended Wallis and introduced her to their own social life. For more than six months out of the year she spent in China she stayed at the Rogers' house, and mixed with a smart, effervescent set of British, Americans and wealthy Chinese. She attended polo meetings. She played tennis—badly. She went on expeditions into the interior which started on horseback, continued on donkeyback and ended by scrambling over rough country on foot. Wallis, who always impressed friends as a rather fragile figure of Southern grace and delicacy, surprised everybody by scrambling around with the best of them.

Early in 1925, however, Wallis decided that she had had enough of China. She said good-by to the Rogers and sailed home, establishing herself for the purposes of divorce in the fashionable and "horsey" area of Warrenton, Virginia, a center of yet more of the parties for which Wallis had developed a great hunger.

By the divorce laws of Virginia she had to reside in the state for a year before her divorce could be heard. So she lived pleasantly in the Warren Green Hotel, consulting lawyers in the daytime, and accompanying a string of dates in the evening.

Life for Wallis at the age of twenty-nine had become a life of pleasure. She did no work, her pastimes were empty, her companionship vapid. But her attributes could be denied by no one. Her impact on men was extraordinary. Her popularity was great. She was clever. She was witty. She was high-spirited, good-natured and kindhearted. All that could bewitch a prince she now possessed, and her charms were set off to their best advantage by the society in which she moved.

What were her dreams of the future? "Don't worry, it might never happen," was one of her principles of life, and it is likely that Wallis, who had never had a proper home of her own, wanted more than anything to become a successful hostess, to have her parties talked about and her cooking appreciated. It was an honest ambition.

But Wallis was being led by unsuspected byways towards her famous role in history. One day she went to Union Station in Washington to buy a ticket to New York. Her reason was that she wanted to go to New York to see her friends, to escape from the drab stores of the capital and revel in the dress shops of Fifth Avenue. But fate was propelling her by degrees towards the Prince of Wales.

Wallis wanted to see Mary Kirk, still her friend and confidante, who was living in New York and worked for her own amusement in a specialty shop on West Fifty-seventh Street. Mary and Wallis had corresponded frequently and saw each other whenever they could.

Mary's French husband had stayed on in the United States after the war to become a successful and wealthy businessman with an apartment on Central Park. Their marriage was eight years old, but though they continued to live together it was dimming fast.

The reunion of Mary and Wallis was joyous, and Wallis stayed in New York for some time. Shopping always brought out the best of her taste and talent. She had very little money at that time, but she made up for it with her knowledge of clothes and her native sense of chic. Some of her friends ran little *boutiques* on the East Side and Wallis would call on them. She would not buy, however, until the end of the season by which time the prices had come down. She would take her pick and then make alterations to the clothes she had bought until they were reborn as new creations. "If I had thought of that in the first place," one of Wallis's New York friends admitted, "I could have sold them originally for twice the price."

Mary Kirk often went shopping with her. They went to parties together, met for tea, and Wallis entered an interlocking circle of friends through which she was to meet Ernest Aldrich Simpson of London and his wife. There is the usual confusion of recollection about how they first met. Some old friends believe they met at a party given for Wallis at Mary Kirk Raffray's house. Others say it happened through Mary Clement, a friend of Wallis's from China, who was also a friend of Mary Kirk's.

Mr. and Mrs. Simpson lived with their small daughter in Greenwich, Connecticut, and maintained a brownstone town house in the smart East Sixties of New York. They were very fond of bridge. Mary Clement, the wife of a naval officer, also liked the game and would call on them, often bringing with her a fourth. On one occasion she brought Wallis.

The Simpsons were on the edge of divorce. Mrs. Simpson—she was the first of four—was an American, the former Dorothea Parsons Dechert, daughter of an ex-Chief Justice of Massachusetts. Simpson was part English, part American, and was one of those not uncommon types who stem from a double heritage yet lavish their loyalty on only one.

He was born and educated in America. His first school was a prep school in Pottstown, Pennsylvania. His mother was American and his father had lived in America for many years while retaining his British citizenship. In spite of all that, Simpson developed into an intensely patriotic Englishman, rejecting his claims to American citizenship when he was twenty-one. He went to Harvard, but England had entered World War I and he left before graduating to join the Coldstream Guards. He finished the war a second lieutenant and through the irresistible influence of the Guards returned more English than ever to America to complete his education and enter his father's ship-broking business.

Simpson was a pleasant English "good sort," an able businessman, something of a dandy, with good taste and a sensitive disposition. Nothing in the whole Windsor story is more incongruous than the fact that he has given the world a name that is a symbol for love both sacred and profane. So many years after the revelation of Edward VIII's love the name "Mrs. Simpson" still touches the mind with a sense of mystery and excitement.

Wallis, who could see that the Simpson marriage would not last much longer, was attracted to Ernest Simpson at their first meetings. When Herman Rogers turned up in New York, she introduced them and told Rogers, "I think I'm going to marry him."

But Wallis also had her mind on other things. Her divorce was coming up in Warrenton, and her Uncle Sol, the main source of her present well-being, was dangerously ill.

With these matters occupying her attention she returned to Washington after fond farewells to Mary. On October 25, 1927, the old railroad magnate died, and Wallis was among the many mourners at the funeral service held at Emmanuel Protestant Church in Baltimore. One of the pallbearers was the famous newspaperman, Arthur Brisbane. Warfield left a fortune estimated at $1,000,000, but bequeathed to Wallis nothing more than a $15,000 trust fund. Friends, knowing Uncle Sol's devotion to his niece, were surprised at the bequest which would yield Wallis, already possessed of expensive tastes, nothing more than a few dollars a week. Sol's generosity to Wallis in the past had made it much easier for her to make a mark in Baltimore. The fact was possibly that Sol, a businessman to the core, felt he had done enough. As a puritan he may also have disapproved of the breakup of his niece's marriage and of her social journeys through Washington and China while still a married woman.

There was a hint of defensiveness in the part of his will which mentioned his bequest to Wallis.

"My niece has been educated by me," he wrote as if on guard against criticism, "and otherwise provided for . . . in addition to provision made herein."

Whatever was going on in old Warfield's mind, it did not seem to distress Wallis unduly. She cheerfully told friends that she would have to go out and get a job for the first time in her life. But before she could consider work seriously there was the second complication which had to be undergone, the business of her divorce from Winfield Spencer.

It was the first of her two divorces, and it was as quiet as the second, nine years later, was to be sensational. It was heard on December 6, 1927, Wallis appearing in the Circuit Court of Fauquier County, at Warrenton, Virginia, before Judge George Lathom Fletcher. Her charge was desertion.

The newspapers did not pay much attention to the divorce of so obscure a couple, but one significant fact emerged. Wallis, filing her petition, testified that her husband had deserted her on June 19, 1922, and had contributed nothing to her support since. Several witnesses also testified. The date was important, not so much because it happened to be Wallis's twenty-sixth birthday but because it signified that Spencer had deserted her *before* she went to China.

No objection was raised and the divorce was granted four days later.

Wallis, having cast off her first husband, and finding herself with almost no income at all, paused to wonder what to do next. There was a suggestion that she might become a businesswoman and sell construction elevators in Pittsburgh, Pennsylvania. She even traveled to Pittsburgh to discuss it. A decision had to be made. Wallis, as she has done all her life when face to face with crises, decided to take a holiday.

She called Aunt Bessie in Washington and together they went to Europe. It was Wallis's second transatlantic holiday. The first time she had stayed in London only briefly and spent most of her time in gayer Paris.

This time she went to London immediately. One of the first people she met was Ernest Simpson, who had transferred his offices to London and was working as a director of the ship-brokerage firm of Simpson and Simpson in association with his father's office in New York.

Simpson was alone now, his wife having left him and returned to New York with their daughter Audrey. He escorted Wallis everywhere, and by the time Wallis and Aunt Bessie were due to return to New York there was an engagement ring on her finger.

Wallis accompanied Aunt Bessie back to New York but stayed only long enough to wind up her affairs in America. Excitedly she told Mary that she was saying good-by to her homeland and intended to settle down in England for the rest of her life. On this, as on other occasions, Wallis's assessment of the future was quite wrong.

The wedding, at the Chelsea Register Office, was quiet. The announcement appeared in the New York *Times* and it took many of Wallis's friends by surprise. It read:

Mr. and Mrs. Charles Gorden Allen of Washington, D. C., announce the marriage of Mrs. Allen's daughter, Mrs. Wallis Warfield Spencer to Ernest Simpson of London on July 21st, 1928, in London. Mrs. Simpson is the daughter of the late Teackle Wallis Warfield of Baltimore, and niece of the late S. Davies Warfield also of the city. She is the former wife of Lt. Commander E. Winfield Spencer of the United States Navy.

So Wallis Warfield Spencer added another surname to the list and set off on a honeymoon which took her to France, Spain, Majorca and Minorca. She was thirty-two and her husband thirty-one. The years were slipping by and the time was approaching when "the most charming American woman in London" was to shake the world.

V

Mrs. Simpson Arrives

When Wallis arrived in London, she hardly knew a soul. Three years later she was a leader in a thriving society. It was a typical Wallis Warfield progression, and as in Baltimore fifteen years before she did it all by herself and made it look easy.

After Wallis and Simpson returned from their honeymoon they found Simpson's apartment at 12, Upper Berkeley Street too small and moved to a large apartment at No. 5, Bryanston Court, Bryanston Square, Mayfair. At first Mrs. Simpson was happy to live fairly quietly, with an occasional theater and night club and, for the rest of the time, evenings at home with her husband who loved to read histories and books about old ships. It seems to have been from the start a marriage lacking in passion, but there is no doubt that Wallis and Simpson were genuinely fond of each other and remained so until the end.

Wallis soon began to meet people. Several secretaries in the Argentine Embassy in London turned out to be old friends from her Washington days, and Wallis and her husband were invited to parties given by South American diplomats.

The English were less easy to know and Wallis had bouts of homesickness at first. She missed Washington and she missed her American friends. Within a year she found herself back in the United States, though there was little consolation in the circumstances of the trip. Her mother was gravely ill.

Poor Alys Montague Warfield Raisin Allen, at the age of fifty-one, could not look back on a great deal of happiness. Two husbands dead:

the first little more than a boy, the second a gay blade, after two years of marriage. Nor had she ever been really able to call her one child her own. Mother and daughter had grown up more like sisters. Wallis had experienced almost no mother influence. They had drifted far apart and even on the deathbed they could not be reunited. Wallis, taking the first train down to Washington after landing, found that her mother had gone into a coma. Wallis kept a constant bedside vigil, but Alys did not regain consciousness and died a week later. Sorrowfully Wallis returned to London.

Her period of mourning was a sincere expression of her sadness, and it was many months before she and her husband began once more to accept invitations. But now Wallis was surprised to see how many friends she had actually made. Through her Latin-American acquaintances she made new friends among the United States Embassy staff. Wallis was immediately popular among her fellow Americans.

The place, the atmosphere and the era were all becoming ripe for Mrs. Simpson. If any one of those factors had been out of position in the London of the early 'thirties, history would have been startlingly different. The war had been over for more than a decade, but London was still tormented by a postwar lunacy. The old aristocracy had been eliminated and into the vacuum they left behind poured the twittering society of bright young things. Royalty, isolated by the flood, could not remain aloof and hardly tried. Instead it stepped down to join the fun. It was a period of social experiment and daring adventure. Such a situation had never existed in Britain before, and it exists no more.

Ghosts alone remain of old days too garish to be remembered as either "good" or "bad"; ghosts of night clubs still standing, but no longer peopled by dazzling celebrities; Mayfair mansions, the scene of unbelievable parties, now deserted or turned into offices; a few elderly ex-playboys still making the rounds, and out-of-date playwrights and novelists unable to make contact with the modern world; the dizzy Mayfair girls in hideous dresses, now transplanted in the austere masks of middle age to New York or the more fashionable British colonial resorts.

But it was remarkable while it lasted. The spirit of abdication was in the air everywhere, abdication from responsibility and authority, loss of faith in the British heritage. The spirit of abdication culminated in the unprecedented act of immolation, the Abdication of Edward VIII, after which scarifying experience the nation rallied, out of necessity, under George VI.

In a society which valued the epigram above faith and hope, Wallis Simpson, the expert, was in a position of advantage. It could never have been done in any other period, but times being what they were Mrs. Simpson shot like a rocket to the very top.

She began to entertain, and she immediately brought to that difficult art a flair that excited the society in which she moved. From the start her dinner parties were original and provocative, spiced by many of Wallis's bon mots on the subject of cooking. "Soup," she said once, "is an uninteresting liquid which gets you nowhere." "The idea," she also said with her special talent for the calculated overstatement, "that everything can be left to a good chef is one of life's most dangerous illusions."

Wallis was true to her principles. In the kitchen as in the rest of the flat Mrs. Simpson was boss and ruled with an iron hand her small empire of cook, kitchenmaid, parlormaid, chambermaid and part-time help. These were the first to come under the spell of eyes that never missed a speck of dust, or a flower out of place. Always able to laugh at herself Mrs. Simpson has turned the sword on her own foibles. "My doctor said he could fix me up if I'd stop moving ash trays three inches," she laughed. It was a genuine compliment to Mrs. Simpson, however, that servants were prepared to take much more from her than they would from many other employers. Domestic servants are proud of their craft and they admire a perfectionist. Mrs. Simpson was a super-perfectionist, and anything less than perfection infuriated her.

She introduced new ideas. Her Southern cooking is still remembered and she is believed by some to have started the now common habit of using a red handkerchief for her lipstick. These she used to give to her women guests. The table in the dining room at Bryanston Square was mirror-topped and Wallis would entertain twelve to fourteen guests at one time, plying them with food and drink in an almost mathematical ration designed to stimulate the best of their conversation.

She worked it out this way: two cocktails before dinner (a third would coarsen the palate). Food perfect but not too much (because that would make the guests heavy afterward). As important as the taste was the appearance. Mrs. Simpson's food had to *look* attractive as well. "Leave it to the chef, and you can be sure everything he cooks will be the same color," she said. Then port and brandy as the guests wished. Every item had one object in view: talk, the best possible talk that could be arranged. "I was always taught," Mrs. Simpson has said, "that even a guest must carry his own weight. My mother taught me that you had an obligation in any gathering: to make other people happy if you could. As a guest or as a hostess you must be sure that others have a chance to put their best foot forward."

The food led to the conversation and whenever the conversation

[45]

showed signs of flagging, Mrs. Simpson would drop a thumping polemic to startle the guests and start an argument. Thus were spent evenings in which the pace never slackened though it sometimes exhausted; in which the vitality of the hostess occasionally devitalized the guests; there were seldom any well-known people among them—just then, anyway—but invariably they were parties to remember.

The qualities which made Wallis a good hostess made her an even better guest. She earned the undying gratitude of some of her friends by agreeing to come and help out when they had some especially turgid guests to entertain. Even the dullest guest could rarely maintain his gravity against Wallis's perpetual exhilaration and high spirits. Parties which seemed doomed from the start turned into triumphs when Mrs. Simpson was there.

Ernest Simpson watched these tours de force, bemused by his wife's genius. Her schooling was only average yet she chattered away in French to make one almost believe she was fluent at it. Never before in her life had she had money to spare, yet her taste in clothes and in jewels was faultless, never too much or too little of anything. Her cooking—both French and American—was a dream, and if she tasted a new dish in a restaurant, she knew no rest until she had learned from the chef its secret. Her feeling for flowers was exquisite. Her love of music was profound and informed, so much so that on more than one occasion she rocked Sir Thomas Beecham back on his pins on the subject when they met at parties. The volcanic maestro never felt he was talking down to a novice when he talked to Mrs. Simpson, though nothing in her education or upbringing gave any clue as to where she acquired her knowledge.

Only in conversation did she tend to put her foot in it by occasional indiscreet references to friends and acquaintances, but even that in the society in which she moved was little more than an occupational disease. She talked incessantly about everything, and people who first met her were impressed at the range of her interests. For conversation's sake Wallis developed the habit of reading all the newspaper headlines and skimming the latest books, but she was heard to better advantage if the conversation did not linger too long on the same subject.

In the course of her expanding relationships Wallis became, in time, a particularly close friend of an American diplomat and his wife, Mr. and Mrs. Benjamin Thaw. Mrs. Thaw was formerly Consuelo Morgan, and her sisters were the two much-publicized Morgan twins Thelma and Gloria, who became respectively Lady Furness and Mrs. Vanderbilt.

Via the Thaws, Mrs. Simpson's name and her reputation as a party-giver reached the ear of the most important American in London, not the Ambassador, Charles Dawes, but the great Lady Cunard.

"Emerald" Cunard was famous for many things during her long reign in Mayfair: for her courage, her snobbishness, her personality, her eccentricity and her services to the arts. The musical soirées which she organized at her mansion at No. 7, Grosvenor Square were celebrated and awaited agog by the gossip writers on the London evening newspapers. She was a patron of music, a director of Covent Garden and an immortal in the passing world of London in the first half of this century. Her wealth was prodigious: among other sources of money, she possessed a fortune in shares in General Electric.

She was born Maude Alice Burke of California and New York. In 1895, when she was eighteen, she had married Sir Bache Cunard, grandson of the founder of the Cunard Line. For the next fifty-three years she was to delight Londoners with her exploits. Disliking the name of Maude, she became Emerald to her friends—"because the name suits me."

During World War II a balloon barrage squad was stationed in Lady Cunard's back garden, and every night after they came off duty Emerald invited them in for supper. This was after the blitz; Emerald prudently spent the period of the intense bombing of London in New York. On her return she closed her bomb-damaged mansion and moved to a suite at the Dorchester where, in 1948, at the age of seventy-one, she died.

Lady Cunard met Mrs. Simpson at a party in 1930 and promptly invited her to a soirée. It was the highest pinnacle Mrs. Simpson had reached in her steady social climb, and people who were there that evening recall that Wallis's entrance was as impressive as might have been expected of her. To an assembly of guests dressed to kill and perfumed to obfuscate, Mrs. Simpson was announced. She carried herself with the beautiful perfection seen twenty-three years later in the mannequin parade at the Duchess of Windsor Ball in New York; she wore a simple black evening gown which she had made herself and no make-up whatever. The courage it took for an ambitious woman, not conventionally pretty, to gamble on this effect of simplicity must have been great.

It worked. Wallis's personality and her engaging self-confidence delighted Emerald Cunard. Wallis knew little about England or English affairs, but she did know human relationships which are universal, and Lady Cunard's guests were as charmed with her as Lady Cunard was herself. Wallis and her husband found themselves invited regularly to Grosvenor Square.

Through this introduction she began to move into the society which made its headquarters at the Embassy Club in Old Bond Street. There are no equivalents today either in London or anywhere else to what this establishment used to represent. It had been made famous in the 'twenties by a restaurateur of genius called Luigi and became the place where London's celebrities drew most of their sustenance, and the gossip columnists most of their news. Luigi died in 1930.

Just as she had done in the Belvedere tearoom in Baltimore in her debutante days Mrs. Simpson made the Embassy Club her home away from home. She also became a familiar guest at the Kit Kat, which had begun to rival the Embassy Club in the 'thirties but which was closed in World War II.

One of the people she met through Consuelo Thaw and Lady Cunard was Lady Thelma Furness, then attracting probably more attention than anyone else in London. Thelma had married Lord Furness, the shipping magnate, in 1923, later, in 1933, divorcing him. Much of an age and much of a temperament, Lady Furness and Mrs. Simpson soon became close friends.

It all happened accidentally. Lady Furness's circle of friends, though not really large, was pretty choice and comprised what was referred to as "The Prince of Wales Set." Most of their conversation revolved round the almost legendary figure of the Prince, and Wallis, who had never met him, would listen fascinated. No one knew the Prince better than Lady Furness. She saw him regularly and many years afterwards admitted frankly that she had been in love with him. An admission of something to this effect was made by the Duke of Windsor in 1954 when he asked a British newspaper not to publish a letter which he had written to Lady Furness.

Thirty miles up the Thames from Westminster, the object of so much admiration and gossip ruled his "court" from a romantic mansion near the river—Fort Belvedere. The Prince of Wales was a small, boyish man of thirty-six, with hair the color of straw and an innocent face animated by sparkling blue eyes and quick, shy smiles. He was eager in spirit, emotional, sincere, erratic, idealistic. For ex-servicemen and the unemployed he had a love and compassion the depth of which they could sense and return. And side by side with many princely qualities he had a disarming naïveté, enjoying electrical gadgets, jazz, the splash of a pebble tossed in a still pool. He had an unabashed admiration for America and the easy, monosyllabic give-and-take of Americans.

He had just returned from the Argentine where he led a successful British trade mission. He was idolized in South America. He was adored in North America, in England, Wales and Scotland. Possibly no other personality of the twentieth century was so universally loved. The richest and the most desirable women in Europe jostled for his favor and the honor of being chosen as the future Queen of England.

But there were flaws, almost invisible as yet, in the picture. Something in his personality sent out a wave that was almost like a cold shiver. The image of his father disturbed his rest. Old King George V, gray and ailing, could sometimes be laughed away as old-fashioned and strait-laced by the Prince of Wales's friends, but he could never be minimized nor could his immense stature as a king and a symbol be diminished. The King bore heavily on the Prince of Wales, much more heavily than he did on any of his other sons, and he dominated a large part of the Prince's consciousness.

Probably in an effort to find a correct perspective for himself as well as to amuse others, the young Prince used to delight his English and American friends with streams of stories about his father, all the stories having one point in common: they showed the King in a warm light and in larger-than-life size.

Even at this time some of the Prince's selections of friends were disturbing the King, and the Prince told guests of an incident when he was driving home from Ascot with his father in the family Daimler.

"I saw you talking to some pretty disreputable people this afternoon, my boy," the King said reprovingly.

"But, Father," the Prince laughed, "I distinctly saw you talking to a young person who has just been divorced."

"I know," the King replied thoughtfully, "but she was such a damned pretty woman."

The father obsession stayed with the Prince to the end of the old man's life. The Prince knew that one day he would have to take King George's place, and sometimes the future seemed to overwhelm him. Once, after a game of polo at Rugby, he threw down his helmet and burst out to his aides, "Oh, God! I dread my father dying! I dread the thought of being King!"

Soothsayers felt the waves he generated as he passed. The Honorable Ralph Shirley, a well-known occultist of the first two decades of this century, predicted as long ago as 1903 that Edward VIII would never come to the throne, or that if he did he would be rapidly succeeded by the Duke of York. This prophecy was actually printed in a periodical of the time called *The Horoscope*.

Cheiro, the famous clairvoyant and palmist, who had a vogue in London before World War I (his real name was Count Louis Hamon, and he died in New York in 1936, aged seventy) wrote this in his *World Predictions* in 1931:

"It is well within the range of possibility, owing to the peculiar planetary influences to which he is subjected that the Prince will give up everything, even the chance of being crowned, rather than lose the object of his affections."

In the early 'twenties a gypsy, in Angus, Scotland, read the hand of a pretty girl called Lady Elizabeth Bowes-Lyon, daughter of the 14th Earl of Strathmore, and told her she would one day become Queen of England.

In the early 'thirties, King George V, a few senior servants of the state, and the Prince of Wales himself, could feel the undercurrent of foreboding. But for the rest of the world the Prince's future seemed to shine with a blinding light.

The Prince's circle of friends was largely American or Anglo-American, and included the Thaws, Lady Cunard and Lady Furness. There was also Lady Honor Guinness and her husband Henry Channon, an American who took British citizenship and later sat as a Conservative in the House of Commons. Among the Prince's English intimates were Lord and Lady Louis Mountbatten, Mrs. Frieda Dudley Ward, and Duff Cooper, married to the beautiful Lady Diana Manners, all gay company, and some with first-class minds.

It was through Lady Furness that the Simpsons first became good friends of the Prince's, though she was not responsible for the first meeting. That came about in the following way:

The Prince, one day, was entertaining Benjamin and Consuelo Thaw at the Fort. As they were leaving he asked them to come back to dinner. Regretfully Thaw was obliged to decline because, he explained, he and his wife had a date that evening to meet Mr. and Mrs. Ernest Simpson.

"Bring them along," said the Prince.

That afternoon he went to Sunningdale to have nine holes of golf with an equerry. The equerry, at the end, suggested another nine, but the Prince declined.

"I can't," he said, "I've got some people I've never met coming to dinner. An American couple called Simpson."

VI

The Prince Falls in Love

This account of the first meeting of Mrs. Simpson and the Prince of Wales differs from that described in the Duke of Windsor's Memoirs. In his book the Duke tells the story in this way:-

> It was during the winter after my return from South America in 1931. I had gone to Melton Mowbray with my brother George for a week-end's hunting. Mr. and Mrs. Simpson were guests in the same house . . . Mrs. Simpson did not ride and obviously had no interest in horses, hounds or hunting in general. She was also plainly in misery from a cold in the head. Since a Prince is by custom expected to take the lead in conversing with strangers and having been informed that she was an American, I was prompted to observe that she must miss central heating . . . a mocking look came into her eyes. "I am sorry, Sir," she said, "but you have disappointed me."
>
> "In what way?"
>
> "Every American woman who comes to your country is always asked the same question. I had hoped for something more original from the Prince of Wales." I moved away but the passage lingered. . . .

The story which the Duchess herself has told to some of her most intimate friends arises from the invitation which the Prince of Wales extended to the Simpsons to come to Fort Belvedere.

The Thaws brought the Simpsons along and introductions were made to the Prince and the few other guests who were there. After that there were cocktails and a dinner totally lacking in imagination.

The dinner over, some of the guests settled down to a game of bridge, while the Prince and Lady Furness busied themselves with petit point which was one of the Prince's hobbies. The evening dragged on with even Wallis's vivacity hardly proof against the insufferable dullness. Finally she rose to her feet and said, in effect, "What kind of a party is this?"

There was a fascinated silence.

"Well," Mrs. Simpson persisted, "can't we dance or something?"

"A very good idea," said the Prince of Wales. He put down his needle and rang the bell.

Immediately footmen entered. Some bore away the bridge tables. Others rolled back the carpets. The guests, in the sudden release of tension, rummaged happily among the Prince's large collection of jazz records and the dancing began. It continued far into the night. It was not the first time that Mrs. Simpson had saved a party from death, but this was a party that changed her fortune.

Whether this version of the first meeting or the Duke's is correct is not really important, though the Duke admits to some confusion by saying ". . . not long after our first meeting at Melton Mowbray we were at a party in London and I am supposed to have asked my hostess, 'Haven't I met that lady before?'"

It is believed to be Lady Furness who made the suggestion which would once have seemed beyond the dreams of even the ambitious girl from Baltimore. "You should be presented at Court."

At first Mrs. Simpson laughed away the idea, but it quickly caught hold of her. She thought it over and put to Lady Furness her two difficulties, one of them a small one, the other possibly insurmountable. For one thing, she said, she hadn't anything suitable to wear and she balked at buying a gown to wear once and never again. For another it would be difficult for her to be presented at Buckingham Palace because she had divorced her husband. Thelma Furness said that she could borrow a gown, and it was pointed out that guiltless parties in divorce were frequently presented at Court. So the American Ambassador agreed to put Mrs. Simpson's name down on the United States list for presentation to King George V and Queen Mary on June 10, 1931.

Thelma loaned Wallis a ball gown and her presentation regalia was completed by a fan consisting of three white plumes, traditional symbol of the Prince of Wales, a customary adornment of this period. She also had an aquamarine crucifix which she wore at her breast. This she had acquired in China and it can be seen on the photographs taken of Wallis in Court dress.

It was as impressive an occasion as Court presentations always are, the King in Court dress sitting solidly on his throne, Queen Mary by his side, under the great Durbar Canopy which they had brought back from India. The scarlet and gold ballroom was brilliant with banked flowers. While a Guards band in the background softly played the latest popular melodies, scores of guests from every corner of the Empire stood around to watch or lined up for their turn to be presented. Behind the throne stood the royal princes each in Court dress scintillating with Orders, the Prince of Wales, Prince George, the Duke of Gloucester, each on the lookout for his particular friends. With them were the Princess Royal, and the old Duke of Connaught, in a state of senility but still appreciative of a pretty face and shoulder.

A number of people were presented though the list now looks rather undistinguished. Only two people still prominent today are easily traceable, one Mrs. Ernest Simpson, the other Mrs. Ernest "Buffie" Ives, sister of Adlai Stevenson.

The Prince certainly noticed Mrs. Simpson, because he is recalled as acknowledging an approving chortle on the part of the Duke of Connaught by telling him who she was and commenting on her grace.

It was the second presentation of Mrs. Simpson's life, the first at the Lyric Theatre, Baltimore, Maryland, U.S.A.; the second at Buckingham Palace. Her old free-and-easy boy friends in Maryland would have been surprised if they could have seen this smart woman, completely self-possessed, make her deep reverent curtsies to the King and Queen, while they, with gracious inclinations of the head, responded to the woman who was to lead their son away from his royal duties and shake the strongest monarchy on earth to its foundations.

"I wouldn't have missed it for the world," Wallis said excitedly that night when Thelma Furness gave a party at her home to celebrate the occasion. And there she again met the Prince of Wales, who complimented her on her appearance. Already the Prince was finding Mrs. Simpson charming although some time was yet to pass before he looked on her with the eyes of love.

By 1933, however, he was beginning to grace the Simpsons' table at Bryanston Court. One society gossip columnist who was present once or twice, wrote ". . . it was noticed for the first time how solicitous the Prince of Wales was of her every need, be it a match, a coat she might have wanted to take off, or some refreshment."

The Prince was at a farewell party given for Wallis before she set out on her first visit to the United States since the death of her mother. While in America she saw Mary Kirk Raffray again; she traveled down to Washington to stay with Aunt Bessie, then she attended the Maryland Hunt Cup in Baltimore. Several old friends recognized her, and at least one ex-beau greeted her with an excited "Hi, Wally! What have you been doing all these years?" Mrs. Simpson smiled slantingly, replied cordially, but generally kept to herself and her family.

In 1934, a whole series of events combined to bring Wallis and the Prince of Wales together. Lady Cunard, who could look deeper into men's souls than most other people, saw what was going to happen before either the Prince or Mrs. Simpson realized it. Whenever she invited the Prince to dinner, Mrs. Simpson and her husband would also be among the guests, and Wallis would be seated close to the Prince. They were amusing dinners, no other salon being more conducive to conversation and romance, with the soft colorings of the walls and carpets, and candlelight everywhere flickering on Emerald Cunard's charming collection of pale Marie Laurencin paintings.

In September, 1934, the Prince invited Mrs. Simpson on a yachting holiday on the Riviera and the first record of the Prince's new love crept into the American press, *Time* magazine reporting:

> Such fun was Edward of Wales having at Cannes last week with beauteous Mrs. Wallace Wakefield Simpson (sic) that he sent back to Marseilles an airplane he had ordered to take him to Paris.

Then Thelma Furness's sister, Gloria Vanderbilt, in October, 1934, became involved in one of the celebrated court cases of the decade, one which became known in time as the "poor-little-rich-girl" case. Gloria had been feuding for some years with her mother, Mrs. Laura Morgan and her aunt, Mrs. Harry Payne Whitney. One night, Mrs. Whitney spirited away Mrs. Vanderbilt's ten-year-old daughter, Gloria, heiress to a fortune worth millions.

Mrs. Vanderbilt sued for her return, lost the case and, with it, custody of her daughter.

Hearing a call for help from Gloria's mother, Thelma Furness and her sister, Consuelo Thaw, immediately made reservations back to New York so that they could appear in defense of their sister.

Before she left, Lady Furness had lunch with Mrs. Simpson at the Ritz Hotel. Mrs. Simpson commented that the Prince of Wales would be lonely.

"Well, be sure to look after him when I am away," Lady Furness said.

"Of course I will, darling," Wallis said. And, as Lady Furness later commented with rueful frankness, "she did."

That night the Prince and Wallis danced together in public in England for the first time.

And that was how it happened. Mrs. Simpson became the closest friend of the golden-boy prince. She had got there almost by default, and it could have happened to several other people. But if luck had helped to carry Mrs. Simpson to her new position of royal favor, she must have been well aware that her abilities alone would have to keep her there above all those beautiful gentlewomen of Europe, bristling with aristocratic connections, pulsating with blue blood, determined to trample with their dainty little feet all over her.

The Prince of Wales, probably for the first time in his life, was really happy. He enjoyed the company not only of Mrs. Simpson but of Ernest Simpson, too. In fact, for a while, the two were inseparable friends. They found a lot in common, swopped stories of their experiences in World War I, and discussed fascinating matters like ships, economics, flowers, trees.

For a while a pleasing and not too emotional relationship existed. Several week ends in a row were spent by the three together at Fort Belvedere. Simpson and the Prince would put on heavy boots and tramp round the estate, attending to the rhododendrons and chopping down any occasional tree that displeased their fancy.

Not sharing their enthusiasm for the raw English out of doors Mrs. Simpson would stay at the Fort assisting the chef and the servants with lunches and dinners. After all his wanderings the Prince was at last enjoying having a home of his own.

The friendship between Ernest Simpson and the Prince of Wales was genuine enough. Unfortunately for Simpson, before the year 1934 was out, the Prince of Wales was hopelessly in love with Mrs. Simpson. It was now Wallis's turn to feel the weight of a force over which she had no control—the Hanoverian capacity for intense love, the kind of love that Queen Victoria had for Albert. Once Mrs. Simpson set the love alight, she couldn't have extinguished it even if she had wanted to, and all the King's Ministers and all the King's Bishops couldn't extinguish it either. In fact Wallis had no desire to stop it. This was success beyond her dreams.

The Prince's London friends were baffled. To worldly men, conscious of all the beauties surrounding the Prince, his love for a happily married, mature American woman was incomprehensible. Prince Christopher of Greece—turning up in London in November, 1934, for the wedding of his niece, Marina, to Prince George, later the Duke of Kent—was seized at a party by the Prince of Wales who said, "Christo, I want you to meet Mrs. Simpson."

Christopher asked, "Who's she?"

"An American . . . she's wonderful."

Christopher noticed how heedlessly the Prince pushed past the other women at the party. He was introduced to Mrs. Simpson and, when the crisis broke, he explored his mind and recalled "a pleasing but not beautiful woman who never stopped talking."

Sir Samuel Hoare also met her and later remembered "not only her sparkling talk but also her sparkling jewels in very up-to-date settings . . . very American with little or no knowledge of English life."

Thelma Furness, back in London, was astonished at a dinner party when she saw Mrs. Simpson lightly slap the Prince's hand. Lady Furness knew he hated familiarities, and realized he must be very much in love indeed.

In February, 1935, the Prince went to the little Austrian resort of Kitzbuhel. Mrs. Simpson was in the party frolicking with the Prince in the Alpine snows, but Mr. Simpson was not. From there the royal party, which numbered a dozen people altogether, visited Vienna and Budapest. Aunt Bessie Buchanan Merryman acted as chaperon and Mrs. Simpson behaved so unobtrusively that there were few opportunities for serious gossip. She was always in the background and never intruded when officials paid their respects to the Prince. Indeed to the outside world she appeared less intimate with him than several other people in the party. Only on occasional evenings were they able to relax. Freed for a few hours from official protocol they escaped to the night clubs of Budapest and danced gypsy *czardas,* some observers recalling the huge diamond which sparkled in Mrs. Simpson's hair.

Mrs. Simpson slowly became a power in the land, a subtle and unobtrusive power, not so much concerned with influencing domestic or international policies of which she knew little and cared less, but important because of the happiness which her presence gave the Prince of Wales.

As such she inevitably became an object of interest to men whose job it was to get acquainted with the people behind the throne. International agents are tough fellows who work and do not play at power. Wallis was an intelligent woman, but inevitably she was inexperienced and she was honored by their attentions.

To one group of people more than most others, unusual happenings in high places had an acute attraction. This was the ruling clique of Nazi Germany. The Prince of Wales was very popular in Germany and it must have seemed to the Nazis that Mrs. Simpson was a person to cultivate in order to advance their own interests. The man who came to try and perform the cultivation was Joachim von Ribbentrop, German Ambassador Extraordinary, later German Ambassador in London, later Foreign Secretary of Germany, later hanged.

The German interest in Mrs. Simpson began a myth that has plagued the Duchess of Windsor unfairly ever since. The myth grew that Mrs. Simpson was a close friend of Ribbentrop's. The story became so widely accepted that the impression is still strong today, particularly in Germany.

Shortly before World War II the Duchess of Windsor was obliged to deny the story specifically. "I cannot recall being in his company more than twice," she said. "Once at a cocktail party at Lady Cunard's before he became Ambassador to Britain, and once at another big reception. I was never alone in his company and I never had more than a few words with him—just small talk. I took no interest in politics." In 1943, at the midpoint of the war, the Duke of Windsor was obliged to deny officially a story in a reputable American magazine that a picture of Ribbentrop hung over his wife's toilet table in the Bahamas.

The rumors were baseless, and there are many facts to prove it, one being that at the time when Mrs. Simpson was supposed to have been friendly with Ribbentrop her time was being dominated by the Duke of Windsor. The story of the picture of Ribbentrop over her toilet table in the Bahamas was pure imagination. Half a dozen women in the Duchess's entourage in the Bahamas had access to her rooms at all times when she was Governor's wife. Not all those women were her friends, but none saw any such picture.

It is probable that the story began in the following way: The Prince of Wales and Wallis were both very good friends of the German Ambassador in London, Dr. Leopold Gustav Alexander von Hoesch, a witty, cultured professional diplomat. He was Ambassador to the Court of St. James, from 1932 until his death at the age of fifty-five, in 1936, when his place was taken by Ribbentrop. Hoesch gave some of the best parties in London, mixing his guests well, serving superb food and hiring orchestras from fashionable West End restaurants to entertain the guests as they dined.

Hoesch was lukewarm about the Nazis, and Ribbentrop knew it. Ribbentrop knew also that Hoesch loved flattery, and he spent a whole afternoon flattering him, telling him how highly his work in London was esteemed by the Führer. Hoesch was delighted. Ribbentrop was obviously a much nicer person than he had always believed. He had organized a dinner for that evening, and the Prince of Wales, Mrs. Simpson and Ribbentrop were all invited. He sat Ribbentrop beside Mrs. Simpson.

The dinner was a notable success. Ribbentrop was at his most charming, and appeared to be very much impressed by the charm and wit of Mrs. Simpson. Next morning seventeen roses were delivered to Mrs. Simpson's flat in Bryanston Square with Ribbentrop's compliments. Every morning from then until Ribbentrop's return to Berlin some days later, a bouquet of seventeen roses was sent to Mrs. Simpson. The "seventeen roses" soon became a subject of gossip in both the British and German Foreign Offices. Hitler himself teased Ribbentrop about it, and asked him what was behind it all.

Mrs. Simpson might or might not have been pleased by the attentions of Ribbentrop. She was living in a world of which she could hardly have dreamed. She was courted and wooed by statesmen, and if some of her friendships were later to turn out catastrophically, it must be emphasized that Baltimore had not trained her for such an existence. Friends, even rich friends, were staggered by her jewels and her clothes. She was once seen to buy eighteen pairs of shoes at one time. The story of her expenditures was reported in some New York newspapers, and the first Mrs. Simpson, living on alimony, was reported to be surprised and annoyed.

As for Ernest Simpson, he liked the Prince of Wales and revered his position as the future King of England. He did not realize how deeply the Prince was in love with his wife, but the Prince's friendship for Wallis dazed him. He could find no weapons in the reserves of his simple philosophy to combat it. Neither indignation, fury, amusement, acquiescence or sorrow would seem to fit the realities of the situation. For most of the time he remained in the shadows in a state of complete indecision. In spite of occasional attempts to assert himself, he remained to the end an inconclusive figure, who never rose or sought to rise to the tragic stature of the two other participants in the triangular drama. In retrospect one has to keep reminding oneself that there was ever a Mr. Simpson in the story at all. Nevertheless he was a good fellow, likable, and the victim of a sharp stroke of fate from which he has today recovered, unembittered and as agreeable and as immaculately tailored as ever.

Mr. and Mrs. Simpson were present at one of the most dramatic scenes of the century, the scene at Friday Court, St. James's Palace, when the Prince of Wales was proclaimed King. The date was January 22, 1936. King George V, his last months clouded with anxiety over his son's impossible love affair, was dead.

George had ascended to the throne on May 6, 1910, and his task had been a severe one. Harold Nicholson, his biographer, wrote:

An unwritten constitution (such as Britain's), although possessing all

ACME

The Brockhurst portrait of the Duchess of Windsor.

Wallis Warfield (center) is pictured with two of her girl friends when she attended school at Oldfields, Virginia, in 1913.

Another picture of Wally taken while at school in Oldfields, Virginia.

The future Duchess of
Windsor, aged seventeen.

utenant Commander Earl Winfield Spencer, (right), first husband of
Duchess of Windsor, shown with his lawyer as he seeks a divorce
m his second wife, Mrs. Norma Spencer.

The late Mary Kirk Raffray Simpson, childhood friend of Wally's who married Ernest Simpson after his divorce from Wally.

Ernest A. Simpson, second husband of Wallis Warfield.

the merits of elasticity and although hampered by none of the defects of rigidity, inevitably contains some zones of uncertainty. When the ship of state enters these uncharted waters, then the most impartial authorities begin to differ on what the correct constitutional procedure really is. King George . . . was often driven by the winds and tides of events into these zones of uncertainty, and was obliged to determine with little more than the stars to guide him, which was the true constitutional course to pursue.

He brought to his job a gift for conciliation, straightforwardness, and an ability to see the truth through the veils that separated him from the rest of his people. In the quarter of a century during which he reigned the world witnessed the disappearance of five emperors, eight kings and eighteen minor dynasties. Despite the convulsions of war and foreign revolutions, the British monarchy emerged more firmly established than it was before.

Four proclamations of the accession of the new King were heard in London: one by the Garter King of Arms at St. James's Palace, the others by Heralds at Charing Cross, Temple Bar and the Royal Exchange. The King had invited a few close friends to the Palace to witness the ceremony, and the Simpsons were among them.

Four state trumpeters in gold-laced tabards paraded on the balcony of St. James's Palace, followed by the Sergeants-at-Arms carrying maces. In the courtyard were guardsmen and bandsmen with their drums muffled in black crêpe. Cued by a fanfare of trumpets, the Garter King of Arms stepped forward and raised a huge scroll. On either side of him stood other Kings of Arms, Heralds and Heraldic Pursuivants with cockaded hats of gold and silver. The proclamation was intoned sonorously.

It was the stuff of centuries. The ceremony over, Mrs. Simpson brought the matter back to the twentieth century and to earth. "Very moving," she said to the new King, "but it has already made me realize how different your life is going to be."

Mrs. Simpson was not the only person to keep her feet on the ground amid the uplifting pageantry. In his offices at No. 10 Downing Street, Stanley Baldwin, the Prime Minister of England, had before him a complete dossier on the life of Mrs. Simpson, which he read with increasing gloom. He knew that a major crisis might be on the way, and so did other people. Dr. Cosmo Lang, the Archbishop of Canterbury, had a good idea of what was going on. The various press lords knew it, too.

Baldwin and Edward VIII had disliked each other intensely ever since 1927 when they crossed Canada together. Their personalities were mutually antagonistic, and the trip had been a trial to both of them. Baldwin was obliged by convention to hide so far as he could his real feelings when he was in the presence of the Prince of Wales, and Edward was misled to some extent by the Prime Minister's avuncular manner. Had he known just how profoundly Baldwin detested him, he would have been both startled and at the same time better prepared for the events to come.

Long before the old King died, when Baldwin first heard of Edward's love for Mrs. Simpson, he had made a significant comment. He had been discussing with opposition leaders the future of the monarchy and he said meaningly, "The Yorks will do it very well," referring to the Duke and Duchess of York who were next in line to the throne after the Prince of Wales.

At the Accession Council where the new King was presented to Princes of the Blood Royal, present and former Cabinet Ministers, Privy Councillors and others, Baldwin was plainly unhappy. He muttered to Clement Attlee his grave doubts about the future, and doubted whether the new King "would stay the course."

Stanley Baldwin was nearly seventy. He was popular in the country, the astutest politician alive, with an unerring sense of timing. He enjoyed being considered the physical embodiment of John Bull, professed to dislike politicians, and liked to imagine himself as a simple countryman, although in fact he hardly knew one tree from another. This artifice produced in his attitude to events a sort of double focus, one public, one private. His public attitude was bluff, honest, forthright. His private attitude was distrustful. His private aims were often good, sometimes bad, and in order to achieve them he did not hesitate to deceive the public, deceive his friends, deceive everybody, in fact, except himself. To his Cabinet Ministers and in time to the public he became the man determined officially to do all in his power to help the King solve his personal crisis "even if we have to see the night through together." But when the crisis broke, friends of his who could see behind the mask realized that his private aim was exactly and diametrically the reverse. He was determined from the start to remove Edward and install his favorites, the Yorks, in his place.

Other people besides Baldwin saw in the impending crisis a convenient field over which to fight personal battles of their own. Lord Beaverbrook, proprietor of the powerful newspapers, *Daily Express, Sunday Express* and *Evening Standard,* was then carrying on a serio-comic vendetta with Baldwin. Beaverbrook blamed the Prime Minister for the rejection of his pet economic policy known as Empire Free Trade. The King's affair gave him a golden opportunity to get back into the fight. By backing the King in any struggle he might have with the Prime Minister, Beaverbrook thought he might have a chance of forcing Baldwin out and Empire Free Trade in. Both men had become used to playing politics with each other. Had they been able to foresee the enormity of the forthcoming crisis, they would probably have been less lighthearted about it. Winston Churchill, by his friendship with the King was also brought into the picture, and he too was eager for a fight. He was now far out in the political wilderness, his fortunes at as low an ebb as they had ever been. As a sincere and emotional monarchist, he had a strong sympathy for the King's plight, and was ready to join any battle on the King's side. If the battle was to be against Stanley Baldwin, so much the better.

And in the privacy of Fort Belvedere the King and Wallis were making plans of their own, plans that looked ahead to one glorious moment when the crown of the Queen of England would be placed upon Mrs. Simpson's head. It must have seemed that the philosophy of the song of François Villon, which had sustained them through eighteen enraptured months of love, had at last come true:

> *If I were King, ah love, if I were King*
> *What tributary nations I would bring,*
> *To stoop before your sceptre and to swear*
> *Allegiance to your eyes, your lips, your hair.*
> *The stars would be your pearls upon a string,*
> *The world a ruby for your finger ring,*
> *And you should have the sun and moon to wear*
> *If I were King.*

But the King was an amateur at political intrigue. He had been the idolized prince too long and it was the only role he knew how to fill. He did not appreciate the forces about to be unleashed under him: Baldwin out to "get" him; Beaverbrook out to get Baldwin; Churchill pawing on the side lines, and below these men, spiralling downwards, plots and sub-plots among politicians and courtiers. Caught in the middle of these powerful professionals, the obstinate, bewitched King and his friend were like babes among the wolves.

They had their chances, but the end is well known. Baldwin got rid of the King. England got rid of Baldwin. The King got Mrs. Simpson and lost his crown, and, in a way, was satisfied even amid the wreck of his dreams. The real loser was Wallis Simpson, who emerged without friends or country, with a husband in disfavor, and a title that mocked her with its indignity.

VII

Mrs. Simpson's Short
but Memorable Reign

"Mrs. Simpson's invitations came to rank as commands. . . . Her position in London is without precedent in history for an American. Nor have those who politically preceded her been remotely like her."

That is the context in which Mrs. Simpson liked to imagine herself. It was written for *The New Yorker* by Janet Flanner, undoubtedly with Mrs. Simpson's permission, and managed to tell the story of Mrs. Simpson's relationship with the King without mentioning either the King or the relationship.

It described Wallis in the full bloom of her reign. From the Baltimore boarding house on East Biddle Street she had now risen to the point where her foot was on the first step of the British throne. The question being asked by politicians, courtiers, foreign ambassadors was: What next?

The King had become two persons, one person when the enigmatic figure of Mrs. Simpson was at his side, and another person altogether when she was gone. The first Edward was assertive, wayward; his ministers found him difficult to handle. He antagonized his staff, especially his private secretary, Major Alex Hardinge, the most unbendingly English of all his counselors. Mrs. Simpson helped him, said *Time Magazine* "to spend thousands of guineas royally, imperially, wildly. . . . Simultaneously she caught His Majesty's servants spending too much for things like bath soap and King Edward sacked retainers right and left on her lightest say-so."

His toughness was inconsistent, haphazard. State documents were left lying around at Fort Belvedere, often mislaid. German Foreign Office heads boasted to British officials in Berlin that thanks to the King's absent-mindedness they knew all Britain's secrets. The King seemed uncaring about anything except Mrs. Simpson.

Away from her he would deflate. He would brood. He neglected his two adoring nieces, Princess Elizabeth and Princess Margaret, making plans with them, then forgetting all about them.

After the manner of lovers, his ways matched those of Mrs. Simpson. He watched her happily as she laughed, joked, talked, spreading her strong expressive hands in acute, sharply defined gestures. Then the King would be restored to his old, bouncy self. Caught in a downpour he was overheard to shout, "Come on, Wallis, let's dodge the raindrops," and he sprinted for his royal Daimler dragging along the protesting Mrs. Simpson.

In private they made their plans. The object was clear, definite and admittedly remote. It was to establish Mrs. Simpson as Queen of England. No compromise was contemplated. It would be done gradually, treading carefully, a step at a time, winning bit by bit the favor of the country, the Empire, the Church, Queen Mary and Parliament. The difficulties in the way were great, but the King held the one trump card. He was the King, and a Coronation was coming up. England would never get rid of her King.

The first step was to make Mrs. Simpson socially acceptable. To do that he invited her and her husband to a dinner party at St. James's Palace, and on May 27, 1936, Mrs. Simpson's name was dignified for the first time in the Court Circular. The guests were an unusual combination. They included Lord and Lady Louis Mountbatten and Lady Cunard, friends and courtiers of the King and Mr. and Mrs. Simpson; Mr. and Mrs. Stanley Baldwin; Colonel Charles Lindbergh, with his wife, just back from an eye-opening tour of Germany, and even then warning British officials that England could never stand up to Germany's air might.

The idea was to break the barrier between Baldwin and Mrs. Simpson. It failed. They could find nothing in common, and to Mrs. Baldwin even more than her husband, the personality of Mrs. Simpson was alien and totally incomprehensible. The thought that this American woman had stolen the heart of her King was shocking to her, and Baldwin's dislike of the King was too deep to be bridged at a dinner party.

The King persisted. On July ninth, Mrs. Simpson's name appeared in the Court Circular again very modestly and this time alone. It was the occasion of another dinner party, and a more formal one than the first. The Circular read:

> The King gave a dinner party at York House this evening, at which the Duke and Duchess of York were present. The following had the honour of being invited:
>
> The Marquess and Marchioness of Willingdon, the Lady Diana Cooper, the Earl and Countess Stanhope, the Countess of Oxford and Asquith, Major the Hon. Alexander and Mrs. Hardinge, the Right Hon. Winston Spencer-Churchill, M.P., and Mrs. Spencer-Churchill, the Right Hon. Sir Samuel Hoare, Bt., M.P., and the Lady Maude Hoare, the Right Hon. Sir Philip Sassoon, Bt., M.P., Captain the Right Hon. David Margesson, M.P., Sir Edward and Lady Peacock, Lady Colefax and Mrs. Ernest Simpson.

Ernest Simpson was absent. Twelve days later on July twenty-first, he went to the Hotel de Paris in the village of Bray, near Maidenhead, and spent the night there with a lady named Buttercup.

The parties took Mrs. Simpson no further than she had already come, but still the initiative rested with the King. Baldwin understood the importance of the King's affair, but he was a man who hated to make decisions before he had to and, not for the first or last time in his career, he decided to do nothing. He took the train to Aix where he went religiously every year and settled down to a happy holiday taking the water.

The King decided to take a holiday, too, and it proved to be an eventful one. The traditional royal vacations enjoyed by his father at Balmoral had little attraction for him and he chose, instead, the Mediterranean. Originally he had planned to stay on the Riviera at the home of the actress, Maxine Elliott, but France was being torn by strikes and the British Ambassador in Paris advised against it.

The King then decided on a cruise, but instead of using the royal yacht the *Victoria and Albert,* he hired the use of the *Nahlin,* a luxury yacht owned by Lady Yule. It was semi-officially explained that the forty-seven-hundred-ton *Victoria and Albert* could not negotiate the shallower waters of the Mediterranean as well as the sixteen-hundred-ton *Nahlin;* all the same a lot of eyebrows, those sensitive arcs of public opinion, were raised at this latest decision of the modern-minded King. Many felt that Edward was once more turning his back ostentatiously on the set ways of his father. The *Victoria and Albert* was slow and old-fashioned. The *Nahlin* was the last word in luxury yachts. John Brown of Glasgow, makers of the *Queens,* had built the ship six years before at a cost of $720,000. It had a gymnasium, a dance floor, a bathroom for each of its eight staterooms. It could do more than twenty knots.

This went part of the way to explaining the King's preference, but the *Nahlin* had another advantage less widely known. Its fifty crew members had been particularly selected for their sense of discretion. Lady Yule, regarded until her death in 1950 as the richest woman in England, detested publicity, and she had a captain who once went so far as to tell an Australian reporter, "We have come from nowhere. We are going nowhere."

The cruise of the *Nahlin* was a milestone pointing in many directions. It marked the high point and the end of Mrs. Simpson's social reign in London. It coincided with the breakup of the marriage between Simpson and Wallis. It precipitated the crisis which from then on progressed nonstop to the Abdication.

Mrs. Simpson, of course, was invited to join the party. Ernest Simpson —now occasionally referred to inside the privileged circle as "the unknown gentleman"—was not. The home in Bryanston Square was broken up, Simpson moving quietly into the Guards Club, and Mrs. Simpson negotiating for some other place to live on her return.

The guests were the King's closest friends, in effect his social court. They included Dickie and Edwina Mountbatten; Duff Cooper and Lady Diana Cooper; Lord Brownlow, a Lord in Waiting and Lord Lieutenant of Lincolnshire, and his wife Kitty; Sir John Aird, an equerry; Colonel Humphrey Butler, a handsome, well-known sportsman, and his wife, the former Gwendolyn Van Raalte; Lady Cunard; Sir Godfrey Thomas, one of the King's assistant private secretaries; the Honorable Mrs. Helen Fitzgerald, Canadian wife of Evelyn Fitzgerald, a London stockbroker; Herman and Katherine Rogers; and Mrs. Gladys Buist, wife of Commander Colin Buist, R.N., an equerry, subsequently equerry to King George VI, and extra equerry to Elizabeth II.

When the crisis was over, this court was to be roasted in a broadcast by the Archbishop of Canterbury in terms so strong that one nobleman threatened him with a libel action. The Archbishop gave him a spoken apology but refused to confirm it in writing, and the matter was dropped.

"An exotic society" the *Times* was to call it. Actually, although the King under the influence of Mrs. Simpson had largely broken with his father's intimates, his choice of friends was not very revolutionary. The subsequent wrath was directed mainly against Mrs. Simpson herself, and against Emerald Cunard, who was blamed by the Royal Family for doing most to bring the two together.

What probably damned the court above all was the simple secret that it shared. Everybody aboard the *Nahlin* knew that the King loved Mrs. Simpson. They were aware of the delicacy of the situation and must or ought to have foreseen the clouds of trouble piling up for them in England. But none could have guessed that within a few months there would be a new King on the throne of England and both the King and Mrs. Simpson would be more or less in hiding in different parts of Europe. For them this relationship clearly had some semblance of permanency, and some of them at least may have thought that in paying court to Mrs. Simpson they were paying court to their future Queen.

On August ninth the King was flown by his pilot, Wing-Commander Edward (now Air Vice Marshal Sir Edward) Fielden, from a private field in Middlesex, to Calais. He traveled incognito, under his recurring, ostrichlike delusion that the stratagems of ordinary people could also disguise a King. Officially he was the "Duke of Lancaster." The destination of the *Nahlin* was officially stated to be the Baltic. Nobody was misled for a moment.

He was seen entering the Orient Express. He was seen and photographed with Mrs. Simpson at Salzburg. He was seen to leave the train at Sibenik in Yugoslavia. The press followed him everywhere. Most of the party went on board the *Nahlin* at Sibenik, the exceptions being Herman and Katherine Rogers who joined it in Athens.

The cruise became the biggest holiday attraction in Europe. The sight of the *Nahlin* in port, no matter where, was the signal for hordes of sight-seers to cram the docks. The Europeans had heard much more than the British about Mrs. Simpson, and were eager for a sight of her.

One man noted the excitement with a troubled mind. Sir Samuel Hoare, First Lord of the Admiralty, was also on a Mediterranean tour in the naval yacht, *Enchantress,* with the object of inspecting British bases at Gibraltar and Malta. At one point the *Nahlin* and the *Enchantress* passed each other. Hoare noticed the excitement of his ship's crew, which had also been picked for its discretion, and he realized for the first time that Englishmen as well as foreigners were beginning to learn the truth. He reminded himself to tell the Prime Minister on his return to England.

Cheering crowds followed the royal party every time they stepped ashore. In the brown fortress town of Trogir in Yugoslavia, a horde of students swarmed round the King and Mrs. Simpson as they walked hand in hand through the narrow streets, cheering them on their way. In Dubrovnik, Mrs. Simpson and Lady Diana Cooper, venturing out on a shopping expedition, saw crowds of people sweeping Edward away down the street amid cheers of "Long Live the King." The breathless, laughing Edward managed to exchange waves with the two ladies but could not stop. At quieter moments the King and Wallis were able to go swimming together off the Adriatic shore (and were filmed doing so). They rowed together (and were filmed again). They strolled through quiet villages, sometimes unrecognized.

From Yugoslavia to Greece: they were driven in style through the streets of Athens, Mrs. Simpson in the same car as the King. One night they made the rounds of the Athens night clubs and danced until three A.M.

The King also went through the motions of his royal duties. He had visited Prince Paul in Yugoslavia. Now he visited General Metaxas and King George of Greece. He inspected the Greek Navy. At the next stop, Istanbul, he was greeted by Kemal Ataturk. Then the royal party left the boat and set out across Europe by rail.

On the way back the party stopped at Vienna, went to the opera and saw "Götterdämmerung," starring Kirsten Flagstad. The King, bored, left the box at one point. Mrs. Simpson went after him and brought him back in time for the final applause.

In the European as well as the American press every activity of the King and Mrs. Simpson was reported in detail. The British press remained silent; even the photographs of the King's progress through the Mediterranean almost invariably showed him alone. Cabinet ministers and Foreign Office officials remaining at home were aghast at the publicity the King's holiday had received. On September fourteenth, the King returned to England, his reputation seriously prejudiced. The rest of the party followed unobtrusively. Stanley Baldwin was still at Aix, and the atmosphere back in England was like the last moments of silence before a great offensive.

Mrs. Simpson went straight to London to organize her life in a new home. She had taken, on an eight months' lease at $160 a week, a furnished, eight-room house at No. 16 Cumberland Terrace, Regent's Park. It was a charming place designed by Nash during the reign of George IV and owned by Cuthbert Steward, a London stockbroker, with a huge lounge decorated in Italian style and a drawing room overlooking the park.

The charged air which Mrs. Simpson now breathed was not the most conducive to sober reflection. The *Nahlin* cruise had been the greatest incident of her life so far. She had progressed up the ladder until she had come face to face with vistas at which ambition reeled, a cloudland of thrones, kings, princes, empires. Kemal Ataturk in Turkey and Metaxas in Greece had treated her like a queen. It was what she had heard over and over again from some of her intimate friends. One woman, in particular, the American wife of a diplomatic official, had kept pressing into her consciousness long before the *Nahlin* trip: "You can be Queen. You are bound to be Queen." It seemed to be King Edward's ambition coming true. Mrs. Simpson was no longer in command of herself.

The King, sensing the Whitehall chill, dined quietly with his mother. Queen Mary gave no sign that she was conscious of the trouble in the air, though she obviously knew all there was to know. Before he died King George V had frankly discussed with the Archbishop of Canterbury, Dr. Cosmo Lang, the matter of his son's friendship, and the Archbishop was convinced that anxiety had hastened the King's death. The Queen Mother must have been deeply disturbed.

There was a moment during the dinner when spirits were lifted. The King told his mother he intended to spend the last two weeks of September at Balmoral, and he saw at once how pleased she was. The Queen probably felt that even Edward could not get into trouble at Balmoral. If she did, she was quite wrong. At Balmoral the King got himself into very serious trouble indeed, and Mrs. Simpson was, of course, the cause of it.

Wallis had not accompanied the King to Scotland. She had been kept in London to deal with the business of moving into a new house and completing arrangements for a divorce. The King had been at Balmoral for four restless days before she was able to join him. She traveled north by train with Herman and Katherine Rogers, and at Aberdeen Station she met the King who had driven from Balmoral to meet them. He smoked a pipe and was muffled, but hundreds of Aberdonians watched him as he helped Mrs. Simpson into the front seat beside him, and the Rogers climbed in behind. Meanwhile, only a short distance away, the Duke and Duchess of York, "on the King's behalf" opened some new buildings of the Royal Infirmary.

It was this which enraged Aberdeen. The newspapers remained tactfully silent, but anger at the King for apparently neglecting his duties in order to meet his woman friend was city-wide and profound. Some demonstrators, combining Anglo-Saxon preciseness with Celtic fire, chalked offensive epithets on the wall. The anger, instead of subsiding, grew, until months later, long after the Abdication, the Provost of Aberdeen issued a corrective statement which did something—not much—to appease the citizens. "Months before the opening date of the Infirmary," the Provost said, "I was in communication with the King through the Scottish Office and the reply I received was to the effect that owing to Court mourning the King had decided he could not perform any such ceremony as the opening of the Royal Infirmary . . . At the same time he was so interested in the opening that he had deputed the Duke and Duchess of York to act for him . . . The fact that Mrs. Simpson arrived in Aberdeen on the same day that the Duke and Duchess of York opened the building was a mere coincidence and whatever may be said about the King's action in coming to Aberdeen on that day it in no way involved any breach of agreement."

At Balmoral the King let the word fall that he intended to cut the domestic staff, and his popularity waned still further; the fond Scottish image of "Bonnie Prince Edward" became even more dim. The King had other things to think about. His *Nahlin* friends had gathered round him for the last time. Mrs. Simpson, the Mountbattens, the Rogers, Mrs. Gladys Buist and her husband were all there. So was the Duke of Kent and his beautiful wife. The Duke and Duchess of York were also there. Nobody ever learned what *they* thought about it.

The King put on the kilt and played the bagpipes. With Mrs. Simpson he tramped the moors round the castle, and one can guess the endless discussions they had about tactics and strategy, how to handle Mrs. Simpson's divorce which was to come up within a month, and how they were to present their position to the British people when the time came.

Taking advantage of a postwar regulation enabling people for the first time in undefended suits to obtain divorces outside London, Mrs. Simpson, on the advice of her lawyers, had taken a small villa called Beech House, near Felixstowe. By establishing residence there she could have her case heard quickly and quietly in the less frenzied atmosphere of Ipswich. Or so she hoped.

By the end of the month, when the royal party was due to return south, a plan of campaign had gradually been evolved. It was a hazardous plan, but if it succeeded, it would end with the crowning of Mrs. Simpson as Queen. Tense but confident the King and Mrs. Simpson left Balmoral to face the battle in London. King Edward VIII never saw Balmoral again.

Mrs. Simpson was installed at Beech House, Felixstowe. From Fort

Belvedere and Buckingham Palace the King sent her supplies of pots, pans and household accessories. Mrs. Mason, the King's personal house-keeper, was dispatched from Buckingham Palace to keep her comfortable, and David Storier, of Scotland Yard, the King's personal bodyguard, to keep her safe. He also sent her something special in the way of presents. It was a big, black Canadian-built Buick, the last word in speed and luxury. With it he sent his chauffeur, George Ladbrook. Mrs. Simpson was thus royally provided for, and what is more she was never out of the sight of the King's servants. With the divorce so imminent the two dared not see each other. Even the King, who recklessly ignored everything and everybody to be near Wallis, realized that, and he fretted alone at the Fort, calling her several times a day for her much-needed counsel and to hear the sound of her voice. Mrs. Simpson never let him down. She was always encouraging, never despondent.

But the strain was very great. Baldwin, they knew, had cut short his holiday at Aix, an important act for a man so set in his ways. They knew he had done so strictly because of the crisis they had created, but they did not know what he intended to do next. The day after he arrived the King summoned him to Buckingham Palace, but Baldwin made no reference to the affair, and the King was left in suspense.

Already Edward was beginning to sag. He performed his royal duties erratically and without enthusiasm. On October nineteenth he invited friends—all male—for the partridge shooting at Sandringham. Sir Samuel Hoare was invited. Hoare, a silent witness to more than one of the King's activities, noticed how nervous the King was. On the first night of the four-day party the blow fell.

The telephone rang at Beech House, and the King told Mrs. Simpson the news. Baldwin had asked for an audience. The King had invited him to join the party at Sandringham, but Baldwin had asked to be allowed to decline the invitation on the grounds that it would be too conspicuous. This was obviously the opening of hostilities—of Baldwin's malevolent intentions neither Mrs. Simpson nor the King had any doubt whatever.

The King agreed to meet him quietly at Fort Belvedere the following morning. He rose shortly after dawn. The other guests were still sleeping when he went down to his car. He left word that the party should go on without him, and set out without security escort across the flat country-side of East Anglia.

All morning Mrs. Simpson waited at Felixstowe for news of the meeting. It was nearly midday before she heard the King's voice, and the report he gave her was encouraging. The King had drawn some optimistic conclusions from the first encounter. He did not know how widespread the alliance against him had already become.

Baldwin did not tell the King that he had spent the week end at the home of Lord Fitzalan. Among the guests had been Alex Hardinge and Lord Kemsley, the press lord. Together they had discussed the King's affair. In consequence Baldwin arrived not only with the latest information, but conscious also that he had the support of the King's private secretary and of the newspaper proprietor most closely identified with the interests of the Royal Family.

From the beginning Baldwin left no doubt as to the reason for the interview. "You remember, Sir," he said directly, "when we came from Folkestone together you said I might speak freely to you about everything. Does that hold good when there is a woman in the case?"

"Yes," said the King suspiciously.

Baldwin's manner became fatherly. He did not mention marriage but suggested that the King persuade Mrs. Simpson not to continue with her divorce action in view of the criticism in the American press and its effect on the monarchy both in Britain and the Empire.

Edward's manner became casual and lighthearted. "Mr. Baldwin," he said. "I have no right to interfere with the affairs of an individual. It would be wrong were I to attempt to influence Mrs. Simpson just because she happens to be a friend of the King's."

The reply sounded a model of judiciousness, rather as though the King and Baldwin were discussing the problem of two other people. Neither was letting his feelings show, and both were deluded to some extent by the other's attitude. Baldwin thought the King had taken his point of view to heart. The King thought he could keep the matter personal and away from the public. It was an odd conclusion for a man who had spent a lifetime in the center of the world spotlight.

The King and Mrs. Simpson were now ready for the second crisis, which they felt would probably come after the divorce hearing. Next time they would be tougher and force Baldwin into a corner. They would have been much less optimistic if they had known what Baldwin was really thinking. The Prime Minister had resolved to play his careful double game, one in public, one in secret. He understood his own difficulties better than the King and Mrs. Simpson understood theirs. When he left the King, he went first to consult his close friend, Geoffrey Dawson, editor of the *Times*. Then he called on Queen Mary. The Queen Mother had moved from Buckingham Palace and was assembling her antiques in the more intimate atmosphere of Marlborough House. "Well, Mr. Baldwin," she is reported to have declared as he entered to discuss the matter with her, "this is a pretty kettle of fish." And in the course of the subsequent conversation Stanley Baldwin was left in no doubt that the Queen Mother was on his side all the way.

VIII

A Window Is Broken

Hardly a word had appeared in the British press about Mrs. Simpson. Not a single word had discussed her love affair with the King. Yet some kind of jungle rhythm was spreading her name across the nation. Mrs. Simpson found this out personally and for the first time when she took the risk of leaving her refuge in Felixstowe to return to London.

Her divorce hearing was imminent, and she decided it was safe to go to Bond Street and have her hair done in preparation for the ordeal. It seemed to be a reasonable risk, but just in case of trouble, she took Storier of the Yard along with her. Ladbrook drove them both to town in the Buick.

She was justified in taking the precaution. A group of newspapermen had been warned in advance of her arrival, probably by some contact or other inside the beauty parlor, and were waiting for her outside. Some pictures were taken, but Storier was able to hustle her indoors without too much trouble. That was the start. Crowds began to gather in Bond Street. The word traveled quickly and accurately: "Mrs. Simpson's inside!" The name and its significance was only vaguely understood by most people, but it was familiar in a disquieting way, and they knew it had something to do with the King. A few in the crowd were wise. In reply to the inevitable, puzzled question of the uninitiated, they said, "She's our next Queen."

Soon hundreds of people were waiting in the street for a glimpse of the mystery woman. Inside the beauty parlor, Mrs. Simpson became frightened and asked Storier what he intended to do. The detective found that there was a back exit, and when Mrs. Simpson's appointment was over an hour and a half later, he sent word out to Ladbrook to take the car round. Ladbrook did, and the crowd followed. Mrs. Simpson, unaware that Storier's plan had failed, emerged and there was a buzz of excitement. Flustered and taken by surprise, Wallis got hastily into the car. She remembered that her bank was just round the corner and ordered the car there. She stayed in the safety of the manager's office until the people finally dispersed. Then she was driven back to Felixstowe.

This was the first of many adventures during two cloak-and-dagger months in the life of George Ladbrook, chauffeur of the King, usually a job which stifles even the most respectable of drivers with its decorum. Ladbrook was a forty-year-old, six-foot, two-hundred-pound giant from Essex, and he held for the King a philosophical English loyalty which he was to demonstrate many times in the years to come.

On October twenty-seventh, a few days after the incident in Bond Street, he was given by the King as tough an assignment as any chauffeur outside a Hollywood movie could be expected to take on. He had to drive Mrs. Simpson from Felixstowe to Ipswich for her divorce hearing and away from Ipswich afterwards, avoiding newspapermen and keeping her out of trouble.

Several days before the hearing was due, newspapermen, most of them Americans, had begun to arrive in town, crowding the hotels, inns and boarding houses. English reporters were arriving, too. Both were preoccupied with unique problems.

In America, interest in the attachment of the British King for Mrs. Simpson was insatiable and was reaching a climax with the divorce action. All of a sudden the Americans had become experts on British divorce procedure. They knew that the King would be free to marry Mrs. Simpson before the Coronation, and were agog to see what would happen next. In Britain, on the other hand, the press lords, for the first and last time in modern newspaper history agreed to suppress all news of the affair, hoping to stave off or avert a crisis too strange and rare for them to visualize clearly. They had done so because the King had appealed to some of them personally. "Mrs. Simpson is being pilloried," he said, "because she is my friend," and he asked that they treat her divorce as they would treat the divorce of any other American woman. The press lords believed him. No other public figure in this age has been treated with so much sensitivity. Speculation all through 1953 in the British as well as the American press on the love problems of Princess Margaret presents the most vivid comparison. Beaverbrook, Rothermere, Kemsley, Camrose and the rest paid for their gullibility in the end, because the King, far from being grateful, came, when the storm broke, to detest the British press.

The British newspapermen arriving in Ipswich were there largely as observers, a decorous role that made little appeal to them. The American foreign correspondents had problems all of their own and felt little enthusiasm for the advantage they held over their British cousins. Foreign correspondents all over the world rely heavily on local newspapers for information. Without local newspapers they are often lost. In this case they were not getting any news at all out of the British newspapers and were having to go out and work for the story as they had not done since they were ordinary reporters.

To Ipswich townspeople nothing could have been more mystifying than this harassed, somber gathering of British and American newspapermen. For them it was a holiday. Once more the mental tom-toms were at work, and the town was jammed with people who seemed to know by instinct that Mrs. Simpson was going to put in an appearance.

Policemen were everywhere, scrutinizing everyone who tried to get into the courthouse. For the first time in memory, local Ipswich members of the bar were denied free access to the courtroom, and even the Mayor, himself an Ipswich magistrate, was held up until he identified himself.

Newsreel cameramen who tried to set up their equipment near the court were moved away. One newsreel group had hired a room overlooking the court, but the police heard about it and took the room over. Tickets were issued to thirty reporters. One New York newspaperman arriving at the last moment was unable to get a ticket. Shortly before two o'clock in the afternoon he clambered over an eight-foot wall into the court precincts. A policeman was waiting underneath for him as he came down.

Inside the courtroom the public seats had been rearranged so that all those which faced the witness in the box were left vacant. Admission was made only to a few seats to which the witness's back was turned. The press seats had also been changed. Normally in British courts the press seats are set so that the reporters face the witness box. The reporters permitted to enter the courtroom found that they, too, had been placed so that they could only see the witness's back.

Mrs. Simpson was wise enough not to come from Felixstowe in her telltale Buick. Instead she hired a sober but fast English car. On the road to Ipswich a photographer's car lying in wait started in pursuit, but by the time it hit sixty-five miles an hour, Ladbrook had left it miles behind. Outside the courthouse, as the car slowed into the garage, a photographer broke the police barrier. A policeman smashed the camera out of his hand, and a police boot kicked it into the gutter.

The Judge, Sir John (Anthony) Hawke, arrived at two seventeen. Hawke had served from 1923 to 1928 as Attorney General to the Prince of Wales, but this was strictly coincidental. He had seen and had clearly been disgusted with the security precautions outside. And he did not know what was going on inside. The door of the counsels' robing room was locked on lawyers engaged in other cases, preventing them from entering the courtroom. A cold in the head did not improve Hawke's temper. The case of "Simpson versus Simpson" was called and Norman Birkett, K.C., on behalf of Mrs. Simpson, rose to say:

"I appear in this case with my learned friend Mr. Walter Frampton. I call the petitioner at once." Mrs. Simpson, looking pale but controlled, in a blue suit and a small, jaunty hat, went into the witness box. A chair had been provided for her, although by the normal practice of the time a woman testifying in her own divorce case was usually required to stand.

In deference to the King's wishes the British press next morning gave the case a minimum of space. The American press covered it in detail, and it is from American newspaper files that the writer gets his picture.

Mrs. Simpson repeated the oath after the clerk, and Norman Birkett began questioning her smoothly and gently:

"Your names are Wallis Simpson? You are now living at Beech House, Felixstowe?"

"Yes."

"Is your town address 16 Cumberland Terrace, Regent's Park?"

"Yes."

"You were married to Ernest Aldrich Simpson on July 21, 1928 at the Registry Office in the District of Chelsea?"

"Yes."

"And I think that afterwards you lived with him at 12 Upper Berkeley Street and 5 Bryanston Court in London?"

"Yes."

"Has there been any issue of that marriage?"

"No."

"Did you live happily with the Respondent until the autumn of 1934?"

"Yes."

"Was it at that time the Respondent's manner changed?"

"Yes."

"What was the change?"

"He was indifferent, and often went away week ends."

[76]

"On Christmas Day, 1934, did you find a note lying on your dressing table?"

"Yes."

The note was produced and handed to the judge. Mrs. Simpson then said that shortly after Easter she received a letter in an envelope addressed to her although the contents appeared to be intended for her husband.

"Having read the letter," Birkett continued, "did you then consult your solicitor?"

"Yes."

"Upon your instructions did they keep observations on your husband?"

"Yes."

"Did they report to you on the result of their observations?"

"Yes."

"Did you subsequently receive information on which your petition in this present case is based?"

"Yes."

Birkett then asked Mrs. Simpson to read a letter which she had written to her husband. She read it quietly but clearly:

"Dear Ernest, I have just learned that while you have been away, instead of being on business as you led me to believe, you have been staying at a hotel at Bray with a lady. I am sure you must realize that this is conduct which I cannot possibly overlook and I must insist that you do not continue to live here with me. This only confirms suspicions which I have had for a long time. I am therefore instructing my solicitors to take proceedings for a divorce. Wallis."

Evidence was produced from employees of the fashionable Hotel de Paris at Bray. They said they had brought morning tea to Simpson, and a woman who was not Mrs. Simpson was with him in a double bed. There must be no provable collusion in an English divorce case and judges usually demand the name of the "other woman." As the evidence continued and reporters waited in vain for the name to be produced, the atmosphere in the court grew more tense. When Birkett finally asked the court to grant the decree nisi of divorce, it was realized that Birkett did not intend to introduce the name at all.

Sir John Hawke, his handkerchief over his streaming nose, had not bothered to hide his distaste for the whole proceeding, and had plainly indicated his belief that the case had been brought to Ipswich just to avoid publicity.

"Well," said Hawke, "I suppose I must come to the conclusion that there was adultery in this case." There was a pause.

MR. BIRKETT: I assume what your Lordship has in mind.

MR. JUSTICE HAWKE: How do you know what is in my mind? What is it that I have in my mind, Mr. Birkett?

MR. BIRKETT: I think with great deference that your Lordship may have in mind what is known as "ordinary hotel evidence" where the name of the lady is not disclosed. With respect I thought that might have been in your Lordship's mind.

MR. JUSTICE HAWKE: That is what it must have been, Mr. Birkett. I am glad of your help.

MR. BIRKETT: The lady's name, My Lord, was mentioned in the petition.* So now I ask for a decree nisi with costs against the Respondent.

MR. JUSTICE HAWKE: Yes, costs against the Respondent, I am afraid. I suppose I must in these unusual circumstances. So you may have it with costs.

MR. BIRKETT: Decree nisi, with costs?

MR. JUSTICE HAWKE: Yes, I suppose so.

It was over in exactly nineteen minutes. Mrs. Simpson was escorted to her car. The newspapermen started to leave but a second case was brought in so quickly that they had no time to get out of the courtroom. The ushers stopped them and called loudly for silence. The reporters complained later that the doors had been locked until Mrs. Simpson's car was gone. As soon as they were released, they made a dash for the crowded street, and then they discovered they had missed nothing.

Ladbrook had taken the car out of the courtyard and had set off for Felixstowe. Press cars started after him, but a police car swung across the road and blocked the route. Mrs. Simpson's getaway was clean.

No investigation was ever made into the unprecedented and unnecessary precautions taken in the Simpson divorce case, precautions seriously at odds with the traditions of British freedom. Nor was it ever officially revealed who gave instructions to the police to be so tough with the reporters. Sir John Hawke was not a party to it, and no official agencies were at the King's command in his private love affair. Theodore Goddard, Mrs. Simpson's solicitor, was certainly the man most directly responsible. It is likely that he approached the police at Ipswich and plausibly suggested the course which they took. But it is also difficult to avoid the conclusion that the ultimate responsibility lay inside Buckingham Palace. The whole affair savors strongly of the way in which the King was conducting these affairs, and it suggests that the King had a very small regard for the word of honour of the British press lords.

* It was a Mrs. E. H. Kennedy, known as "Buttercup."

This incident ties in with many others to show that the King, despite his long training for the job, had only the vaguest notions of his own power. He did not understand his limitations, and gave orders which, although they might be obeyed, were backed by no authority.

In the end the police achieved nothing except to establish a somewhat sinister precedent. The Americans were not prevented from reporting the case in full, the police measures merely giving them added color material. The British press did not report the case in full, not because of the police but because of policy.

And even if policy had been different, the British press would have been inhibited in its reporting of the case by the Judicial Proceedings (Regulation of Reports) Act 1926 which banned the publication of anything other than a bare skeleton of the case. In other words, had the police taken no precautions at all, the British reports of the Simpson divorce case would have been exactly the same, and the American reports would have been less lurid. All the incident did was to give a misleading veneer of force to the King's cause, and this veneer was recalled with anxiety by some, a few weeks afterward, when Sir Oswald Mosley and his Blackshirts were demonstrating against Baldwin and in the King's favor in the East End.

With the divorce an accomplished fact the person of Mrs. Simpson paralyzed the administration of the country. In Buckingham Palace, Major Alexander Hardinge was reading a letter which had been shown to him by Geoffrey Dawson, summing up the state of opinion in America. Hardinge was horrified. He, more than any other of the King's advisers, was baffled by Mrs. Simpson's personality. Had she been an English-woman he would have known how to handle her. But for Hardinge, above all, her "Americanness," was an impossible barrier. He did not understand her thought processes nor the things she talked about. Hardinge was so worried by the information given him by Dawson that he spent a fortnight drafting a letter to the King, a letter which was to have vital consequences.

Mrs. Simpson's shadow also darkened the cabinet room at No. 10 Downing Street. Stanley Baldwin was face to face with an urgent and critical situation. The result of the divorce meant that the King would be free to marry Mrs. Simpson in six months' time when her decree nisi became absolute. This would only be about two weeks before his Coronation scheduled for May twelfth. Baldwin's predicament was made worse by the fact that no one could be quite certain of the King's rights. Nothing like this had ever happened before in England's history, and even the greatest experts on constitutional law could do no better than grope uncertainly through the legal darkness. The English journalist, Hannen Swaffer, has revealed* that Baldwin, in the strictest confidence, asked the only two lawyers in his administration for their opinion, and both were either afraid to answer or did not know. Later he put the question to an expert member outside his own party, and received the most discouraging answer. The member believed that the King could wed any woman of his choice. He thought that the action of Henry VII after the defeat and death of Richard III (1485) had established a precedent that the King could order her crowning or not as he chose.

It was possible, then, that the King had it in his power any time after April 27, 1937, to marry Mrs. Simpson without consulting anybody, then return to Buckingham Palace and summon his Cabinet to meet the empire's new Queen. It was one thing for Baldwin to deal with a King standing pat, as he was doing at the present time on a technical situation that might never happen. It was quite another to deal with a *fait accompli,* a King already married and on the throne. The problem as it presented itself to Baldwin's mind presupposed of course that the King, determined to marry the woman of his choice, would not hesitate to resort to any means in order to get Mrs. Simpson accepted as Queen.

Wallis returned to London. She had no more use for the house in Felixstowe. She was slightly unnerved, and at the same time exhilarated. She was bewildered by the furore in Ipswich, and staggered by the attention her affairs were receiving in America. She realized, possibly for the first time, that she was attracting more publicity than any other woman on earth. It was a position where the most hardheaded and logical of women would be carried away. She was forty years old and had never been a celebrity before, and it was all new and unbelievable. The effect on her was mixed. She was alternately flattered and frightened by it, pleased one moment, appalled the next. But all the time the crown and the throne hovered a measurable distance before her. It was a fairy tale come true.

Now she was able to see the King again. She moved to Fort Belvedere with Aunt Bessie, and the two lovers walked the gardens of the mansion combining in their conversation visions of romance, ambition realized and a glorious future.

Meanwhile the letter which Major Alexander Hardinge was assembling was completed. It was sent on November twelfth and reminded the King that if the Cabinet submitted advice and the King rejected it, the ministers must resign. He appealed to the King to send Mrs. Simpson out of the country. Baldwin knew that Hardinge was writing the letter

* *Daily Herald,* March 27, 1954.

and encouraged it. Before he submitted it Hardinge showed it for approval to Geoffrey Dawson, an unexpected act in this case for a man who is supposed to be the King's closest personal aide; at the same time a courageous act for an honourable man deeply disturbed.

Dawson was a character who was moving closer and closer into a picture which would seem to involve him only indirectly, as a journalist, if at all. He was a brilliant writer, and as editor of the *Times*, a newspaper over which the proprietor exercises no policy control, he was the most important journalist in Britain. In 1952, sixteen years after the Abdication, Dawson's part in the crisis was made the center of a controversy by a sensational broadcast which Lord Beaverbrook made over B.B.C. television. Beaverbrook was reviewing the fourth volume of the *History of the Times,* and, basing his conclusions exclusively on statements made in the appendix on the Abdication, asserted that, after Baldwin, Dawson was chiefly responsible for forcing the King to abdicate; that he did it "by methods many would condemn," and that "he pursued his quest with a vigour that seemed more like venom."

Beaverbrook described Dawson as "a man of middle height with a good head going bald . . . and a rather flushed face. He liked to dine in important company. He had an excellent taste in port wine . . . and could be depended on for three full glasses."

Dawson was sixty-one. He was conservative in outlook, discreet, untiring at his job, and snobbish. He seldom spoke to Labour M.P.'s and felt himself under no obligation to be polite to servants. He was cordial only to people whose company he liked. But the most important single fact about Dawson's character was that he lacked the courage of independence, and he was at his strongest when he attached himself to people whom he considered knew more than he. His first mentor had been Lord Milner, former British administrator in South Africa, who died in 1925. Later he attached himself to Lloyd George, and subsequently he was to become the devoted and adoring disciple of Lord Halifax. At that particular time he was lavishing his loyalty on two men, Stanley Baldwin and the Archbishop of Canterbury.

This habit was not unusual, of course, or even necessarily undesirable for a newspaper editor. Dawson's great predecessor on the *Times,* John Thadeus Delane, had been Lord Palmerston's protégé, and the friendship of important men has always been found invaluable to an editor. In the crisis coming up, however, Dawson's devotion to Baldwin became something more. The alliance between the Prime Minister and the editor of the *Times,* with the Archbishop of Canterbury lending his support in the background, gave the impression sometimes of an invincible force.

Whether or not Beaverbrook was justified in his attack, Dawson was the latest character to join the select group of personalities in this drama. To the talents of King Edward, Wallis Simpson, Stanley Baldwin, Lord Beaverbrook, Queen Mary, the Archbishop of Canterbury, he added his own gifts of clear thinking and the ability to write history in daily journalism, failing to add what, amid all this brilliance was possibly most needed and certainly most lacking, a sense of Christian charity.

Wallis disliked and feared Dawson above all. She had already read the innuendoes which he was inserting in the *Times* for her eyes and the King's eyes alone. To the still-ignorant public his references could have had little significance. One of his editorials, for example, appeared to deal with nothing more than the philosophy behind the appointment of a Governor-General to South Africa. But to Mrs. Simpson and the King the warning could not have been plainer:

> It is the position—the position of the King's deputy no less than that of the King himself—that must be kept high above public ridicule, and it is incomparably more important than the individual who fills it. The King's deputy like the King himself should be invested with a certain detachment and dignity, which need not at all preclude his contact with all sorts and conditions of people, but which are not so easily put on as a change of clothes.

Wallis and the King were furious about Hardinge's letter and guessed immediately that he had shown it to Baldwin or Dawson or both. The battle they knew was getting hotter, and the King sent for Baldwin.

He played his trump card and handed the Prime Minister an ultimatum. "No marriage, no Coronation," he said, and added, "I am going to marry Mrs. Simpson, and I am prepared to go." Baldwin said he found this "grievous news."

Edward, of course, had no intention of going. He knew something about the fate of ex-Kings. Some of his closest European relatives had been tumbled from their thrones and he had witnessed the living purgatory of their lives in exile in the dreary round of the Continental seaside resorts.

There could seldom have been a stranger contest than that now going on between Baldwin and the King. They were like two men with their backs to each other, firing at each other over their shoulders. The King was pretending that he was willing to go, and was in fact determined to stay. Baldwin was pretending that he wanted the King to stay, and was determined to make him go. The King believed that by his ultimatum he had put himself in an unassailable position. The opposite was true. He had put himself at Baldwin's mercy. Edward's battle slogan was "No marriage, no Coronation." Baldwin's was "The Yorks will do it very well." The two statements, instead of clashing, dovetailed. Added together they meant that the King was on the way out.

Stanley Baldwin drove straight from Buckingham Palace to the House of Commons, and asked Geoffrey Dawson to meet him there. Baldwin, Dawson reported later, looked exhausted.

The King, feeling himself surrounded by enemies, realized he needed help. He heard with dismay that Beaverbrook was on his way to the United States on the S.S. *Bremen* in his annual quest of winter sunshine, and appealed to him by cable to return. Beaverbrook replied that he would turn round with the ship. The King knew he could rely on the sober but powerful support of Lord Rothermere, and his son, Esmond Harmsworth.

The King then called on his family one by one, and told them the facts. George, the Duke of Kent, though he subsequently turned into an enemy, was sympathetic. The Duke of Gloucester was dazed. The Duke of York, face to face with the strong possibility of becoming King, was appalled. The King, leaving his brothers behind, then told his mother and begged her to meet Mrs. Simpson. The Queen refused and next day told Stanley Baldwin all about it.

The world's statesmen, briefed day by day by their London ambassadors, were following the developments enthralled. One of the few foreigners indelicate enough to try and intervene was Joachim von Ribbentrop, then the German ambassador in London, who felt himself an interested party. He had heard "from a reliable source" that Edward had declared he would consider the coming Coronation only side by side with ("zusammen mit") Mrs. Simpson. "I was very depressed and racked my brains for a possible way in which to influence the course of events," Ribbentrop wrote in his diary. "King Edward VIII had shown himself a potential advocate of Anglo-German understanding, therefore it lay in our interests that he should remain King." He asked for an audience, but the court advisers did not appear to feel that it was any of Ribbentrop's business. He was pointedly told—probably by Alex Hardinge—that the King was not at home. The palace door was slammed shut on outsiders; and the German ambassador, having made his little effort to nose his way in, bowed out.

Still the nation continued to go about its work unaware of the battle going on around its King. The business of the monarchy went on, the Court Circular announcing arrivals and departures. The King went abstractedly to South Wales to tour the distressed areas. To unemployed miners he made a comment. "Something must be done," he said, to ease their misfortune. It was a dangerous remark for a reigning King to make to desperate men, and it was received with horror in Whitehall. Was the fellow trying to start a civil war just to get his own way? The King protested. It was, he said later, the very least remark he could have made in the circumstances, but it was one into which could be read political significance, particularly in view of his conflict with the Prime Minister. Once more the King had blundered. Once more he had shown how not to be a King.

King Edward VII had been a King of grace and sophistication. King George V, according to his biographer, Harold Nicolson, never once said or did the wrong thing in his reign of quarter of a century. He was responsible for the widespread impression that being a King was easy. Now King Edward VIII was making it look too hard for a man to handle. He was blundering repeatedly, speaking out of turn, claiming rights for himself which no King could claim, giving orders he had no right to give, ignoring functions he should have performed, losing his head. The folly of his remark to the miners was soon revealed. First they felt elation at the thought that the King himself had taken note of their plight; then, when he abdicated in order to marry, apparently not caring who, if anybody, did the something that "must be done," they felt a personal sense of desertion, and bitterness against him in South Wales became very deep. The monarchy, which had been so powerful only a few months before when Edward came to the throne, was already shaky.

There was one consolation. Ministers had developed the habit of blaming Mrs. Simpson for all the King's mistakes. She could hardly be blamed for this one.

On the night of November 30, 1936, London glowed red with an evil omen of spectacular proportions. The Crystal Palace, built in 1851 by Prince Albert, went up in flames. It was a tremendous conflagration. The Abdication crisis had only a fortnight to go.

No one sensed the witchery in the air more clearly than Beaverbrook when he returned to England on November twenty-first. He found the King in terror of Geoffrey Dawson who he believed was holding an article attacking Mrs. Simpson, waiting for the right moment to print it. (Dawson wanted to break the press silence and use it just before Beaverbrook's return in order to spike the *Express* proprietor's guns; Baldwin dissuaded him.) Mrs. Simpson's emotions still careered from the heights to the depths, but she continued to give heart and combativeness to the King. Baldwin under the strain of the double game he was playing was almost at the end of his tether, buoyed up only by Dawson's support. So long as Mrs. Simpson went on holding up the King while Dawson held up Baldwin the battle would go on. The press lords, in fact, were briefing their editors to that effect, and were preparing to keep the story running up to and beyond Edward VIII's Coronation.

But now the King and Mrs. Simpson were full of a new idea, an idea which the author believes originated with Winston Churchill although it was subsequently credited to other sources. It was characteristically Churchillian, and it was just the solution Edward was seeking. The King acting as a private person would marry Mrs. Simpson morganatically. Mrs. Simpson would not take the rank of Queen, nor would her children, if any, succeed to the throne. But she would be the King's wife, probably with some title like the Duchess of Cornwall or the Duchess of Lancaster. The practice of morganatic marriage had been common enough in Continental countries, but what precedents applied in Britain were remote and vague.

The King sent for Baldwin on November twenty-fifth and put the idea to him. The Prime Minister had already heard about it from Esmond Harmsworth, and he was prepared for it. He warned the King cautiously that he did not give it much of a chance, but the King impatiently packed him off and told him to submit it to the Cabinet and the Dominions anyway.

Baldwin's forebodings were deep, and he had no intention of letting the King get out of the trap this way. His distrust of Mrs. Simpson was infinite. He guessed that she would never be content for long with the inferior position given her by morganatic marriage. He told the Cabinet of the King's proposal, and the same fear occurred to his ministers. Neville Chamberlain, the Chancellor of the Exchequer, went home and wrote in his diary, "I have no doubt that if it were possible to arrange a morganatic marriage it would be only a prelude to the further step of making Mrs. Simpson Queen with full rights." Sir John Simon, the Home Secretary, was even more emphatic. "The lady the King marries necessarily becomes Queen and her children would be in direct succession to the throne," he wrote.

Nevertheless this was probably Baldwin's severest moment. If the King insisted on the morganatic marriage proposal, Baldwin would be obliged to resign. The King would then ask Winston Churchill to form a government. Churchill would have to go to the country and there would then be an election which the King might well win, particularly if he presented his case as that of a lonely and modest man who wanted to marry and did not even seek to make the woman of his choice Queen.

From any point of view an election on such an issue would be a disaster to the nation and the monarchy.

The Archbishop of Canterbury had immediate views on the subject. Dr. Lang was being careful to avoid any direct involvement in the situation, but he did not hesitate to assert in private that the circumstances in which the King hoped to be crowned would make the ceremony meaningless. It would, he said, be "pouring all those sacred words into a vacuum."

The Government, however, was given very little time to deliberate on the matter because on December first the secret was let out. Newspapers seized on an oblique criticism of the King's church-going habits at the Diocesan Conference in Bradford to break to the nation for the first time the full story of the crisis, the King's love affair, and Mrs. Simpson. The criticism was made by the Bishop of Bradford, the Right Reverend A. W. F. Blunt, who later denied reports published at the time, that his speech had been approved in advance by the Archbishop of Canterbury.

Mrs. Simpson and the King were rocked by the sudden appearance of the story in every newspaper. "They don't want me," was the King's first mortified cry when he picked up the *Birmingham Post*. That night Beaverbrook called and told the King that the Cabinet had turned down the proposal for a morganatic marriage, that the facts were known in Fleet Street, and that the London press would come out with "sensational disclosures" on Thursday morning.

The world was collapsing about the lovers, but there was still plenty of fight left in them. Mrs. Simpson's worst fears concerned the intentions of Geoffrey Dawson who, she knew, was preparing to attack her in the *Times*. The King, as apprehensive as she was, and still completely at sea regarding the things that can be arranged and the things that cannot rang the Prime Minister at No. 10 Downing Street and imperiously ordered him to forbid Dawson to publish the article.

Wearily Baldwin tried to explain to the King that the press of Great Britain was free and he had no more authority over the *Times* than over any other newspaper. The King could not see it. Were not Baldwin and Dawson working as a team? He insisted.

In the end Baldwin called Dawson apologetically and said that the King would be satisfied if he (Baldwin) read over the intended article. Dawson grumbled, but he sent a proof of the article to Downing Street at midnight, by which time Baldwin had gone to bed. It was not, however, the article the King most feared.

Now that the story was out in the open the King and Mrs. Simpson found themselves with many powerful allies. The *Daily Express* and the

Daily Mail were going all out in their support—Rothermere's *Mail* more forcefully in fact than Beaverbrook's *Express*. No one could accurately assess public opinion, but there was no doubt that sympathy for the King was widespread, and even the *Times* was forced to admit later that the overwhelming majority of readers' letters on the subject were in favor of the King's marriage. The King's position was undoubtedly strong, and he was determined to stay. In his memoirs he represented himself as a man always half prepared to abdicate. The facts would suggest more that he was ready to fight to the end for both the throne and the woman. If he played his cards right now, he was almost immovable.

But one thing was wrong. Mrs. Simpson's nerve was beginning to crack. Threatening letters were reaching her and there was a report, probably from a crackpot, that plans were afoot to blow up the house in Cumberland Terrace. Reporters waited outside the house day and night, trying every trick they knew to get in and see her. Mrs. Simpson was forced to abandon the front part of the house altogether. She entered and left by the kitchen which had a door leading to the garage.

One evening, just as the crisis was beginning to blow hot, servants were terrified to hear someone *inside* the garage beating with a club or hammer on the kitchen door. No one dared to open the door and challenge the intruder, and when someone said shakily, "Who's there?" there was no answer. When finally the door was opened, the marks of the battering could be plainly seen. On the same day a window was broken in the dining room. The invaders had penetrated to Mrs. Simpson's inner retreat.

It was too much. Mrs. Simpson had planned a dinner party for ten. She cancelled the party and called for the Buick. To servants who asked what should be done with the food she replied, "Eat it yourselves," and with Aunt Bessie, and her little dog, Slipper, she left for the sanctuary of Fort Belvedere. She was on her way out.

IX

Plans, Plots, and
a Nocturnal Meeting

Mrs. Simpson did not stay long at the Fort. With the crash of breaking glass her nerve was shattered, her pretensions were destroyed and she was gone from England by nightfall on December 3, never, except for the most fleeting visits, to return.

Away from England, Mrs. Simpson's tired, clever brain revived, and some of the clearest and most concise thinking of the few remaining days left of the drama came to her. Unfortunately, though her sense of reason was restored, she had underestimated the madhouse left behind her in London.

Mrs. Simpson had not recovered from the incident when she reached Fort Belvedere and she was overwrought. "I cannot stay here another day with all this going on," she said. But the King had worked out plans which he now went on to reveal to her. They were his own plans. He had consulted nobody. They were unworkable and had almost no hope of succeeding. But conceived in love they were also boyish and inspiring.

The idea was to spirit Mrs. Simpson very quietly out of the country to the safety of France, undetected either by the press or the public. The job might have been handled better by Scotland Yard, or the French Foreign Office, working tactfully in co-operation with the French Sûreté. But the King preferred to do it in his own way and had evolved an extravagant plan which resulted in one of the most futile but at the same time one of the most exciting flights of romantic history.

Mrs. Simpson would travel to the Riviera where they had friends. False names would be used and false trails would be spread to divert reporters. Any communication between Mrs. Simpson and the King would be in code. If they talked to each other by telephone, or cabled, the King would be referred to as "Mr. James," after St. James's Palace; Mrs. Simpson would be "Janet"; Lord Beaverbrook was "Tornado"; Stanley Baldwin was "Crutch." According to the Duke of Windsor's story Winston Churchill was referred to by his initials.

The King was aware that he had little time to lose. The uproar was increasing. He had another important meeting coming up with the Prime Minister. A great debate was due in the House of Commons in which the King suspected his major support would begin and end with Churchill. After that, nobody knew what would happen.

At lunchtime that day the telephone rang at the Villa Lou Viei, the mountain home, near Cannes, of Herman and Katherine Rogers, who were at that moment entertaining an English guest. The butler announced that the call was from London. Surprised but not realizing the momentousness of the occasion, Rogers picked up the receiver in the lunchroom with both his wife and guest listening in. He nearly dropped the phone when he was told that His Majesty the King was coming on the line.

Without preamble the King asked if Rogers would take Wallis as a guest. "I want to get her out of the country," he said.

Rogers said of course he would.

The King went on, "It might be necessary for you to move on from Cannes and get her even further away from England. Would you be prepared to do that?" Rogers said yes, and the King then gave a guarded outline of his plans and mentioned when Rogers could expect Mrs. Simpson.

Rogers was a thoughtful man when he put down the telephone. He had been reading the papers, and he knew he was letting himself in for something big. He did not realize yet how big. After his holiday at Balmoral some months earlier Rogers had written thanking the King warmly on behalf of his wife and himself, expressing the sincere hope that if there were anything he could do in return, he was at the King's service. Now the King had taken him up on his offer. Rogers was pleased but disconcerted. "I hardly thought I'd ever be in a position to help a King of England," he later confessed to a friend.

First of all he swore the English acquaintance to secrecy—not too hopefully. Who, after all, could resist repeating a sensational conversation he had overheard with the King? In later years Rogers was impressed to learn that the acquaintance had kept his word and had not repeated to a soul a hint of what he had overheard.

Next he checked his wallet. There was not much money there. He agreed with his wife that he should go to his bank in Cannes and get out all his cash and if necessary borrow more. "I might have to go to Cairo and beyond for all I know," he said. And while he was sending for his car, Katherine Rogers went to prepare the bedroom.

Meanwhile in London the King considered his next problem, the selection of an aide to accompany Wallis on the difficult trip to the south of France. There were few people left in the Court that the King could trust any more, and almost automatically he turned to Lord Brownlow, one of his Lords in Waiting, and a close friend both to the King and to Mrs. Simpson. Peregrine Brownlow was thirty-seven at the time, a witty, handsome, quick-thinking man whose worldliness did not affect his sense of idealism or his unquestioning devotion to the King.

Brownlow was called by the King on the telephone, and told of the plans for getting Wallis out of the country. He was asked to come at once to the Fort and tell no one, not even his wife. The vigor and tempestuousness of the King's call left little time for contemplation. Brownlow put down the telephone and must have mused on the strangeness of human affairs. Less than twenty-four hours before the incident of the brick he had been at a meeting called by Lord Beaverbrook to try and solve the crisis. Walter Monckton and George Allen, the King's lawyer, were also there, and they agreed that the best method would be to persuade Mrs. Simpson to give the King up. The crisis, it seemed to them, must die on the spot, and Baldwin would be frustrated in his showdown with the King. The big question at the time was how to approach and "get at" Mrs. Simpson, who was always under the King's watch.

This was later to be referred to—without too much bitterness—by the Duke of Windsor as "the conspiracy." And here was the King himself putting Mrs. Simpson in the hands of one of the conspirators-in-chief. Although the aims of the men around the King seemed sometimes contradictory there was no question of loyalty in their own minds. All were united in their determination to keep the King on the throne. Of the consequences to Mrs. Simpson they were totally indifferent.

Actually Lord Brownlow was not the King's first choice as the most suitable person to escort Mrs. Simpson to the south of France. He first approached an American journalist named Newbold Noyes, then in London representing the Associated Press, to take the job on. The selection

Wally, when she was Mrs. Ernest Simpson, is shown in her Bryanston Court (London) apartment, where she first entertained her future husband, King Edward VIII.

U.P.

Wally and the King walk hand in hand through the streets of Dubrovnik, Yugoslavia, during the famous holiday cruise aboard the Nahlin in 1936.

ACME

ACM

King Edward visiting with workers in Wales, during his tour of inspecti
of depressed areas of South Wales that caused so much comment in Brit
Government circles in 1936.

Francis Stephenson, the "Common Informer," who on December 9, 1936, made the last assault on the nerves of Mrs. Simpson and the King, when he appeared in court and said he had reason to show why Wally's divorce from Simpson should not be confirmed. He went to his grave without explaining his actions.

The late Geoffrey Dawson, who was editor of the London Times *at the time of the Abdication. A close friend and supporter of Stanley Baldwin, his editorials in the* Times *were most violent in opposition to the King.*

The King and Stanley Baldwin just prior to the "crisis."

The King seated before the same microphones into which he made his emotional Abdication speech.

was odd though not quite as odd as it sounded. Noyes was married to a second cousin of Wallis's, so he could be considered remotely "in the family." But Noyes, who was deeply respectful of the monarchist tradition, and felt himself personally and emotionally involved in the crisis, declined.

Brownlow threw a few changes of clothes into his suitcase, absently adding to the pile a novel which he seemed to think he might have time to read. The afternoon was gray and cold and rain smacked against the windows of his dressing room. He put on a heavy coat with an astrakhan collar, a style he had picked up from the King, and locked his bag. He was just checking his passport when his wife, the beautiful Kitty Brownlow, who died early in 1953, came into the room. It was a slightly embarrassing moment, as Brownlow had sworn silence to the King, but he survived it.

Brownlow's Rolls Royce was then called for and he drove from his London house to the Fort, arriving in time for a tense tea. The lights were on because the afternoon was so dark, and this added to the air of gloom. Around the tea table were the King, Mrs. Simpson, Aunt Bessie and Major (now Sir) Ulick Alexander, Keeper of the Privy Purse, a loyal King's man, who continued to serve both King George VI and Queen Elizabeth II in the same capacity until 1953.

Over tea the King eagerly outlined his plans. Brownlow and Wallis were to leave straight away, not even stopping at Cumberland Terrace in case her flight were suspected by the newspapermen on watch there. With them would travel the ever-reliable George Ladbrook and a trusted young Scotland Yard detective named H.J. (Jimmie) Evans, who would travel as "valet." Evans was an experienced hand at looking after royalty. One of his great assets was that he was smooth, good-looking and well-spoken and totally unlike the traditional flat-footed London bobby. This immaculate appearance of Evans was to serve the party well in the adventures which lay ahead.

In Dieppe they would pick up the Buick which had been sent on in advance, and from then on it would be south to Cannes as fast as Ladbrook could make it.

The story of the parting is told by the King:

> The separation was all the harder to contemplate for the reason that there was no way of telling how long it would last. Nothing was said between us as to when or where we would meet again. . . . Long afterwards Wallis confided in me that only on this last day at the Fort did she begin to comprehend what abdication really involved. . . . Until then it had only been a word—a possible remote alternative. . . . When in the dark-

ness she left the Fort with Perry Brownlow for France, it was with the hope that she would see me again, but never expecting that she would. . . . I watched them go. With dimmed lights and the Scotland Yard man in front, the Rolls took the back drive down towards Virginia Water, and the public road through Windsor Great Park some distance beyond. . . .

The King was left alone to attend to other business with as much concentration as he could muster. It had been an eventful day—more eventful than he was yet able to realize. And he still had to see Stanley Baldwin later in the evening.

It was now possible to review events that had been pushed into the background by Wallis's flight. For some days the King had been working on a new approach; to broadcast to the British people explaining his love. "Neither Mrs. Simpson nor I ever sought to insist that she should be Queen," he wanted to say. "All we desired was that our married happiness should carry with it a proper title and dignity for her, befitting my wife." He would go on to offer to withdraw from Britain for a while until the issue was settled. The Duke of Windsor believes the idea of the broadcast originated with Mrs. Simpson.

Once at the microphone he understood his talents well enough to know that he could put his message across. The difficulty was how to get there in face of Stanley Baldwin's probable disapproval.

He had already made quiet overtures to the B.B.C. That morning he had sent Sir Godfrey Thomas to Broadcasting House to talk to Sir John Reith, Director-General of the B.B.C. about it. The King knew and liked Reith and hoped he would be receptive to the idea. Reith at least proved sympathetic. He poured out a stiff whisky and soda for Thomas who was close to collapse, having worked nonstop on the King's behalf since the crisis began. Thomas, rallying, asked Reith if the King could broadcast at short notice from Windsor.

Reith replied, "Of course," but asked, "Has the Prime Minister agreed to it?"

Thomas was on his guard at once and said that so far as he understood, "it could only so be done," and he left it at that. He returned to Fort Belvedere to report to the King.

Now the King thought about Winston Churchill, the one man, he knew, who would help him. But he was separated from that immense, wise and sympathetic figure by a great gulf. Baldwin again. The Prime Minister would have to give his permission before Churchill could be consulted, and the King could guess bitterly and in advance what Baldwin's answer would be to such a request.

Baldwin and Churchill had been adversaries too long and it was unlikely that the Prime Minister would allow Churchill—"my opposition" Baldwin sometimes called him—to join the fight with official blessing on the side of the King. Only that afternoon Churchill had challenged Baldwin in the House of Commons, and asked for an assurance that no irrevocable step would be taken before a general statement had been made to Parliament. Baldwin would not be drawn.

But if Churchill could not be consulted directly, he could always be consulted indirectly, and this the King had resolved to do. He sent a copy of his proposed speech that morning to Lord Beaverbrook at Stornoway House, asking him for his comments, and requesting that he show it to Churchill. Beaverbrook immediately called Churchill and suggested they meet and study the speech together. Churchill was obliged to decline. He had to go to the Albert Hall in the evening to address a meeting of an organization called Defense of Peace and Freedom, but he promised to join Beaverbrook immediately afterwards and go over the speech with him.

The meeting to which Churchill had been called had nothing whatever to do with the King's affair, but the national preoccupation with the crisis was so great that the most unrelated events seemed to be sucked into it. When the meeting was over, the audience of five thousand rose to sing "God Save the King." As the last notes died away a woman shouted, "Long live the King." There was a moment of surprised silence, and then a tremendous cheer shook the huge hall.

It was an incident which could not be ignored or underestimated. It showed that although the nation as a whole remained almost disturbingly quiet, a chance word could fire the masses and sweep events out of the control of the participants, with unimaginable consequences.

Afterwards the two close friends, Beaverbrook and Churchill, radiating between them more energy, dynamism and antic genius than any other two people in the world, settled down to apply themselves to the King's speech.

Meanwhile Baldwin had arrived at the Palace. His car pulled up outside promptly at nine, and he tried to slip in unseen by the back door. But people were everywhere and they watched in silence as he hurried inside. The King had already been furnished with one important piece of advice by Beaverbrook. It was: *Don't show the speech to Baldwin.*

Tell him about it, urged Beaverbrook, and insist on your right to make it. But don't let him know what's in it. The important thing is to get the microphone at all costs and say your piece.

The King, illustrating once more why he was the despair of his friends, immediately read the speech to Baldwin. The Prime Minister listened bleakly. This was an ugly new development for him, and he did not like it at all. He commented that he would have to consult his colleagues, but he personally thought the broadcast was "thoroughly unconstitutional."

Now more than any other time in the crisis the hatred between the two men rose to the surface. There was an outburst from the overwrought King, and a moment that came closest to frankness in all the dealings the monarch and the Prime Minister had had with each other.

"You want me to go, don't you?" the King cried. "Well, before I go, I think it is right for her sake and mine that I should speak."

Baldwin was not deluded by this rhetoric. The King had said a lot about "going," but nothing was clearer than his present determination to stay. The speech Baldwin had just listened to was no speech of farewell. It was a fighting speech, aimed at getting public opinion on the King's side. Baldwin had not yet heard of the demonstration in the Albert Hall, but he knew that public opinion was precariously poised and ready to crash down in one direction or the other. He absorbed the King's words and replied to them with care.

"What I want, Sir," he said, "is what you told me you wanted, to go with dignity, not dividing the country, and making things as smooth as possible for your successor. To broadcast would be to go over the heads of your ministers and speak to the people. You will be telling millions throughout the world—among them a vast number of women—that you are determined to marry one who has a husband living. You may by speaking, divide opinion, but you will certainly harden it. . . ."

Baldwin went on to give the King a remarkable warning, which must have seemed to the King almost a threat. He reminded Edward that Mrs. Simpson's divorce did not become absolute until the following April, and that if the King associated too closely with her before then it was possible that some "muddleheaded busybody"—Baldwin's words—might seek to delay or prevent the divorce by some sort of intervention with the divorce authorities. It was to frighten the King away from making the broadcast that Baldwin made this statement. Later, at another crucial moment when the King appeared to be making a comeback, the very thing that Baldwin warned might happen, did happen.

King Edward began to see his hopes of the broadcast fade. He counterattacked, and for once, miraculously, scored a point. "May I consult Winston Churchill?" he asked abruptly.

Taken by surprise, Baldwin said yes. The interview was over. Baldwin went pensively home. He did not know, of course, that only a few hours earlier the King had said good-by to Mrs. Simpson. Neither Baldwin nor the King were aware of the Beaverbrook "conspiracy," soon scheduled to go into operation. The big events of the crisis were still to come.

x

Mrs. Simpson Departs

The car had quickly left the lights of London's suburbs behind and traveled through the rainswept darkness towards the coast. On the main highway to Newhaven the party had an unpleasant experience. A police car pursued them and indicated to Ladbrook that he should pull up to the side of the road. The policeman did not recognize Mrs. Simpson in the back of the car, but a quick glance at Evans's Scotland Yard badge convinced him that he had put his nose into something that it would be healthier for him to ignore. He waved the car on. Had the King warned the Government of Mrs. Simpson's flight, such an incident would have been avoided. As it was it proved to be one of the lesser scares.

The party got on board the boat without trouble, and Lord Brownlow conducted Mrs. Simpson to the cabin that had been reserved for them. The zealous Evans stood guard outside as unobtrusively as he could. At Dieppe, Ladbrook collected the Buick, and a grinning French customs officer stuck the car's papers under Brownlow's nose. "Mr. Harris" realized, with horror, that they were still in Mrs. Simpson's name. The secret was cracking already. The *douaniers* crowded round and with knowing winks and wise nods led the party discreetly through the crowds of waiting tourists to the street outside. Brownlow was relieved to be rid of this complication so easily, but he was not reassured. Too many French porters and dock workers were looking on. Still, there was nothing he could do about it, and he ordered Ladbrook on to Rouen. As soon as the Buick moved out of sight through the streets of Dieppe, the porters, buzzing happily, dispersed to sell their information to the local press.

The car reached Rouen by dusk. The town was full of visitors, and Brownlow had to make his way through a swarm of French actors and actresses in the lobby of the Hôtel de la Poste to get to the reservation desk. Brownlow was worried about Mrs. Simpson who was suffering acutely from the strain of parting, and he was relieved when he found that there were still vacant rooms. The hotel was pretty busy, he was told, because it was accommodating a touring company of the Comédie Française. Mrs. Simpson was able to make her way to her room unrecognized, but she could guess what would be the King's state of mind without her and she insisted over Brownlow's protests that she must call him.

This was responsible for the next crisis. The only available telephone was on the room clerk's desk in the middle of thick clusters of French actors. It was asking for trouble to phone from there, but Mrs. Simpson insisted. After the usual delays the call was put through, and Wallis spoke to the King. The actors listened, fascinated, some of the girls in the company wept openly. Brownlow chafed anxiously and glared a Guardsman's glare at the actors. It might have petrified a Guard but the actors were too much absorbed in the conversation to take any notice whatever. The line was good, and Mrs. Simpson, who probably never realized there was anybody else in the lobby, was noticeably lighter in spirit after the call was made.

The party was up early next morning, but already a few Rouen reporters were in the lobby interviewing the actors who were giving a splendid performance of the "*coup de téléphone de Madame Simpson à son amour*" with sighs, sobs and gestures. Through the mist of histrionic tears Brownlow and Mrs. Simpson were able to slip unnoticed out of the hotel.

Outside, however, the situation was bad. Ladbrook had driven up to the hotel in the Buick which was immediately surrounded by excited passers-by. Of all the mistakes the King made in his plans for Mrs. Simpson's escape, the Buick was undoubtedly the greatest. Already it was the most famous car in the world, even the number plate, CUL 547, being as familiar to many newspaper readers as their own telephone numbers. In France, American cars of any description attracted attention at this time, and the Buick was unmistakable.

Brownlow had to push to get through. As he helped Mrs. Simpson inside, a French girl, aged about eighteen, and dressed, so far as various memories can recall, as a Girl Guide, turned her Leica camera on Mrs. Simpson. Evans sitting inside the car reached out and splayed his hand over the aperture. The girl laughed, evaded his hand and aimed the camera once more at Mrs. Simpson. Evans then knocked it out of her hands, and it fell to the pavement and smashed. "I thought it might have contained acid," he said later.

The crowd's holiday good humor faded, and there was a loud murmur of indignation mixed with some really angry muttering. The crowd began to close in and pressed round the car. There was a scuffle and a middle-aged man screamed that he had been hit.

The crowd now became ugly, and there were some tough characters there who were obviously not a bit reluctant to cause trouble. It was an unpleasant spot for the English party to find itself in, particularly for Brownlow and Evans with their precious charge. Brownlow said to Ladbrook, "For heaven's sake, get us out of here!" The Buick pushed through, and to everybody's relief put the crowd behind. Soon it was on the high road and making good progress, and the incident faded gradually from their minds. Mrs. Simpson's morale had been much higher since she had made the telephone call, but her concern for the King's welfare remained. Abdication, she knew, had been uppermost in the King's mind at their parting. As Brownlow was a confidant and intimate in the Abdication drama they discussed the matter, and Mrs. Simpson insisted once more on phoning the King on arrival at Évreux which was the next town on their route.

Brownlow protested. "It's asking for trouble," he said, "to keep phoning from hotels and restaurants. Let's go to the local police station at Évreux. I'll explain to the police what's up, and you can phone safely."

But Mrs. Simpson was determined to act under the instructions of the King, who had urged absolute secrecy, and she was fearful of bringing French officials into the adventure.

Brownlow was obliged to agree to the call, and Mrs. Simpson demanded some paper to write down the message. Brownlow had no paper but remembered the novel he had brought with him from England, fished it out of his bag and tore out the flyleaf. On it Mrs. Simpson wrote the words, "On no account is Mr. James to step down."

The King was at Buckingham Palace when Mrs. Simpson got through from Évreux, but the line was dreadful. However the King strained to hear what she was saying, he could not catch a word, and what was worse he could not get through to her a message of his own. Earlier that day he had been called up by a friend, Bernard Rickatson-Hatt, then editor of Reuter's, that the press was on to her, and although the Buick had given them the slip they knew roughly where it was, guessed the destination was Cannes, and were heading there as fast as she was.

How had the news leaked? The fact was that Wallis unwittingly broke the secret herself. A few days earlier she had entertained Newbold Noyes and another American journalist, Otis Wiese, at cocktails at the Fort. Over strong Old-fashioneds they had discussed the situation, and she promised them another interview later. But immediately afterwards the story had broken in the newspapers, and the brick had been thrown through Mrs. Simpson's window. Plans for flight followed, but Wallis, with Southern politeness, first called Wiese at the Ritz Hotel to cancel the interview. "I don't have to tell you why," she said, and told him why. That night American newsmen were on the watch at all British ports of exit for France. Though Wallis and Brownlow, with the confidence of ignorance, had slipped through unseen, the newsmen had rallied in France and were closing in relentlessly.

Neither Wallis nor the King could make any sense to each other at all over the telephone. No phone call since the instrument was invented could have probed more profoundly into the depths of human frustration. The King said in his book that he nearly hurled the receiver against the wall.

Nor was the anxiety limited to the King and Mrs. Simpson. Brownlow and Evans were having a most embarrassing time of it. The party had stopped at the Hôtel du Grand Cerf at Neveux. There Brownlow found to his relief that there was an enclosed telephone box in the lobby. His relief did not last long. The walls were like paper and Mrs. Simpson, having to shout to try to make herself heard, was audible all over the crowded lobby. Many of the hotel guests were English and American, the hotel being a very popular resort place until the war; it was shelled flat shortly after D-Day.

To prevent Mrs. Simpson's call becoming the public property it had been in Rouen, Brownlow and Evans, probably feeling utter fools, stood outside the box and talked loudly to each other. As the line inside proved hopeless, the two men talked louder and louder. People present must have wondered for years and possibly still do today why two distinguished-looking young Englishmen stood so long in front of a telephone box talking gibberish at the top of their lungs.

Whatever the temporary loss to the dignity of the British aristocracy and the Metropolitan police force, Brownlow and Evans at least succeeded in jamming out Mrs. Simpson's call from the guests. She left the box unrecognized, and they headed for the car. But they could never seem to get over one obstacle before meeting a bigger one. Although it was many months before the sense of Mrs. Simpson's message reached the King, the King's message to Mrs. Simpson was made too desperately clear within a matter of minutes. As she was leaving the hotel, the first British newspapermen began to arrive and spotted her.

This was the advance guard. Ladbrook bustled and in no time at all the party was in the Buick and away, the reporters left behind. For two hours they drove on a superb highway at one of Ladbrook's fastest licks. Brownlow was pleased at escaping the reporters so easily. The party had become quite a cheerful one by this time. Mrs. Simpson in the excitement of the flight was regaining some of the famous verve that had been unhappily missing in the last few trying weeks, and kept everyone in the car amused at her comments on the passing French scene.

Then two catastrophies hit them simultaneously. "Blimey," said Ladbrook, "I've hit the wrong road." And Mrs. Simpson said, "Oh, I've left the note behind." Here were two serious problems dumped into Brownlow's lap, of which the more serious by far was that of the note, "Under no circumstances is Mr. James to step down." The first solution would be to drive back to Évreux, pick up the note and get on to the right road, but Brownlow and Mrs. Simpson agreed that such a move would be to invite utter disaster, as the town by now would be infested with newspapermen of all nationalities.

It was agreed after a brief conference to abandon the note. Optimism reasserted itself. It was after all a cryptic and not particularly incriminating message, and even if a reporter did find it, it might not mean anything to him. And probably it would be found by a hotel employee and destroyed.

They underestimated the wit of the hotelier, who, shortly after Mrs. Simpson's departure, went into the telephone box and found the note. He read it, having already recognized his visitor, and saw the significance. He framed it and kept it to show his favorite customers. A year or so later Harold Nicolson, the writer, stopped briefly at the hotel for lunch, discovered and retrieved the hotelier's prize and returned it to Mrs. Simpson, who by that time was the Duchess of Windsor.

Having made his decision, Brownlow told Ladbrook to carry on until they got back on the right road. They found themselves back on their planned route just north of Blois. The little town was deserted when they arrived, for which discovery they were most thankful, and they reserved rooms at the Hôtel d'Angleterre. But some form of mental radar was attracting their pursuers, and less than half an hour after their arrival the first press cars were nosing speculatively into the town. By late evening there were more than thirty newspapermen in the hotel, most of them British and eager to make up with as much sensation as possible for all the months of enforced silence. There were also a fair number of Americans and a few Frenchmen.

Jimmie Evans was the first to spot them, and he had a big slice of luck. Wallis, Lord Brownlow and Ladbrook had retired to their rooms, but Evans went to the bar. As he sat enjoying a glass of wine, half-a-dozen British reporters came in. They did not recognize him and they began to talk. Evans listened with deep interest. They had bribed the concierge: the first move Mrs. Simpson made they would be alerted. They had all the exits watched. They also said something about the Buick . . . blocking the Buick. Evans paid for his drink and went upstairs. He told Lord Brownlow what he had heard, then entered Ladbrook's room. The chauffeur had dropped his immense bulk onto the bed, a French beret still on his head and a cigar in his mouth. Evans told him to hold himself ready. Ladbrook sighed.

The first reporter reserved rooms, and by the time the others turned up the hotel was full. None wanted to move to any other hotel, so those unable to get rooms cheerfully elected to sleep on chairs all night in the lobby and wait for any appearance Mrs. Simpson cared to make.

Brownlow had to think hard. He worked out a tentative plan. To the concierge he said quietly—but sibilantly enough to be overheard—"We will have breakfast at eight. It is very important that we leave this hotel at nine o'clock." As he waited for the elevator to take him to his room, he heard a Fleet Street newspaperman on the telephone to London. "Don't worry," he was bellowing—and Brownlow began to see virtues in wafer-thin walls—"we've got them trapped. They are leaving at nine." Impassively optimistic Brownlow returned to the hotel room at the door of which Evans stood guard and told Mrs. Simpson the news.

In time all the reporters made their calls to London and New York, and as even the latest sleepers made their way to bed silence finally enclosed the hotel. The scene in the darkened lobby was like a refugee center, with newspapermen lolling on chairs and couches. The luminous watch on the wrist of the unsleeping Detective Evans said three o'clock when Brownlow, heavy-eyed, crept silently along the corridor to awaken Mrs. Simpson. His call was unnecessary. She was ready and she emerged a revelation. Not a hair was out of place. She looked bright and wide-awake and appeared as if she had stepped from the bath and the attentions of a score of maids. Her clothes were as chic and as faultless as if she were about to go to a Mayfair cocktail party. She gave Brownlow an alert smile, and together the three adventurers set out to run the gauntlet of the snoring reporters.

They tiptoed downstairs and through the lobby, stepping over motionless bodies. If one reporter had awakened they would have been lost. Almost too easily, it seemed, they were outside in the bitterly cold night, behind them not a single newspaperman had been disturbed in his slumber. They congratulated one another with triumphant winks, then crept round to the back of the hotel where the Buick was garaged. They had cheered too soon.

Parked directly in the path of the Buick the reporters had set another car with the hand-brake firmly applied and every door locked. Mrs. Simpson's party seemed effectively stymied.

"What," Mrs. Simpson wanted to know, "do we do now?"

Ladbrook who was scratching his head at the scene when they arrived said, "Leave it to me." He ordered the other three into the car and started the motor. The car moved forward and pressed its bumper against the locked vehicle. In the still night air the racing engine seemed to make the sound of fiends, but there was still no move from the hotel. Very slowly, the car began to budge. Ladbrook kept pushing, and in the end, the reporter's car, bumped, dented and seriously diminished in salable value, had been pushed out of the way. Once more they were off and racing south into the dawn along empty highways, complimenting themselves on their victory with a fervor that was all the more heartfelt because they knew that it could not last.

The weather had turned out bad. Snow was falling and the roads were treacherous, but the Buick kept going. For most of the time Brownlow and Wallis sat in the back and chatted, mostly about the crisis they had left behind them and how the King was making out alone.

An important change was coming over Mrs. Simpson. The King had sensed it in the last words they had together when she told him she was realizing for the first time what abdication meant. The woman whose almost inhuman sophistication never failed to stagger childhood friends when they saw her again, seemed to be rediscovering the fact that she was once Wallis Warfield, remembered as one of the nicest girls in Baltimore.

Wallis Simpson had a kind heart and her sympathy was easily touched. She was beginning to understand that the King's cause was hopeless and that perhaps only through her renunciation of him could he remain on the throne.

Brownlow for his part must have been thinking of his second mission on this expedition, about which the King knew nothing, but though the thoughts of both people were almost certainly running along the same lines, the moment had not yet come when they could be discussed openly. Mrs. Simpson had recovered her good spirits along the road and was now trim and in possession of herself, usually amusing, particularly when fatigue seemed to weigh upon the other occupants of the car.

She laughed through one incident which came close to farce. Brownlow was muffled against the cold in his heavy overcoat when a sudden bump threw him against the side of the car. There was the sound of breaking glass. The bump had broken a small bottle of whisky in his pocket and the fumes spread everywhere. At first it was a joke ("Before breakfast too!") ("Hope the reporters don't catch us now!"), but the aroma quickly became too overpowering for laughter. Finally Mrs. Simpson put her foot down.

"Perry," she said, "I cannot stand this. You'll have to put your coat somewhere." Brownlow protested weakly about the cold but Mrs. Simpson was not moved, so he stuffed the coat in the trunk of the car. He spent the rest of the journey wrapped up in a couple of rugs.

When Ladbrook tired, Brownlow took the wheel. There were no signs of reporters as they flashed through village after village, but Brownlow and Mrs. Simpson guessed that they had not shaken them off for long. However their luck held good as far as Moulin where they stopped for an early breakfast. Here Brownlow composed a telegram to send to the Rogers who, he knew, would be waiting for them in the greatest of anxiety at Cannes.

He re-worded it more and more vaguely until he was finally satisfied that it would arouse no suspicion. It said something like "Having wonderful time. You might see us tonight but don't wait up." He put no signature on it and handed it in to the cable office. Once more he underestimated the capacity of the French to read between the lines even in English. Rogers received the cable all right—after he had read it in print in the local Nice paper that afternoon.

Brownlow did not hear of that until later. The roads continued free of press cars, and the fugitives were in excellent spirits all morning. Ladbrook at one point was seeking the "Route Bleue" to make a turning. As they passed a crossroads Mrs. Simpson said absently, "Isn't this it, the Route Royale?" then collapsed in laughter at the joke which she insisted was on her.

About fifty miles before they reached Vienne, the press hit them again in huge numbers. And this time they could not be shaken off. Local inhabitants in the Rhône Valley villages poured out to watch the mysterious caravan of cars tearing through, a big black American car in the lead, and a stream of other cars of all sorts of nationalities following.

Probably the best-known thing about Vienne is the Restaurant de la Pyramide, sometimes called Chez Point, the world's most famous eating place. Brownlow and Mrs. Simpson decided to stay there for lunch, and Ladbrook drove the car into the garage while the press remained outside. They entered the restaurant via the wine cellar, and Brownlow asked for a private room. The headwaiter was desolate, but all he had that was not occupied was the banqueting hall.

"It'll do," said Brownlow, and he and his charge were conducted to a huge echoing room. They sat at the long dining table, posting Evans outside and had an excellent light meal consisting of pâté, salad, chicken and white wine. Brownlow and Mrs. Simpson were both excellent conversationalists with highly developed senses of humor. The press men waiting outside became something of a joke and lunch was spent merrily, the absurdly large room adding to the somewhat hysterical laughter.

They had managed to enter the restaurant without much harassment. But the sight which greeted them as they left was positively terrifying. The struggling crowds of reporters and photographers had been reinforced by newsreel camera squads, and Mrs. Simpson's appearance was the sign for the cameras posted on the top of cars to start whirring.

As the Buick started up all the other cars got into line behind. At Avignon later that afternoon they paused for a snack in the car. Obligingly the press cars pulled up behind them, and all the newspapermen also took advantage of the occasion to have snacks, too.

They did not stop again. The car went on until two thirty the following morning. Fifty-six hours after leaving England, it arrived at the foot of the narrow winding mountain road leading from Cannes up to the Villa Lou Viei. It was an appropriate sanctuary. It had once been a monk's residence and parts of it were over five hundred years old. The Rogers had bought it some years before.

No one, of course, in the brightly lit house was thinking of sleep. The Rogers had had a harassing time. For more than twenty-four hours they had been watching more and more newspapermen arrive until now there were more than five hundred encamped just beyond the small private road that led from the house to the main mountain road. Herman Rogers knew that Mrs. Simpson was going to have a hard time breaking through. The road from Cannes is so winding that it needs a constant use of the wheel, and even at comparatively slow speeds the tires scream on the turns.

He took comfort, however, in the gendarmes at the end of the pathway, who were keeping the reporters at bay. And out in Cannes harbor other friends of the King and Mrs. Simpson had rallied. The *Nahlin* was there and so was the yacht *Sister Ann*, property of the French sewing-machine heiress, Mrs. Reginald Fellowes. Both kept steam up in case Wallis was obliged to escape by sea.

Brownlow was the first in the Buick to spot the reporters, now reinforced by hundreds of sight-seers, and he realized that the end of the six-hundred-and-fifty was going to be the severest test of all.

"Wallis," said Brownlow, "if you don't want to be photographed, the only thing to do is to get down on the floor." Mrs. Simpson did so, and Brownlow told Ladbrook to outdo himself and to head for the house for all he was worth. The Buick streaked through a vivid white blaze of flash bulbs into the villa grounds, and the gendarmes formed a line as it passed to bar the way. Mrs. Simpson was safe at last.

The anxious Rogers hurried out of the house to greet them, but when he opened the door of the car, he had a nasty shock. "Hello, Perry," he said, then, "My God, where's Wallis?"

"Here I am," said Wallis, somewhat disheveled but cheerful as she climbed from under a car rug. With great relief Rogers led his guests inside, where Katherine Rogers was waiting with food and badly needed stiff drinks.

Outside, the newspapermen and photographers, deprived of their coup, dispersed with not very good grace. No one had succeeded in even seeing Mrs. Simpson. A few of the more unscrupulous characters in the newspaper business in London, however, were not going to be defeated as easily as the men on the spot had been. Noticing in the cabled pictures that there was no sign of Mrs. Simpson, at least one art editor decided it was a mistake and cheerfully introduced one by composite photography. It duly appeared the following day. It showed Mrs. Simpson in different clothes from those she was wearing at the time but, after all, one couldn't have everything.

The reporters, whose equipment is the written word rather than the visual image, had rather a better time of it, and a very touching picture of Mrs. Simpson's arrival was recorded. As long after the event as 1948 one London newspaper biographer of Mrs. Simpson was still under the impression that watchers at the gate would "never forget her tragic face, pale under the Mediterranean moon and half-closed weary eyes." Actually Mrs. Simpson was crouched on the floor, and if her emotions have been correctly remembered, she was rather enjoying it.

Sleep came with varying ease to the people besieged that night in the sixteen-room Villa Lou Viei. In the servants' quarters Ladbrook and Evans slept the sleep of men satisfied with a job accomplished as well as it was within their power. Mrs. Simpson, on the other hand, was as wide awake and as alert as she had been throughout the flight. She was still apprehensive, however, for her personal safety, and asked Lord Brownlow to sleep in an adjoining room. This was a dressing room which the Rogers had turned into a makeshift bedroom, and Mrs. Simpson arranged for the connecting door to be left half open.

The story of what happened after everyone in the house had gone to bed was repeated with hilarity at breakfast next morning and has been repeated many times since by mutual friends.

Both had retired, Brownlow so weary that he did not even take his clothes off. He simply threw himself fully dressed on the divan bed. As he smoked a last cigarette he called Mrs. Simpson.

"Wallis," he said quietly in case she was asleep. A sound from the next room indicated that she was not, and Brownlow said something to this effect:

"We've had a tough journey together, and I'd like to ask you a favor. I think you might feel I'm entitled to a little privileged information. Tell me the story. How did it all happen? What made the King fall in love with you? How did you do it?"

Brownlow's cigarette was out, and he was fighting against sleep even while he spoke.

After a while Wallis said, "All right, I'll tell you." She started to speak.

The next thing Brownlow remembered was the start of sudden awakening. For a moment, as so often happens after the first sleep of utter fatigue, he did not realize where he was; then he heard Mrs. Simpson's voice saying, "And that, Perry, is the whole story. What else could I do?"

So the world's strangest love story was told freshly and purely, as, after all the subsequent years of fact and rumor, it can never be told again, possibly not even by the Duchess of Windsor herself. It was meant for the ears of one loyal friend, who slept through it all.

Brownlow, awake again, was somewhat vexed with himself. But being a gentleman he could hardly say, "Sorry, would you mind starting at the beginning again?" Instead, regretfully but philosophically he turned over and went back to sleep.

XI

Climax--and Defeat

The night of Thursday, December 3, 1936, was the turning point in the crisis. That was the night when Wallis left, the night five thousand people in the Albert Hall cheered the King and a "King's Party" appeared to be forming, the night when the King confronted Baldwin with his intention to broadcast. At midnight that night Godfrey Thomas had called Sir John Reith on the telephone and told him that the King might broadcast on the following evening. It was the high-water mark of Edward's fortunes.

Twenty-four hours later he was a beaten and a broken man.

What happened to cause such a change? The first pregnant hours of Friday gave no indication of the great break to come. In fact, it seemed as if the King's cause was strengthening by the hour, and at 10 Downing Street the news looked bad. The Cabinet had heard with gloom about the Albert Hall demonstration, and of the nationwide sympathy for the King as revealed in readers' letters to the *Times*. An alarming rumor had reached the Ministers that Windsor Castle was being wired for sound by B.B.C. engineers. They received yet another shock when Baldwin opened his business of the day.

The Prime Minister had guessed he was in for trouble when the time came to admit to his colleagues that he had given the King permission to see Winston Churchill, a man both feared and disliked by the orthodox Conservatives who formed the bulk of Baldwin's Cabinet. Having foreseen trouble, he decided to forestall it in a manner peculiar to his tangential personality.

"I made a bloomer last night," he said sheepishly and told the Cabinet what had happened. Duff Cooper, the War Minister, an acute observer of the Stanley Baldwin character, watched the performance fascinated. "Baldwin adopted, with the vocabulary of the schoolroom, the appearance of a penitent schoolboy 'owning up' to a delinquency," Duff Cooper later recalled.

As Baldwin had admitted his error, his colleagues could hardly take him to task about it. But a week later, when the drama was completed, and the Prime Minister had finished making his triumphant speech to the House of Commons describing the Abdication, Duff Cooper provoked a sequel. He congratulated Baldwin and said to him, "So it wasn't a blunder after all."

Baldwin was flushed and elated. He laughed. "My dear Duff," he exclaimed, "I never thought for one moment that it was a blunder, but it seemed to me the best way of presenting the matter to my colleagues that morning."

Baldwin immediately felt he had gone too far. "The laugh faded, the mask fell, and he hurried down the corridor in solemn silence." At that moment Duff Cooper remembered a Frenchwoman whom he had once met at a party, and who did not recognize Stanley Baldwin standing nearby. "That man must be an actor," the Frenchwoman had commented.

The Prime Minister's cause sagged even further that afternoon. Once more Churchill demanded an assurance that no irrevocable step would be taken. Churchill had been informed that the King had permission to consult him. It was a conflict to give him obvious joy . . . Cavalier against Roundhead; Royalist against Puritan; dashing rebel against relentless constitutionalist. The romantic nature of the struggle may account for a sense of fantasy in Churchill's counsel.

He dined that evening in Fort Belvedere. The situation, as it was unfolded to him, shocked him. About Mrs. Simpson he prudently said not a word. He concentrated on the constitutional aspect, and his exposition must have been masterly because as he put his points, his audience, the King, Walter Monckton, Ulick Alexander, George Allen, listened, rapt. No crisis could possibly arise, he said, until Mrs. Simpson's divorce was confirmed in April. Baldwin had no authority to confront the King with a choice of abdication. If there was disagreement, it was the Government not the King whose responsibility it was to resign. His case was unanswerable and exposed the dubious nature of the Baldwin campaign. It had only one weakness, and the King apparently did not enlighten Churchill on it. The alternative of abdication had been introduced not by Baldwin but by the King, not once but repeatedly, and as a threat. Baldwin was merely holding the King to his word.

Winston Churchill traveled back to London that night stimulated and heartened by the situation as he found it. He drafted three messages. One was a letter to the Prime Minister stating that the King was in no fit state to give a decision. It would be "cruel and wrong" he said, to extort one. He wrote out a statement to give to the press, pleading for "time and patience" and urging tolerance and delay in reaching a decision over the King's affair. Finally he wrote a letter of "half-humorous advice" to the King, suggesting, according to the Duke of Windsor's Memoirs, that he should withdraw into Windsor Castle, pull up the drawbridge and admit no one.

Churchill wrote his notes in good heart and good conscience. He was looking forward to a fight and a long fight. It is certain from the tone of his messages that he did not think for one moment that the King was on the point of giving up.

Yet even as he wrote, Stanley Baldwin, at No. 10 Downing Street, seemed to receive a telepathic flash. From sources which even now cannot be disclosed, the author has proof that Baldwin on Friday night knew that the King was licked, and the crisis was over. Something or someone had told him that a secret ravage was working on the King, a ravage that had escaped Churchill's notice, but which was making Edward sag like a pricked balloon. Mrs. Simpson's departure had wrecked him.

The following day the King sent Walter Monckton to Baldwin with the news that he intended to abdicate. The King's friends were amazed, but Baldwin was ready for it. At once he established a Cabinet Committee, under Sir John Simon, the Home Secretary, to draw up the Abdication documents, then he went off to tell the Duke of York to stand by.

The King's friends witnessed his collapse and were in despair. The greatest blunderers of all were now proved to be the conspirators, and they had blundered in the most foolish way imaginable. They had ignored the personality of the woman in the case. They thought they could be loyal to the King alone, and seemed to consider Mrs. Simpson little more than a nuisance, someone to be got rid of or otherwise put out of mind. The fact was that not one of the King's supporters liked or bothered about Mrs. Simpson, and this weakened their argument fatally. Churchill scarcely mentioned her. His entire campaign was for delay and the avoidance of irrevocable decision. If he gave any opinion at all on whether or not the King should marry, it seems to have been a guarded hope that the King would get over his infatuation once the crisis died down.

Beaverbrook's simple solution for many difficulties over the years had been "Never resign; wait until you are fired." Now his theme was, keep the King on the throne, because once he was off it, he could not get back on to it. He knew that there was a core to the crisis far more important than the personalities of Edward VIII and Mrs. Simpson. It was nothing less than the future of Great Britain and the Empire. Idealism has driven Beaverbrook in many strange directions in his career, none stranger than this. His passion was the British land and the British people. His obsession was a policy of British Imperial isolationism, and he identified Edward with his own cause, partly because Edward was the personification of his beloved Empire, partly because he could just not bring himself to trust the Empire to Baldwin.

One of the tragedies in the conflict lay in the fact that Baldwin and Beaverbrook might have been allies had their personal enmity been less strong. The essence, as seen by the author, is that Baldwin's fight, however he fought it, was for the preservation of the Kingly symbol, the unity of the British nation, the dignity of Parliament, the loyalty and reverence of the British Empire. Victory for Lord Beaverbrook's man would have meant at best a nation sullenly divided, and an Empire that might have cut its ties rather than pay homage to Wallis Warfield Spencer Simpson Windsor as Queen or even as first lady.

Baldwin in fact was fighting Beaverbrook's fight. Such is the sadness of rivalry in small matters, that Baldwin even today, nine years dead, is the one man Beaverbrook seems unable to recall with magnanimity.

The King's supporters thought that, once Mrs. Simpson was out of the way, King Edward would become more amenable to their advice. Instead he lost all reason and thought only of following her. Baldwin, as usual, was wiser than his enemies. He had learned much about Edward's personality from the miserable tour of Canada nine years earlier. Working from an unsure position, he based everything on his assessment of Edward's obstinate, wayward temperament. He never made a mistake.

Baldwin had realized more quickly than anyone else the vital fact that the King was beaten from the moment Mrs. Simpson left his side. Edward lost his courage, his morale and his will to fight. This total collapse was without doubt the most important single factor in his Abdication after three hundred and twenty-five days as King of England. And its very suddenness illustrates more clearly how closely Wallis and the King actually came to victory. If Wallis had kept her nerve and continued to stay close to him, invigorating him and giving him encouragment, he might have gone on fighting indefinitely and possibly won. It would have been a bitter, empty victory, but he might have forced his will on the country.

Even now the die was not completely cast. The King could reverse his decision before the Cabinet Committee got seriously to work on the complicated and unprecedented construction of the Act of Abdication. But Edward, after many months of daydreaming about what he would do for himself and his intended bride, was now face to face with many bitter truths. Forty years of popularity that came close to idolatry, built up by every device of propaganda and wishful thinking, had evaporated in a week. The Government was against him. The Labour Party sided with the Government. The Dominions, for whom he had worked so hard, were solidly opposed to him. Britain, far from rallying to his support, seemed stifled, the people silent. If he overcame all his present obstacles, took his case to the country with an election, and won, the Archbishop of Canterbury would certainly refuse to carry out the ceremony of the Coronation, and the Church of England would certainly refuse to marry him.

As far as Edward VIII was concerned, once he reached the throne with his domestic life unresolved, the avenues that were available to him were few and distasteful. He could remain celibate, something which is demanded of priests, but never of Kings, who are indeed required to be just the opposite. He could make a "cold" suitable marriage which would have revolted him. He could tread the more traditional royal path of forming a semi-permanent relationship with a mistress. A sufficiently dedicated King would have taken the first or second course. A practical King might have chosen the third. A King better organized in his own life would never have let himself get into this position in the first place.

But King Edward VIII was in love as few men in history had been in love. Mrs. Simpson was the one light in an existence that otherwise was unbearable to him, and both he and she indignantly rejected a relationship without marriage. Having come so far there was no way out. Abdication, the grenade which the King hoped to pitch into Baldwin's tent, was stuck in his hand. Baldwin had cleverly left the King without the freedom even to do what Baldwin was ostensibly urging him to do: to change his mind and stay on the throne. To renounce Mrs. Simpson would have been to brand himself not only a weakling, but also as the most forsworn man who ever sought the hand of a lady.

Spiritually he was left without comfort or guidance. The Church of England remained remote and disapproving, the Archbishop of Canterbury a dark eminence hovering in the background. The Archbishop knew how deeply Edward hated him, but he knew too how desperately alone the King was. The Archbishop was troubled. He was aware, at least to some extent, that his own attitude did not altogether square with the teachings of Jesus. "I am disposed to think," he wrote later in his diary, "I might have written to Edward VIII if only to liberate my conscience." After some soul searching, however, the Archbishop made it all right with himself. "Almost certainly," he added, "this would have invoked, even if any reply had been given, the sort of slight which I personally would have understood, but to which the Archbishop of Canterbury ought not to be exposed." So Lang left Edward to deal with his soul in his own way.

The King began to go to pieces. He felt bitterly that he was a King who was ruler of nothing, lord of nobody, a King who could do no right. Contemporary accounts of him speak of a man who raved, wept, called himself a fool, and then in moments of quiet said, "My brother will make a better King than I." He waited helplessly for Baldwin to push him off the throne.

Baldwin, having made sure that the King would not keep the crown, went on to make sure that he would not get anything. The King, through Walter Monckton, asked the Cabinet for a few favors, the most important one being that when the Abdication Bill was submitted to Parliament, a second Bill should be presented at the same time making Mrs. Simpson's divorce absolute forthwith and avoid the delay of six months between the decree nisi and the decree absolute. Baldwin promised that it would be done, but when he presented the idea to the Cabinet he bowed immediately to their protests. The Cabinet insisted that the Divorce Bill would never get through Parliament, partly for religious reasons, and partly because it would have sounded too much as though Parliament and the King were making a bargain over the Abdication.

Then the King pleaded with the Prime Minister to be fair to Mrs. Simpson. When the time came for Baldwin to review the Abdication to the House of Commons, would he please pay tribute somewhere in the course of his speech to her impeccable behavior in times that were trying to say the least. Baldwin did not say he wouldn't, but he didn't.

The last hope of the King's supporters now rested in the success of the "conspiracy," which had widened to the extent that it was a secret to almost no one except the King and Mrs. Simpson. Nearly all the King's friends had been put into the picture, and most of his enemies, too. Even the Prime Minister knew all about it: Beaverbrook had kept his friend Sir Samuel Hoare informed, and Hoare, in turn, told Baldwin, who was reported—by Hoare—to be "sympathetic." Hoare revealed this development many years later, and nothing illustrates more vividly the unexpected ways in which personal loyalty carried the various participants in the crisis. For a moment we actually have the enemies Beaver-brook and Baldwin, men working for opposite ends, now partners in the same plot. Baldwin then carried the confusion even further by calling Theodore Goddard, Mrs. Simpson's tricky solicitor, to Downing Street for a secret conference. The certain truth was that while Baldwin gave Hoare the impression that he was not opposed to the "conspiracy," he was really very uneasy about it, and to Goddard he outlined a plan which was shortly to become clear.

Ironically enough, Wallis Simpson, in her retreat at Cannes, was need-ing very little persuasion. She was beginning to see the issue more clearly than she had ever done before. In the five, six, seven, sometimes eight telephone calls she had every day with the King, she repeatedly told him to hang on, not to abdicate whatever he did.

The French switchboard operators listened in eagerly. At first they were delicate enough just to listen in a little from time to time. Gradually they grew bolder, and listened in to everything, romantically ignoring other calls. Then they would repeat the entire conversation—inaccurately —to the French newspapers.

Finally Brownlow, who was still in charge of Mrs. Simpson's safety and welfare, lost his temper and stormed out by car to call on the Prefect of the Alpes-Maritimes Department. The Prefect, who controls the dis-trict politically, was immediately fearful of repercussions and called Paris. Within a matter of hours the French Foreign Office flew down skilled and trusted telephone operators to replace the over-romantic girls, and the King and Mrs. Simpson were able to hold their last conversations before the Abdication in privacy.

The little party of friends in the Villa Lou Viei were now literally besieged. The British and American correspondents outside had banded together to hire the largest car they could find, which happened to be a gigantic Hispano. This they kept with the nose sticking out across the Rogers' private path. Unless the Hispano backed up no vehicle could get into or out of the grounds. The engine was always kept running and the correspondents' aim was to scrutinize everyone leaving or coming to the house. If Mrs. Simpson or Rogers ventured out, the Hispano would let them pass, then keep on their tail everywhere they went.

The reporters were trying every trick they knew. Gendarmes had to drag out of neighboring houses photographers with telephoto lenses, and one newspaperman was hauled down from the roof of the Villa onto which he had somehow managed to climb. The Villa at the time was being redecorated and plumbers were also working there. Two reporters dressed themselves as plumbers and tried to bribe the real plumbers to let them into the house. They then discovered that Provençals are the hardest of all Frenchmen to bribe. They failed and to the accompaniment of the guffaws of the rest of the reporters, the two men returned sheepishly to their hotel to change back into ordinary clothes.

One American woman correspondent, using the names of mutual friends, put Herman Rogers under a social obligation to see her. She suggested an interview at her hotel, and he reluctantly agreed. The correspondent had arranged it cozily and informally with a log fire, a bottle of whisky and two glasses. She was attired, for comfort, in a filmy negligée. Rogers, who was a particularly handsome man, had been feeling rather distrustful of the whole business, and spoiled the effect by bringing his wife along. . . .

Extra postmen were put on the round to carry the flood of letters arriving at the Villa Lou Viei by every mail. They represented every shade of opinion from encouragement to threats of death. It was hopeless trying even to sort them.

In 1952, Rogers, moving from the Villa Lou Viei to a smaller house nearby, found in an attic a dozen crates of letters, which he burned. He estimated that it amounted in all to about one tenth of the volume of mail which arrived all told.

It was the never-ending mountain of mail more than any other single item that was influencing Mrs. Simpson. She was terrified by the abuse and opprobrium she was receiving, and she began casting around in her mind for some way to divert the anger away from herself. Renunciation had already occurred to her, but she could not face this except as a last desperate resort. She did not realize how hopeless the King's cause had become, and she still hoped.

The idea came to her to make a tentative statement of withdrawal from the King's life, not a renunciation, but a cautious plea to ease her present unsympathetic position, in which she appeared to be solely responsible for toppling a King from his throne. In one of her telephone conversations with the King, he agreed that she should issue the statement. Edward, absorbed in his own mental problems, as well as the Act of Abdication now near completion, did not realize that Mrs. Simpson was on the threshold of saying good-by to him forever.

On Monday, December seventh, Brownlow called a press conference at the Hotel Majestic in Cannes. He announced crisply in his best Guardsman's manner: "What I have to say tonight is divided into two sections, separate and distinct. First a denial, secondly an official announcement. The denial is as follows: Mrs. Simpson has given no interviews of any sort or kind or made any statements to the press whatsoever other than the statement I now make on her behalf. [This in answer to a few wild French claims of "exclusive interviews."] The following is the official announcement of Mrs. Simpson: Mrs. Simpson throughout the last few weeks has invariably wished to avoid any action or proposal which would hurt or damage His Majesty or the Throne. Today her attitude is unchanged, and she is willing, if such action would solve the problem, to withdraw forthwith from a situation that has been rendered both unhappy and untenable."

The reporters faded away, and Mrs. Simpson was left with a few hours of peace in which she could explore the miseries of her position. In a walk through the Villa grounds she asked Brownlow his opinion. Brownlow replied frankly that he thought she had put herself in a position whereby the British people, rightly or wrongly, would never forgive her.

Wallis could remember the brick flung through her window, and she could well believe him. The vision of the crown and the throne at last faded into nothing. So did morganatic marriage. The man who loved her could not even keep the throne for himself if he married her. The masquerade was over and the love affair was heading for a classically unhappy ending. Wallis Warfield had started from nothing and reached the society of emperors. She had achieved what few women of history had achieved, but she abdicated when she fled England.

Only one thing would save the King and preserve his throne. Renunciation, followed by flight. At long last Wallis Simpson saw it all. Few people today realize how deeply the plans were laid for what was to be the second and final escape of Mrs. Simpson, or how closely they came to being carried out. They were evolved in great detail. Mrs. Simpson would issue a formal statement of renunciation, via Perry Brownlow. In the meantime Evans, the detective, would be sent on ahead into Nice and make reservations in the Blue Train to Genoa or Brindisi, whichever port could offer earlier ship bookings. They would then sail together somewhere too remote for her to be recalled by the King. Ceylon was discussed and even China where Wallis had lived thirteen years earlier. Once Mrs. Simpson was safely installed on the other side of the globe, Brownlow would return home.

They agreed that the King must hear news of the renunciation from Mrs. Simpson herself. It would be a painful moment, but it was intolerable to think that the monarch should first hear the news from the press.

Quite suddenly, however, before they could make another move, Mrs. Simpson found herself beset on all sides by people determined apparently to force her to do what she had decided to do voluntarily. Immediately the waters of the "conspiracy" turned muddy. Everybody was getting in the act, and no one knew what anyone else was doing. Theodore Goddard, at the end of his mysterious interview with Stanley Baldwin, flew through foul weather to France, force-landed at Marseilles, drove nonstop to Cannes, and turned up exhausted and unexpected at the Villa Lou Viei. Because he was in poor health he traveled with a doctor and sent the waiting reporters scattering with crazy rumors. The King called frantically from London: "Don't see him; he's a Baldwin man." Mrs. Simpson protested she couldn't refuse to see him after he had traveled so far.

Officially Goddard had come, on the Prime Minister's behalf, to persuade Wallis to renounce the King. Actually Baldwin wanted no such thing. It was merely an excuse to get a man into the Villa Lou Viei to find out what was going on. Information was what he was after. What he succeeded in achieving was nothing less than sabotage. The picture which Mrs. Simpson had seen clearly in the calm, sympathetic company of Lord Brownlow, became confused. Then Esmond Harmsworth (now Lord Rothermere) arrived from nowhere to add his voice to the same plea: "Renounce the King." It was reported that Ernest Simpson was trying to get through to his ex-wife with the same message. It was the solution the world was yearning for. But Wallis was now in a panic.

On the same day Winston Churchill rose in the House of Commons and was howled down. It was, as the *Times* said, the worst rebuff in modern political history. Baldwin had successfully crushed an incipient Parliamentary King's Party. He had put the autocratic Government Whip, Captain David Margesson, on the track of Conservative M.P.'s whose sympathy seemed to be with the King; officially Margesson set out merely to sound opinion, in fact he diverted it firmly into line with Baldwin. This was a job at which Margesson was unsurpassed, and he succeeded. Nobody rose to support Churchill who, gesticulating defiantly, his voice lost in the uproar, finally slumped back in his seat defeated. Many observers of that scene believed that Churchill's career was finished.

Events were now moving so fast that they were out of date before the newspapers could grasp them. Next morning (Tuesday) Fleet Street was still coping with Wallis's statement to the press. The *Times* treated it with uneasy contempt, and the editor was clearly determined that the King was not going to wriggle free in this manner. They printed the story in small type under the Parliamentary debate. Under the story of Wallis's offer to withdraw and linked to it by a row of dots they ran the following paragraph without headline: "Thelma Viscountess Furness arrived in Southampton on the liner *Queen Mary* yesterday from New York."

It was an acid joke to please a society in acid mood. Exit Mrs. Simpson; re-enter Lady Furness. It was typical of Dawson's temperament, but he quickly decided that either it was not funny enough or else it was too funny, for after the first edition the item was moved to a less explosive part of the paper and readers of the later editions missed the double-entendre.

Geoffrey Dawson's editorial on the adjoining page was the most withering and ripped to shreds the last remnants of Mrs. Simpson's aspirations. Answering a last plea for morganatic marriage by the *Daily Mail*, Dawson wrote:

> There has, as Lord Rothermere says, been no suggestion at any time and from any quarter that the lady for whom the morganatic exception is recommended should become Queen. Yet in law—apart from the fact that she is not legally free to re-marry—there is nothing to bar her from becoming Consort and Queen in the full sense. The disqualification here is not, as on the Continent, one of law, but of fact. What is demanded is statutory recognition of the fact that she is not fitted to become Queen. The Prime Ministers of the Empire are to be asked to propose, and the Parliaments to accept and ratify, a permanent statutory apology for the lady whom the King desires to marry. The Constitution is to be amended in order that she may carry in solitary prominence the brand of unfitness for the Queen's Throne. . . .

Lord Beaverbrook, in London, could see all round him the collapse of the King's cause, and he was aware of the hash being made of the conspiracy on the Riviera. His handling of Mrs. Simpson's statement was in significant contrast to that of the *Times*, and typified the conflict of the press.

Beaverbrook went all out on the statement. Making a mountain of propaganda out of a molehill of news was a familiar game to him. He had done it many times in the past and he did it again now. The *Daily Express* brought out its blackest type for the headline "End of the Crisis." The words were ironically chosen.

The crisis was indeed almost over, and ending on a note of din and confusion. Yet inexplicably, as events succeeded, overlapped and crossed each other during these last hours, Stanley Baldwin began to have last-minute alarms, and appears to have feared an eleventh-hour reversal. It was probably the result of the strain of the previous weeks and the victory that now seemed so very close. Sometime earlier Baldwin's Cabinet had sent an address to the King, saying:

"Ministers are reluctant to believe that Your Majesty's resolve is irrevocable, and still venture to hope that before Your Majesty pronounces any formal decision Your Majesty may be pleased to reconsider an action which must so deeply distress and so vitally affect all Your Majesty's subjects."

To this the King had replied, "His Majesty has given the matter his further consideration, but regrets he is unable to alter his decision."

It seemed safe enough, but Baldwin was not so sure. Mrs. Simpson's statement had attracted wide attention, and the Simpson press, as it was being called, was making a lot of noise about it. Baldwin was due to see the King that evening (Tuesday), and he was determined not to let him get out of the trap. "Only time I was ever frightened," Baldwin admitted later. "I thought he might change his mind."

He need not have worried. Edward, he found, was calm and inflexible, almost gay, in spite of the *Times* editorial of that morning. But next day the King received the most crushing blow of all. It must have been for Wallis Simpson the most difficult moment of her life. She told him of her intention, and he heard her out, stunned. "It's too late," he cried. "The Abdication documents are being drawn up. The Cabinet is meeting at this moment to act on them." Mrs. Simpson weakened at the sound of the King's despair, but still the escape plans stood awaiting her final decision. Esmond Harmsworth momentarily stiffened her resolve, and she called the King once more pleading for him to give her up. In this call it is clear from the King's memoirs that the scene was a climax of emotion, and it culminated in the King's steady warning that wherever she went, he would follow. Mrs. Simpson was beaten. The King's love, as Theodore Goddard told Baldwin, was too much for her, and she threw in her hand. The brief tempest of conjecture which had followed Wallis's statement died and with it the last hopes of the British Empire that it would keep its King.

It is remarkable, in retrospect, to note how little compassion was shown for Mrs. Simpson's plight at this time. Cut off from the outside world, her only link being telephone calls from a sometimes hysterical King, she sought only to be let off the hook. She was being blamed for the crisis. She was accused of ambition and selfishness; and what was most terrifying of all was the fact that both her enemies and her friends believed that the solution was in her hands, that she had only to lift the telephone to renounce the King and resolve the crisis. In fact this was something she was completely helpless to do. The King would not let her go. He was now positively eager for the great act of self-sacrifice.

The last assault on the nerves of Mrs. Simpson and the King was made on Wednesday, December ninth. A seventy-four-year-old solicitor's clerk named Francis Stephenson, of Ilford, Essex, "intervened" at the Divorce Registry at Somerset House and said he had reason to show why Mrs. Simpson's divorce should not be confirmed. It was an odd coincidence. It was exactly as Baldwin had forecast in his warning to the King the week before. Had it happened a day or so earlier when Baldwin feared the King might be wavering, the intervention might have altered considerably the character of the crisis, as it sought to prevent the King marrying Mrs. Simpson, on the throne or off it. Now, however, the crisis was too far gone for anything to be done about it.

On this same Wednesday the skies opened over Cannes and the rain came down in sheets drenching the thousands of sight-seers waiting outside the Villa Lou Viei. The following day the King abdicated.

A few more scenes were still to be played before Edward left for his exile. He had drafted the notes for a short farewell speech to the British people, calling in Winston Churchill and his unfailing muse for the final polish. The meeting between the defeated King and the apparently beaten statesman was a moving one, and gave Churchill the moment to invest the whole crisis past and present with its one note of sheer nobility.

As he said good-by, tears in his eyes, he recited half to himself, tapping out the rhythm with his stick, the words which Andrew Marvell wrote to a King who lost not only his throne but also his head:

> He nothing common did or mean
> Upon that memorable scene.

It was utterly Churchillian to go out into a future which would seem black enough to embitter any man, his parting words being a little couplet in tribute to the man in whose cause he had given everything he had. And if Churchill was at his most magnificent, Edward recaptured for a flash the boyishness of his Prince of Wales days.

He picked up the autographed photograph of himself that he had given Churchill and tore down the drive after him. "Hey Winston!" he shouted. "You've forgotten the picture."

That evening, all his bags packed, he said good-by to Fort Belvedere, the place where he had been young in love. Away from his sight dust sheets were already being put over the furniture, and the chintz curtains were being taken down.

He was driven to Windsor Castle where he was to have dinner with his family before making his broadcast. As a farewell meeting it went off better than it might have done. The ex-King probably did not realize how completely he had been written off by his family. Perhaps the family did not realize it either just yet. The crisis had been so sudden and cataclysmic that it was difficult for members of the family to adjust themselves to it. Although the scepter had passed from David to Bertie, neither could reconcile themselves to their new positions, and tonight David was still the senior, Bertie the junior. The ex-King talked little about the job he had given up. He recommended his valet to his brother, "a good fellow," and chatted about family matters. George VI was polite, possibly unaware himself of the deepness of his anger. The Duke of Kent, a young man of high intelligence and artistic imagination, was the least composed and closest to breaking down. Gloucester was distrait, and showed most resentment. He had made a career of the Army and now realized he would have to give it up to help his brother, the new King, in his task. Queen Mary was impassive, invulnerable. Her bitterness was the deepest of all, but that night she revealed the least. The dinner marked the last time in which Edward was admitted as part of the family. So far as the Royal Family was concerned the story was finished. For the rest of the world, waiting by their radio sets, the emotional climax was about to come.

A limousine traveled through the night along the Great West Road from London to Windsor. In the back sat Sir John Reith, a steely, handsome Scot, head of the B.B.C., and a good man for the part he now had to play.

Windsor Castle was ominously black and strangely deserted. There were no sentries or guards to be seen. Reith's car passed unchallenged, unrecognized, under the main archway and pulled up at the foot of the private apartments. Reith got out, but was given no opportunity to knock. He had hardly reached the doorway when the door opened silently and the light from the corridor streamed out into the courtyard. The superintendent admitted him without a word. The housekeeper stood in the corridor, her eyes on his face. Reith was shown up to the King's modest three-room apartment in the Augusta Tower. The engineers had done their job, the B.B.C. was ready, and Reith settled down in the King's bedroom to wait. A servant came in and put a match to the fire, and Reith stared into the flames.

He was interrupted in his reflections by the arrival of the superintendent who said that the King was approaching—the "former King" he meant—and would Sir John go down to welcome him. Reith thought it hardly correct to welcome the ex-King to his own apartment, but a glance at the servant's distraught face made him cut short his refusal. Edward did not seem at all surprised to see him. He wore his famous coat with the astrakhan collar, and puffed at a big cigar.

"Good evening, Reith," he said amiably. "Very nice of you to come over yourself for this." Walter Monckton was by his side and was introduced.

What was there to say? Reith decided to act as though nothing had happened. He discussed the broadcast cheerfully. "Madrid has just called," he said. "Civil War or no Civil War, they want permission to relay your broadcast." Edward laughed.

The former King walked into his suite, and saw some of the furniture was under dust covers. For a moment the thin veil of aplomb dropped, and his face went gray. So soon? Then he recovered himself. He remembered he had personally ordered the furniture to be covered. He had planned some redecorations and had not expected to leave so abruptly.

There were still some moments to go. Reith suggested a routine voice test, and handed the former King a newspaper to read from, tactfully turning the front page down to the table and presenting him with the sports page. But the Abdication was in the news everywhere. Mechanically the ex-King started to speak and found he was reading a speech by Sir Samuel Hoare, who that day had told a tennis organization that the new King was an enthusiastic tennis player. Involuntarily Edward stopped, looked up at Reith, and grinned. Reith noticed that the typescript of Edward's speech had been untidily prepared with many corrections and erasures. He recalled that Edward, as Prince of Wales and King, always pasted each page of his speech meticulously and personally on to large sheets of cardboard.

The red light went on. "This is Windsor Castle," Reith said to the listening world, "His Royal Highness Prince Edward." Reith then slipped out of the chair and Edward took his place, banging his foot against the table leg as he did so and making a noise that perplexed millions. Reith left the room noiselessly. Monckton was waiting for him outside. "Glad you behaved as you did," Monckton whispered. "Pretending nothing had happened. Right approach." Reith looked at Monckton and saw the tired eyes behind the rather owlish glasses. He remembered the haggard face of Godfrey Thomas in his office the week before. He realized how utterly the King's men had given themselves to the cause that had been lost that day. The ex-King was speaking:

At long last, I am able to say a few words of my own. I have never wanted to withold anything, but until now it has not been constitutionally possible for me to speak. A few hours ago I discharged my last duty as King and Emperor, and now that I have been succeeded by my brother, the Duke of York, my first words must be to declare my allegiance to him. This I do with all my heart. You all know the reasons which have impelled me to renounce the throne, but I want you to understand that in making up my mind I did not forget the Country or the Empire, which, as Prince of Wales, and lately as King, I have for twenty-five years tried to serve.

But you must believe me when I tell you that I have found it impossible to carry the heavy burden of responsibility and to discharge my duties as King, as I would wish to do, without the help and support of the woman I love, and I want you to know that the decision I have made has been mine and mine alone. This was a thing I had to judge for myself. The other person most nearly concerned has tried up to the last, to persuade me to take a different course. I have made this, the most serious decision, only upon the single thought of what would in the end be best for all.

This decision has been made less difficult to me by the sure knowledge that my brother, with his long training in the public affairs of this Country and with his fine qualities, will be able to take my place forthwith without interruption or injury to the life and progress of the Empire, and he has one matchless blessing, enjoyed by so many of you, and not bestowed on me, a happy home with his wife and children.

During these hard days I have been comforted by Her Majesty, my mother, and by my Family. The Ministers of the Crown, and in particular, Mr. Baldwin, have always treated me with full consideration. There has never been any constitutional difference between me and them, and between me and Parliament. Bred in the constitutional tradition by my Father, I should never have allowed any such issue to arise. Ever since I was Prince of Wales, and later on when I occupied the Throne, I have been treated with the greatest kindness by all classes wherever I have lived or journeyed through the Empire. For that I am very grateful. I now quit altogether public affairs, and lay down my burden. It may be some time before I return to my native land, but I shall always follow the fortunes of the British race and Empire with profound interest, and if, at any time in the future, I can be found of service to His Majesty in a private station, I shall not fail.

And now we all have a new King. I wish Him and you, His people, happiness and prosperity with all my heart. God Bless you all. God Save the King.

It was probably the most emotional night in the history of radio. An American woman correspondent arriving in London that morning had been warned earlier by a British politician friend to stay out of the West

The Duke and Wally in the grounds of the Chateau de Cande, near Tours, France, just prior to their marriage.

The Reverend Robert Anderson Jardine, who defied the Church of England by officiating at the marriage of the Duke and Duchess, is pictured with his wife as he arrived in the United States a few months after the wedding.

Herman Rogers, friend and spokesman for both the Duke and Duchess of Windsor, to whose Riviera Villa Wally fled prior to the Abdication.

Mr. and Mrs. Charles Bedaux, at wh Chateau the Duke and Duchess were m ried. His connections with Nazi Germ subsequently caused the Royal Cou considerable embarrassment.

wedding picture of the Duke and Duchess with the best man, Major Edward Metcalf.

The Duke and Duchess meet Herr Hitler at Berchtesgaden during their imprudent trip to Germany in 1937.

The Duke and Duchess in Paris just after war was declared in 1939.

End as the police expected trouble. The politician underestimated the massive receptivity of the British people. London, far from exploding, seemed uncomprehending. The crowds outside Buckingham Palace stood silent. Later the arguments stilled by the King's speech were resumed in homes and public houses, sometimes with heat but rarely with violence. Sadness, coupled with wonder and relief at the quietness of one's own reactions, seemed to be the national note. From Buckingham Palace courtiers two authentic quotes of the time were preserved.

One, from a man: "We have seen in him the last of the Stuart charm in the Royal Family. History may never be able to estimate its loss."

And the second, from a woman: "I loved Edward with all my heart, and I would have died for him. But when a King fights Parliament, Parliament always wins—thank God."

Wallis Simpson sat the speech out at the Villa Lou Viei with Herman and Kitty Rogers and Perry Brownlow. She was dry-eyed, but the moment the speech was over she went silently to her room and closed the door. Ernest Simpson listened to the speech in a friend's home in the West End of London. As Edward ended with the words, "God Bless you all. God Save the King," the radio rumbled into the sonorous tones of the National Anthem, and Ernest Simpson rose to his feet and stood to attention.

Edward left the microphone as though he were in a daze. He had not the slightest idea what was going to happen to him next. He did not even know where he was going, and there was some vague impression in his mind that he was going to Zurich, although Mrs. Simpson had made plans for him to go to Austria. . . .

King George VI had created him Duke of Windsor.

A butler helped the Duke on with his coat. Together the four brothers walked to the door and shook hands. Edward disappeared into a night that was raw and wispy with mist. With Walter Monckton waiting for him and Slipper, Mrs. Simpson's small dog left behind in her flight to France, snuffling on the front seat, the Duke climbed into the car which started off in the direction of Portsmouth. He had declined the sympathetic offer of Samuel Hoare to accompany him and to give him whatever ceremony was fit for an ex-King. He wanted to slip away quietly and undetected at night so that he could be out of the country by the time his brother was proclaimed King next day.

The arrangements to receive him at Portsmouth were makeshift and went wrong. At first some official at the Admiralty had arranged for the former King to go to France in the naval yacht the *Enchantress* which had taken Samuel Hoare to the Mediterranean some months before. But it was hastily felt by some other official that the name was ill-chosen in the circumstances and switched orders to the destroyer *Fury*, of the 6th Flotilla, Home Fleet, without however informing all the officers on the dock, who were consequently in some confusion.

None of the newspapers had heard of the King's impending departure, which was a relief, but on arriving at Portsmouth docks, he was driven through the wrong gate. While a small Guard of Honour was chilled to the bone waiting for him at Unicorn Gate the Duke's car had passed through Main Gate guarded by a single stamping sentry. The sailor recognized the former King and straightened into a salute which the Duke acknowledged. The car continued into the dockland and got lost. A passing watchman was asked the way and gave incomprehensible directions. The Duke thanked him.

A policeman who had seen the car pass phoned Admiral Sir William Fisher, Commander in Chief, Portsmouth, waiting with the Guard of Honour. Fisher got into his own car and drove off in search. He found the Duke's car stopped, the chauffeur baffled. Smiling the Duke apologized.

Fisher led the Duke back to the *Fury*. It must have been difficult for the Admiral to know what to say, but he found words. "Your broadcast, Sir, was deeply moving," he said hesitantly. "It must have made a great impression on all who heard it."

The Duke smiled slightly. He waited cheerfully on the dock while Slipper attended to necessary matters, then carried the dog under his arm up the gangplank. On board ship the last remnants of King Edward's court were assembled. Sir Piers (Joey) Legh, his equerry, was to accompany him to Vienna, with Storier of the Yard, and a valet. Sir Ulick Alexander and Sir Godfrey Thomas were to cross the Channel with him. Walter Monckton was saying good-by to him in Portsmouth.

Admiral Sir Roger Backhouse, Vice-Admiral Sir Dudley North and the commander of the ship, Commander C. L. Howe, welcomed him aboard. The Duke went immediately down to his cabin, and invited the flag officers to join him. The officers protested. "You must be terribly tired, Sir," said Backhouse. "Perhaps we should say good-by now." But the Duke insisted they come down. "Just for a moment," he said. The officers did and farewells were made.

The night had become clear and calm as the *Fury* sailed at two, Monckton, a solitary figure in civilian clothes among the impersonal blue and gold of the Royal Navy waving good-by from the dock. *Fury* anchored for the night in St. Helen's Roads, and that morning at six-thirty set out for Boulogne. Meanwhile the dawn of a new day and a new reign was breaking over London.

The former King had succeeded in leaving his realm quietly. On the windy wharf at Boulogne he said good-by to his friends, and summed up the events of the preceding months simply and frankly. "I always thought," he said to one of his friends, "that I could get away with a morganatic marriage."

His was not the only last word on the subject. Stanley Baldwin, characteristically, made two.

His narrative to the House of Commons describing the events of the crisis and his efforts to dissuade the King from marrying Mrs. Simpson, provided him with the greatest triumph of his career. At the end he looked up from what he called his "scrappy notes" and said, "I am convinced that where I failed no one would have succeeded."

A few weeks later Lord Brownlow returned to London and called on the Prime Minister. Brownlow had also failed in his mission to separate Mrs. Simpson from the King, but he was in good conscience. He had done his best, and he could have used Baldwin's words to the House of Commons as his own. He told Baldwin the whole story. The Prime Minister, puffing his pipe, listened silently. At the end he said jovially, "My boy, if you'd succeeded in your mission, I'd have clapped you in the Tower of London."

THE WINDSORS

XII

The Morning After

Behind the Duke the waters closed, and in England so smoothly did the new reign take over that the Abdication, which some feared might produce a revolution and the disintegration of the Empire, was quickly made to look almost unimportant.

In Berlin, Hitler complained to his ministers that Edward VIII had been squeezed out because he was pro-German. Apart from this gem of top-level Nazi thinking, the world reactions to the Abdication were somewhat inconsequential. Major Howard W. Jackson of Baltimore offered the couple the keys of the city and in Washington Don Felipo Espil, now Argentine Ambassador to the United States, clucked admiringly. "My! My!" he said, "who'd have guessed our little Wallis would come so far!"

Americans were as divided as the British on the subject. Sinclair Lewis in the New York *Post* begged Edward to come to the United States. "We are a funny people, David Windsor," said Lewis unctuously, "because we believe in righteousness. We believe that a man must have his own conscience and his own life. We believe perhaps that the most important thing that has happened in the last one hundred years is whether David Windsor should have his own life or not." William Allen White, distinguished editor of the Emporia (Kansas) *Gazette* said that Edward should have told the British people from the balcony of Buckingham Palace, "You are all a bunch of white-livered hypocrites."

H. L. Mencken, the American sage, and a Baltimorean, moreover, took a different view. "The King is an idiot," he said, "and the Abdication showed it. He ought to go to Hollywood. If he is too dumb to make good there, he could go to Washington."

From Jamaica, Lloyd George cabled the Duke:

BEST CHRISTMAS GREETINGS FROM AN OLD MINISTER OF THE CROWN WHO HOLDS YOU IN AS HIGH ESTEEM AS EVER AND REGARDS YOU WITH DEEPER LOYAL AFFECTION DEPLORES THE SHABBY AND STUPID TREATMENT ACCORDED YOU RESENTS THE MEAN AND UNGENEROUS ATTACKS UPON YOU.

Later Ribbentrop's wife claimed to have heard Winston Churchill say at a supper party at Lord Kemsley's, "Had Lloyd George not been abroad they would never have succeeded in making Edward VIII abdicate. Alone I was too weak."

In the correspondence columns of the London newspapers some readers urged that once Mrs. Simpson became the Duchess of Windsor bygones should be considered bygones and the couple should be allowed to return quietly to England. Others wrote bitterly condemning the ex-King for placing a woman above the Empire. Seventeen years later readers were still writing in the same vein.

A mood of introspection settled on the people of the British Empire. Even the newspapers were muted after the Abdication. But quite suddenly into this valley of calm poured an extraordinary assortment of high dignitaries of the Church of England, howling in pursuit of the former King.

It was headed by Dr. Cosmo Lang, the Archbishop of Canterbury, in a statement of such un-Christianlike vindictiveness that the Church has still not shaken off the painful effects of it. He condemned the King for wanting to marry a woman who had divorced her husband and rebuked the King's friends whose ways of life he said were "alien to the best interests of the people."

Other bishops scurried to get into the act. The Bishop of Durham said hopefully that if the marriage were taking place in the diocese of Durham, he would consider himself in duty bound to inhibit any clergyman within his jurisdiction from officiating at it; though there seemed little reason to think that the Duke had even momentarily contemplated Durham as the place in which to get married.

Then the Bishop of Fulham made a statement which carried more bite. He controls the chaplains on the continent of Europe, and he told reporters with urbane obscurity that his "directions to them would be followed with complete loyalty," his instructions being not to marry the Duke to Mrs. Simpson.

Such remarks stung some people to reply. In Parliament, John Mc-Govern, Glasgow Socialist, bawled, "Let the bishops get out and deal with the means test instead of kicking a man when he is down." And H. G. Wells commented that he thought Mrs. Simpson would be "a far nicer-minded and altogether cleaner house companion" than the Archbishop of Canterbury.

The Archbishop was, in fact, disconcerted at the unfriendly impact of his speech, so he hastily made another one urging people to forget the Abdication, after which he did his best to woo some of the more outspoken British correspondents away from their hostility with a Gargantuan banquet of pheasant in Lambeth Palace.

Throughout the incident the Archbishop kept his piety for his private diary. "My heart aches for the Duke of Windsor," he wrote. "Remembering his childhood, the rich promise of his services as Prince of Wales . . . I cannot bear to think of the life into which he has passed." Later he admitted he had been unwilling to crown King Edward. He saw King George VI and wrote "For an hour we talked together with the utmost ease about 'the crisis,' about the poor Duke of Windsor and then about arrangements for the Coronation. What a relief it was after the strained and wilful ways of the late King to be in this atmosphere of intimate friendship, and instead of looking forward to the Coronation as a sort of nightmare to realize . . . that to the solemn words of the Coronation there would now be a sincere response."

Fort Belvedere, the Duke of Windsor's old home, described so movingly in his memoirs, was left deserted except for a housekeeper. Weeds grew and choked the rhododendrons he had tended with such care, and the lawns, unmown, became a derelict jungle. For a long time the Duke kept the furniture under dust covers, but as the years passed and the possibilities of his return became more and more remote he moved the furniture out bit by bit, so that today it is scattered over the Windsors' homes everywhere from Paris to the Waldorf-Astoria.

The real-estate aspect of the Abdication involved others besides the staff and trustees of Fort Belvedere. Shortly after the Abdication the charming D. B. Merryman estate with five hundred acres (five times as many as Fort Belvedere) at Hayfields in the Washington Valley near Baltimore, was put up for sale. As Mrs. Simpson was related by marriage to the Merrymans, the estate agents put out a few feelers in the direction of the Duke to find out whether he would like to buy it. And up in Alberta, Canada, the manager of the EP Ranch (EP-Edward Prince), the Duke's own ranch, wondered whether it should be spruced up for the arrival of the owner and his bride as permanent residents. It was a decrepit windy shack, but the Duke had always been proud of it, and it was the only home he had left. But neither the quiet respectability of the former nor the dedicated discomfort of the latter made any appeal to the Windsors, and from the Duke came no word.

Ernest Simpson crossed the Atlantic to be united with Mary Kirk Raffray now divorced. To his surprise and alarm he found himself a hero in America and momentarily disappeared under a squealing swarm of bobbysoxers. He escaped to Connecticut where he married Mrs. Simpson's childhood friend.

An idyll—tragically short—began with both Simpson and Mary really happy. To the delight and mild surprise of friends, all of whom liked Simpson a lot but scarcely thought of him as the life and soul of the party, it was seen that Mary adored him. She also fell in love with England in a way that Mrs. Simpson had never done.

Mary made no secret of the fact that she was determined to give Ernest Simpson a son to make the marriage a success. She did so in 1939 when she was forty-three. It hastened a dormant cancer condition. Mary went to New York in 1940 to take her baby out of the way of the bombs. There she learned that her illness was incurable and said simply, "I want to die in England." She was given a priority passage back to blacked-out Britain, and a few months later she died. She is buried in the cemetery at Wells, in Somerset.

Simpson was deeply affected by her death. He rejoined the Guards in World War II and served for three years in India. It was not until 1948 that he married again, for the fourth time but to his first English wife. The fourth Mrs. Simpson was the beautiful former Mrs. Avril Joy Leveson-Gower, younger sister of the famous Mrs. Barney, who was found not guilty on a charge of murdering a Chelsea artist in a famous case in the early thirties and died some years later in a Paris hotel room. The Simpsons live happily today in Kensington, Simpson wealthy both by inheritance and by his own business efforts.

The Duke must sometimes find himself bewildered at the proliferation of marriages surrounding the Duchess. He is her third husband, and her two previous husbands between them have had eight wives.

Stanley Baldwin continued his controversial career under a new King. We have explored at some length the torments of both Mrs. Simpson's and Edward's position. But Baldwin had endured as great an ordeal as either. For nearly a year he had fretted and worried as First Minister to a King he distrusted. So far as he could tell, the instability of the monarchy would continue well beyond his (Baldwin's) death. Then Edward had offered him a pistol marked "Abdication" and Baldwin had, thankfully, shot him with it. Baldwin never had any regrets about this. As he saw it, Edward had assumed the monarchy when it was at its peak of popularity, and abandoned it eleven months later in an utter mess, leaving a shy but courageous younger brother to restore it.

The Duke of York was proclaimed King George VI. No man ever stepped into a tougher job. He had to prove not only himself, but also the institution of monarchy which had been sprung on him. How much luck and how much rationalization there was in his almost immediate popularity it is difficult to say. But in the new King, with his diffident manner, his shy smile, his sudden startled-stag expression, his reverence for his own position and his single-minded determination to live up to it, there was an atmosphere of goodness and refreshment. His apple-cheeked wife and adorable daughters helped. Baldwin's forecast was quickly justified. The Yorks did it very well.

Before returning to the story of Mrs. Simpson, one incident remains to be cleared up to wipe the slate of England clean of the Windsors' affairs. It was a strange incident, the ultimate secret of which went to the grave in the mind of an incredibly old man.

Francis Stephenson, the seventy-four-year-old solicitor's clerk, had "intervened" with the King's Proctor slightly more than twenty-four hours before the Abdication, stating that he was going to show why Mrs. Simpson's divorce decree nisi should not be made absolute. The intervention was pushed to some extent into the background by the other sensations of that memorable day. But even after the Abdication the matter remained on the books, and until it was removed Mrs. Simpson could not obtain her decree absolute and marry.

The act of intervention was a little known fact of law, yet during the Abdication crisis it had occurred to at least two people. Baldwin had warned the King that someone might take advantage of it. A week later Stephenson, coming from nowhere, known to nobody, did take advantage of it. The revelation of the power of a private citizen in a divorce case was startling.

The British people heard, most of them for the first time, that any person can interfere in any divorce. He simply goes to the Divorce Registry at Somerset House in the Strand. He pays half a crown and states he has reason to show why a particular decree should not be made absolute. His "appearance" is noted, and notice of it is sent to the solicitors of the petitioner (the petitioner in this case being Mrs. Simpson). According to law the intervener must file an affidavit within four days, giving his reasons, though even if he fails to do so, his "appearance" remains on the records and the decree cannot be made absolute until it has been formally removed in court.

In order to get an "appearance" removed the King's Proctor—the man who "polices" divorces to make sure there is no collusion between the two parties—has to appear in Court and ask for directions. The petitioner's lawyer must also appear and request the "appearance" to be removed from the register. Altogether the act of intervention is quite a business, and it remains, with alterations, on the books today except that the period between the decree nisi and the decree absolute has been cut from six months to six weeks.

Francis Stephenson turned overnight into a world-famous and, to some, a sinister figure. Whether he was a praiseworthy citizen doing his duty, or a publicity-seeking meddler, he was acting within his rights. Stephenson made his "appearance" and filed his affidavit, and then when the matter came up in the Divorce Court in March 1937, he withdrew as abruptly as he had intervened.

The Attorney General, Sir Donald Somervell, K.C., was in Court for the occasion. He represented the King's Proctor and applied to Sir Boyd Merriman, President of the Divorce Court, for directions in the case. Sir Donald pointed out that the King's Proctor had seen Stephenson, and Stephenson had stated that the suit was a collusive one (meaning that there had allegedly been collusion between Simpson and his wife in arranging their divorce). Stephenson, said Sir Donald, stated also that there had been conduct on the part of Mrs. Simpson which, unless the court exercised its discretion in her favor, disentitled her to the relief she sought. Then Sir Donald added, "Mr. Stephenson told the King's Proctor further that he had no evidence to support his allegations and that they were based on rumors which he had heard from friends and news which he had seen in the press."

Stephenson stood up in court, a stooped, insignificant man with drooping mustaches, but confident and precise. He announced that he withdrew his notice, and Sir Boyd Merriman ordered it to be struck out. Stephenson's affidavit setting out the reasons for his intervention was not read out, but several interesting facts emerged during the hearing. One was the first mention in court of the name of the corespondent in the Simpson suit, Mrs. E. H. Kennedy.

Another was the frank discussion of why Mrs. Simpson had moved to Felixstowe before the divorce, the reason allegedly given by Stephenson that she hoped to slip the divorce through quietly without the publicity which would have attended a London divorce. Mr. Norman (now Lord Justice) Birkett, K.C., representing Mrs. Simpson said hastily on this account, "I think it only fair and right to say at once that as far as Mrs. Simpson herself is concerned in all matters of procedure she acted on advice.

"Expedition was the primary consideration. Mrs. Simpson at the time was suffering from ill health. A very great nervous strain was imposed upon her. The matter of expedition was carefully considered by her advisers—I don't mean by her solicitors only, I mean solicitors and counsel." (Meaning Birkett himself.) "Reading was the appropriate Assize town. The adultery was at Bray. It was ascertained at Reading there would be no divorce suits. Ipswich was considered and a residence was taken at Beech House, Undercliff Road, Felixstowe, where Mrs. Simpson resided during the trial and intended to reside for some time afterwards. After the trial certain circumstances arose. . . . Mrs. Simpson cannot expect to be free from those things (rumors and gossip) but if it is in anybody's mind at any time that the reason for removal of this trial to Ipswich was to avoid a London trial I am here to say that the only reason for removal was that of expedition."

Sir Boyd Merriman acknowledged Birkett's honesty. "You have put it quite frankly that the Felixstowe residence was taken in order to qualify for trial. I understand."

With the intervention withdrawn, the way was cleared for Mrs. Simpson to get her divorce made absolute, and the storm in the teacup died. Stephenson retreated into the endless jungle of London suburbs leaving behind him two questions still not properly solved. Why did he intervene originally? And, having intervened, why did he so quietly withdraw?

Stephenson was no ordinary crank. He had a good brain, an above-average knowledge of the law, and a self-confidence which enabled him to have his say without either losing his head or being frightened by the uproar he created.

In the beginning he gave out a story that he was "so moved" by the King's Abdication speech that he felt he could not continue with the intervention. Later he admitted bluntly, "I withdrew because I was told to." Next the question must be asked, "By whom?"

That was the secret locked in the old man's mind. Stephenson, nearly ninety, and a widower, lived in a single room in a boarding house in the wilderness of fading stucco houses known as Tulse Hill in South London, and clung with complacent glee to his secret knowledge.

"One of the newspapers sent a pretty girl to me a few years ago," he was fond of telling friends. "She handed me a blank check and said I could fill it in if I told her the inside story of my intervention. But what do I need money for at my age?"

The central figure of one of the strangest incidents in the Abdication crisis talked in rambles, interspersed with many mysterious chortles, and long pauses for the wandering of the mind. He talked freely about his intervention, but he was so old that it was impossible to give too much credit to his stories. But he gave no word on why he intervened or why he withdrew the intervention. "I don't want to involve a lot of people," he said usually.

Whatever the fact or legend of the Stephenson business, he certainly caused deep distress to an overwrought couple.

XIII

Forlorn Wedding

After putting England behind him the former King traveled quietly to Vienna where he was greeted by the British Ambassador, Sir Walford Selby.

The Vienna police had made elaborate arrangements to make sure that the Duke of Windsor was not pestered by photographers, but the Duke saw them and said patiently, "Let them come." Afterwards, escorted by police, he set out into the Austrian countryside, and to the Castle Enzesfeld, twenty-five miles from Vienna.

It was the home of the Baron Eugene de Rothschild and his American wife. During the war it was occupied first by the Germans, then by the Russians, but is now restored to the Baron minus a few art treasures. As soon as he arrived the Duke was on the long-distance telephone to Cannes and to Mrs. Simpson still cloistered in the Villa Lou Viei. From then until May when Mrs. Simpson's decree nisi became absolute the telephone was to be their only means of communication. They dared not see each other and risk another incident like that created by Francis Stephenson. It was a heartbreaking separation, but both Mrs. Simpson and the Duke were exhausted by the events of the previous weeks, and for several days they did little in their respective retreats but sleep, venturing out only occasionally, and hardly bestirring themselves except when the time came for their two long-distance calls every day.

Only once was the Duke stirred out of his torpor. That was when he heard the remarks of the Archbishop of Canterbury. Not unnaturally they whipped him to a fury. He blew off by challenging Kitty de Rothschild to a round of golf and went plodding round the course slashing savagely and ineffectually at the ball, losing heavily. The following Sunday he dourly read the lesson in the local church.

As the weeks passed Mrs. Simpson found herself occasionally able to wander into town on shopping expeditions without being buffeted by sight-seers and newspapermen. She appeared pale but self-possessed, and was beginning to regain the ten pounds she had lost during the anxiety over the Abdication. Gradually in her telephone talks to the Duke their wedding plans began to form, although the difficulties in the way seemed endless.

Difficulty number one was the matter of the church service. The Duke was desperately anxious to have the wedding blessed by the Church of England, but there seemed to be no way round the Church's "hands-off" attitude. Difficulty number two was the alarming business of Francis Stephenson and the King's Proctor. Stephenson's intervention, if carried through, could prevent the marriage altogether unless they were to flee to Mexico or some other land with less rigid divorce laws. Difficulty number three was that even if the Stephenson intervention was withdrawn—and Mrs. Simpson's lawyers were reassuring—would the decree absolute come through on schedule? Difficulty number four was to find a place where the marriage ceremony could be held, and difficulty number five was to find another place for them to make their home.

One by one the difficulties were overcome, and if Wallis blundered in many of her decisions, she could be excused to some extent because she received no help from the Duke who was remote and ineffectual in Austria.

Her best move was when she found an ideal place to live. She entertained Sir Pomeroy and Lady Burton at dinner. Burton was an American-born, British-naturalized newspaper executive who died in 1947, aged seventy-nine, and Wallis arranged to rent from them their Riviera home, the Château de la Croe, a radiant tropical house near Antibes with stone terraces grading gently down to the Mediterranean. This she planned to occupy as a holiday home. For a town house she opened negotiations with agents in Paris.

Next she turned her attention to the wedding itself and in so doing she quickly came in contact with two extraordinary personalities, the Reverend Robert Anderson Jardine and Charles Eugene Bedaux, the first an aggressive, ambitious little man of God, vicar of St. Paul's Church, Darlington, the second a business tycoon who later became a traitor both to the country of his birth and the country of his adoption. Both the vicar and the industrialist had one point in common which brought them together with the Windsors. They had a total disrespect for authority.

Of all the many unfortunate acquaintances which the Windsors have made, Bedaux was by far the most unfortunate of the lot. He was dishonest and he was volubly pro-Nazi in his conversation whenever he was not being volubly pro-Bedaux. A French-born American citizen, he was a business operator of the E. Phillips Oppenheim school to whom frontiers and trade barriers seemed to present no obstacle.

He had perfected in the United States a scheme of industrial efficiency which made him millions in all sorts of countries—and Bedaux preferred traveling with large chunks of currency of whatever country he was in, rather than rely on orthodox bank accounts. Bedaux has been classed with operators like Ivar Kreugar who turned matchsticks into a gigantic financial empire, went bankrupt in 1932 and later shot himself; Serge Stavisky, whose frauds involved nearly $30,000,000 and who was found shot in 1934, whether by suicide or not was never settled; Alfred Loewenstein, the iron and coal magnate who fell out of a cross-Channel plane in 1928.

All died violently and Bedaux followed the rule. He was picked up in Africa by the liberating Americans in 1943, taken to Florida to be charged with treason for trading with the Germans, and there he poisoned himself. Bedaux's reputation was well known in 1937 and, even allowing for the man's great personal charm, any association with him was bound to give rise to criticism.

The attractiveness of his way of life could not be denied, however. He owned a storybook castle in Touraine, a gray, turreted place called the Château de Cande, built on a hill slightly more than eight miles from Tours, amid woods thick with lilies of the valley, violets and wild strawberries.

Bedaux had met Herman Rogers and his wife two or three times. He had followed the Abdication with the same avidity as the rest of the world, and had a special sympathy for Mrs. Simpson and her sufferings at the hands of the press. Bedaux had had similar trouble himself. A few days after the Abdication, Bedaux, being in New York at the time, cabled Rogers and offered them and Mrs. Simpson the Château de Cande as a holiday home and a refuge. It would be empty, he pointed out, as he did not plan to return until the following March. There was no reply to his cable and Bedaux, as thick-skinned as he was philosophic, forgot all about the matter.

Rogers's omission was not due to bad manners. The Abdication and Mrs. Simpson's flight to his home had given him a trying time. He was harried by the press between whom and Mrs. Simpson he was acting as a combination of public-relations officer and buffer. Though he was handling his job well, there were moments of confusion, and this was one of them. Mrs. Simpson was not so much thinking in terms of a holiday home as of some place in which she could possibly get married.

She had received more than one offer—Sir Pomeroy Burton had put the Château de la Croe at her disposal for the ceremony, and an American called Gerald Murphy who had been to Yale with Herman Rogers offered his house at Cap d'Antibes. Both offers were appreciated, but it was the sixteenth-century castle in Touraine that appealed to Wallis.

Bedaux was somewhat taken aback when he found belatedly that his castle which he had offered to Mrs. Simpson and the Rogers for a holiday had been selected over his head as the place where Mrs. Simpson should marry her Duke. But the times and circumstances being unusual and full of hazards, he readily understood the confusion and he received the news of his honor with delight. He hurried back to France from New York to prepare for the event.

It was stipulated at first that Wallis would have the Château to herself and that the Bedauxs should stay elsewhere. That, however, did not prevent Bedaux from being there to greet her and hand over, so to speak, the keys.

When Mrs. Simpson arrived at the end of March with the Rogers and Aunt Bessie, Bedaux's thirty servants, in knee-breeches and their most satiny uniforms were lined up to greet her. The Bedauxs waited at the top of the stone steps. Mrs. Simpson was shown to a suite which included, apart from antique furniture worth a fortune, a pink marble bathroom with gold attachments. Comfortably ensconced in the Château the party said good-by to the Bedauxs who were off to stay in Paris, and settled down to wait for the Duke who would join them as soon as Mrs. Simpson's decree became absolute in another six weeks. If they thought they had seen the last of the Bedauxs, they could not have been more wrong.

But first there was a poignant incident. Mrs. Simpson had brought with her Slipper, the cuddly little Cairn terrier. He had been given to the Duke when he was King, and when the uproar began, the happy little dog seemed to represent peace and contentment to the harassed couple.

Gamboling with the charming foolishness of small dogs in the grounds of Cande, Slipper was bitten by a viper and died. All sorts of themes could fit the sudden death of such a beloved dog. It could point to the trials and tribulations of the Windsor marriage, or to the progress of

Bedaux towards treason and suicide. At any rate, coming as it did after the strain which Mrs. Simpson had borne so resolutely, it was the last straw, and she broke down when the little dog was brought in.

It was the kind of situation in which Charles Bedaux appeared at his best. He bought her another dog called Pooky which in time took Slipper's place in her affections, and spent a long, muddy lifetime rolling happily in every piece of dirt he could find.

Bedaux had reappeared rather quickly on the scene to which he was supposed to have said farewell. Actually Mrs. Bedaux had been in the habit of driving to Cande on occasional week ends to take things back with her to Paris. Herman Rogers recalled later that Mrs. Simpson's kind heart was troubled at the inconvenience to which her affairs had put the Bedauxs. In the end they were invited to return. They protested, but did so.

Though Wallis was deeply upset by Slipper's death, she quickly recovered her composure. In the ebb and flow of life she had learned the virtues of patience. Not so the Duke of Windsor, who fretted at Enzesfeld and had to be restrained by all the powers of Rothschild's persuasion from catching the first train to Mrs. Simpson, without whom he had scarcely made a move in three years. The reunion dominated his thoughts. Forgotten were the years of service as Prince of Wales and his brief illumination as King. His Abdication hardly bothered him. He thought only of his intended bride. But the period of waiting did him good. The Duke had always had a valuable recuperative gift of sleep, and Major Edward Dudley Metcalfe, his aide, coming into his bedroom one morning and seeing the window open, the snow blowing in and the Duke of Windsor asleep like a tousled boy, marveled at the stresses which the human spirit could survive.

The Duke moved out of Enzesfeld at the end of the winter and rented a house, the Villa Appesbach, on the lake at St. Wolfgang, near Salzburg. Here he ruled with a passionate economy. He signed an agreement paying rent of sixty dollars a week, but stipulated that he did not want the house's tennis court or private motor launch which would have involved something extra. He slashed his total of servants to seven, supervised his own shopping, preferring to travel to Salzburg where the prices were lower than to shop in neighboring St. Wolfgang. He kept his calls to Mrs. Simpson to the evening period when the charges were $1.50 for three minutes instead of $2.00 in the daytime.

The lid was finally lifted on May 3, 1937, and from then on the events which had been blocked ever since the Abdication started to move swiftly. On this date Mrs. Simpson's decree was made absolute, and the

Duke was at last free to join her. Mrs. Simpson's lawyers hurried from the Divorce Court in London to the telephone and at ten thirty-three A.M. they telephoned her the good news. At ten fifty A.M. she was connected with St. Wolfgang, and at four P.M. the Duke was racing for Salzburg Station by car, followed by other cars piled high with eight trunks, two golf bags and a litter of suitcases.

An aide, left behind to settle the accounts, goggled slightly at the telephone bill, then recovered himself and paid—$3,760.

At four forty-five the Duke was occupying three private suites in the Orient Express bound from Salzburg to Paris. With him were his equerry, Captain Greenacre, Chief Inspector David Storier of the Yard and an assistant named Gattfield. Dotted along the train were a dozen or so British and American correspondents, typing madly.

At nine twenty-three on the morning of May fourth, Mrs. Simpson's Buick was waiting at Verneuil, thirty miles from Paris to pick up the Duke as he arrived. An interesting transformation: twelve months before it was the King's car and the King's chauffeur which called to collect Mrs. Simpson. Now the former King waited for Mrs. Simpson's car and driver. The train was on time and soon the Buick was traveling along the dusty lanes of Touraine to Cande. There a squad of five French detectives under an inspector and a Scotland Yard man prowled the grounds. Reporters were encamped around the gates as they had been ever since Mrs. Simpson arrived, kept at bay by gendarmes reinforced by the powerful figure of Madame Robinet, the concierge, at the gatehouse of the Château.

For the occasion the resident reporters had been joined by plane loads of the hard-eyed women correspondents which British and American newspapers invariably select to specialize in stories of true love and romance. The local hotels were jammed with as many as three correspondents per room. One or two of the French journalists raised a cheer as the Duke shot through and were acknowledged by a fleeting wave.

At the top of the stone steps leading into the Château the Duke and Mrs. Simpson met for the first time since before Mrs. Simpson's flight from England six months before. As the Bedauxs and the Rogers supervised the Duke's tower of luggage, the Duke and his intended Duchess walked arm in arm into the Château. They had much to talk about.

He had brought her gifts from Austria: a Tyrolean costume, wooden ornaments—and an engagement ring, that glittering little band of good intentions which had signified so much in the Abdication crisis, but had somehow been forgotten in the substance until now.

After lunch the Duke and Mrs. Simpson walked through the woods of the estate, making plans that now they were together seemed easier, Mrs. Simpson stooping once to pick him a flower.

On May eighth a statement was issued from the Château announcing that the marriage would take place on June second. On the same day Wallis changed her name by deed poll to Mrs. Wallis Warfield, a move rather plaintively designed to free herself from the association of the name of Simpson. It failed. Even the name of the Duchess of Windsor failed to do that.

On May twelfth a silent party sat in the gun room of the Château de Cande and listened on the radio to the Coronation of King George VI. The Bedauxs were there, Aunt Bessie, the Rogers and Dudley Forwood, the Duke's new equerry, a distinguished public-school man. Side by side on the couch sat Mrs. Wallis Warfield and the Duke of Windsor. There was much good in this little band of international sophisticates, even in the potential traitor Bedaux, and among the others was represented not only wealth and ambition but also loyal friendship and selfless generosity. Yet they seemed in this setting to be isolated from a rejoicing world. They went on listening as the voice which was to become familiar to every hearth throughout the Empire was heard for the first time as the voice of the King, hesitant, apprehensive, but deeply moving.

Somewhere in the castle a telephone rang. It was a reporter wanting to know if the Duke of Windsor cared to comment on his younger brother's speech. The Duke asked Rogers to pass on a brief message to say that he thought the speech was inspiring. The occasion was too great for pat speeches of praise.

The excitement of the Coronation died gradually away. Sixteen days later, Lord Brownlow, accompanied by a mutual friend, Brigadier Michael Wardell, arrived at Cande, having flown from London with bad news. He carried with him an official notice which was to be formally published in the *London Gazette*. The notice read:

> The King has been pleased by Letters Patent under the Great Seal of the Realm bearing date the twenty seventh day of May, 1937, to declare that the Duke of Windsor shall, notwithstanding his Instrument of Abdication . . . and his Majesty's Declaration of Abdication Act, 1936, whereby effect was given to the said Instrument be entitled to hold and enjoy for himself only the title, style or attribute of Royal Highness, *so however that his wife and descendants, if any, shall not hold the said title, style or attribute.*

It was the concluding statement which caught and held the attention. "The Duke is not going to like this intelligence," Brownlow had said to

Wardell on the way, and indeed dinner at the Château that night was a depressing meal. No one could think of anything else to talk about. Wallis, when she married, would be entitled to the forms and addresses appropriate to the wife of a Duke. She would be addressed as "Your Grace." She would not be entitled to the address of "Your Royal Highness," and she would not be entitled to a curtsy on formal occasions. The discussion went back and forth endlessly, but it is doubtful if any of the people at that table realized how profoundly the fortunes of the Duke of Windsor and his intended bride had been changed by the announcement.

The Duke's consideration of this ruling, however, had to be put aside under pressure of arrangements for the marriage. And now the second interesting character of the period turned up, the Reverend Robert Anderson Jardine. In his parish Jardine conducted four services every Sunday and had become known as "the poor man's preacher." He was a small man, independent, and moved by a feeling of deep irritation at the ways and affectations of bishops. He also adored publicity and the two combined to the point that when he heard that the Church was bringing pressure to prevent the Duke's marriage being blessed by the Church, he sat down and wrote to Herman Rogers offering his services to the Duke.

By this gesture Jardine thumbed his nose at the bishops and satisfied his conscience. He expected no answer and forgot the matter. To his surprise he received almost by return a telegram from George Allen, the Duke's legal adviser. The telegram read:

REFERENCE YOUR LETTER TO HERMAN ROGERS AT CHÂTEAU DE CANDE. WILL YOU PLEASE TELEPHONE ME AT WEST WITTERING, SUNDAY, ABOUT 1.30. A. G. ALLEN.

It is depressing to list the Windsors' category of mistakes, but here was another one. It was all very well to appreciate the offer of a clergyman to come forward despite the Church's ban, but was that what they really wanted? Should they not have inquired first what kind of a man it was who could blithely defy the bishops? If they had, they might have discovered that in Church of England circles Jardine was unpopular and regarded, even before this incident, as something of an opportunist. It would have been better, perhaps, to have sought in Canada or the United States for an Episcopalian clergyman who could perform the ceremony without involving an act of rebellion against Church heads.

Soon Jardine was on his way to the Château where the Duke and his intended Duchess were absorbed in wedding plans that seemed to get steadily more complicated and unhappy. The Duke, anticipating snubs, had decided to issue no formal invitations at all. He relied on his trusted friends to turn up if they could. He quickly heard that no member of the Royal Family was to be present, nor was any official of the British government, though the British Ambassador in Paris had said soothingly that somebody might come down "in an unofficial capacity." An impressive list of reasons why they could not come were given by friends whom they had expected. Even friends who had stood by them during the crisis were sending their regrets.

The excuses depressed the ex-King profoundly, more so perhaps because he understood that the confusion and conflict of loyalties among his old friends was genuine and mortifying to them. Many of his most trusted allies from his old Court had now accepted appointments with the new. And in the new Court suspicion against the Duke of Windsor and his intentions had a real force. The thought that some Britons might still look to him as their leader rather than the new King was a worrier. His remark "something must be done" to the Welsh miners was still remembered.

The attitude was shown in strange and un-English ways. One British official who wanted very badly to attend the Windsors' wedding wrote personally to the King to ask his advice. He received no answer. This puzzled him until later he became convinced, for reasons that satisfied him at least, that a scheming courtier had intercepted the letter on its way to the proper authorities and destroyed it. Whether such violent means were necessary it is difficult to say. The King was certainly not encouraging the officials around him to go to the wedding.

Other friends of the Duke turned for counsel to the various elder statesmen who knew more about the background of the Abdication. Baldwin, Churchill, Lord Beaverbrook, Lloyd George were all approached for advice. One perplexed British peer approached two of those gentlemen for their opinion. One told him emphatically "Go." Another said, "Whatever you do, don't go." Which left the peer not noticeably clearer in mind.

At the Château the ceremony seemed likely to be rather makeshift, a likelihood which increased when Jardine arrived and saw what he had to use for the Holy Service. The castle was not equipped for the convenience of the Protestant Church so Bedaux put his services at Jardine's disposal to improvise a suitable setting for the ceremony, and a most unlikely alliance sprang up between the two men.

Bedaux, the humorous cynic, took an immediate liking to Jardine. They understood each other from the start, and both recognized implicitly the fact that they were there for all they could get out of the Windsors' wedding. When Jardine announced that he needed a holy table Bedaux and he scoured the house, and Jardine ultimately settled on an oak chest. More rummaging was necessary to find a piece of cloth to cover it, and it was Mrs. Simpson who emerged dusty and breathless from her boxes with a piece of embroidered silk which Jardine proclaimed satisfactory.

Next there was the problem of the cross. Jardine did not have one. Bedaux gave a wave of the arm that encompassed the entire Château and said with an agnostic grin, "Take your pick." But Jardine's puritan mind shuddered at the Catholic crosses with vividly colored figures of the Lord crucified, and declined. A plain cross, he insisted, no crucifix. Bedaux shrugged and set to work. Finally he located a Protestant church in the vicinity and the problem was solved.

And so the ex-King of England was married to a woman who had two former husbands still living by a renegade clergyman in a room of a castle owned by an international scoundrel. The pathetic nature of the ceremony was felt by the guests, some of whom had been friends of the groom when he was the most idolized prince on earth; a time which must have seemed an eternity ago, but which in fact had come to an end when he became King less than eighteen months before.

The wedding itself went without a hitch, in spite of the confusion caused by friends not knowing whether to come or not. Sixteen guests turned up in all, more than half of them American friends. The guests included the Rothschilds, the Bedauxs, the Rogers, Sir Walter Monckton, George Allen. There was also Lady Selby, wife of the British minister in Vienna, Dudley Forwood and a few others. Aunt Bessie was Wallis's only relative present. Only one friend of the Duke's deliberately defied an official ban. He was Hugh Lloyd Thomas, a former secretary of the Duke's, then with the British Embassy in Paris.

Mrs. Simpson looked suitably charming in her long "Wallis-blue" dress made in Paris. A brooch of clustered sapphires and diamonds was at her throat, and a crucifix dangled from a bracelet of gold and sapphires. Her earrings were of sapphires.

She carried no flowers, but there were flowers by the hundreds in the huge, high-ceilinged drawing room.

According to the law the Duke and Mrs. Simpson first had to go through the civil ceremony which was performed at the Château by Dr. Charles Mercier, the Mayor of Monts, superb in an outsize tricolor sash. At this ceremony the Duke slipped the ring on his bride's finger, and by French law they were married.

After that they walked hand in hand down the corridor to the music

[146]

room where the Reverend Robert Anderson Jardine waited to bless their marriage in the Church of England. The Duke had fought hard for that blessing as he has fought hard for everything concerning the prestige of the woman he married for love. This was one of the few battles in which he could claim the victory.

Herman Rogers had been selected to give the bride away. Major Edward Dudley ("Fruity") Metcalfe supported the Duke as best man. Waves of organ music were heard throughout the ceremony, played by Marcel Dupre, one of France's leading organists, on the organ which Bedaux had brought over from America at a cost of $40,000.

People who were there remember that both the Duke and his bride looked pale and tense. The Duke's reply "I will" to Mr. Jardine was so high-pitched that the guests in the music room were startled. Mrs. Simpson faced the occasion better. Her response was soft, almost inaudible, but with no trace of nervousness. The words of the wedding service were spoken in full. The Duke and Mrs. Simpson knelt on the Château's brocaded satin cushions, and at the end the organ gently toned the hymn "O Perfect Love."

The business was over. There was the usual escape of tension as the champagne corks popped. The Duke gave his bride a tiara of diamonds, and Bedaux turned up with a statue representing "Love" sculptured by Fanny Hoefken-Hampel, a popular German artist. Neither the Duke nor anybody else kissed the bride. Outside, Madame Robinet, the gatekeeper, hurled a bottle of champagne against the gates in accordance with a local custom, to christen the marriage, and the patient newspapermen outside the castle gave Herman Rogers a gold fountain pen in token of his tactful liaison work over the past six months.

Mrs. Simpson was now Her Grace, though not Her Royal Highness, the Duchess of Windsor. It was the cue for the hard-eyed sisterhood of the press to go up in a spray of platitudes. "Prince Charming and the Beggarmaid," "Cinderella," "Wed in exile," "Off to live happily ever after," "The King who gave up everything for . . ." et cetera.

The Duke and Duchess said good-by to their guests and climbed into the Buick with good old George Ladbrook at the wheel, off on a honeymoon to the Castle Wasserleonberg in Carinthia, home of Count Paul Munster, an Austrian nobleman who married Peggy Ward, cousin of the Windsors' friend, the Earl of Dudley. Wasserleonberg was to be followed by a three-month honeymoon schedule taking in Salzburg, Venice, Budapest, Prague, Paris.

They were fairly well cushioned against the exigencies of exile. Servants loaded two hundred and sixty-six pieces of baggage, including one hundred and eighty-six trunks, into the train to arrive ahead of them. The habit of traveling much and traveling heavy became a characteristic of the Windsors in the years that followed.

XIV

The New Life

The Duchess had gambled away a throne. She now began the long lonely saga which even today shows no sign of ending. The tide of the Abdication had receded leaving her stranded, and her life assumed a harsh pattern of isolation with no connection at any point to her previous experience. At the height of her power she had been an obscure figure. Now she had lost her power and was world famous. Once she had been genuinely popular, the great houses of England open to her. Now she was an outcast hated by her old friends. She had married a King and lost her social position.

A terrifying future yawned ahead of her. Her husband did not even know how to put a coin in the telephone box. She was totally responsible for his well-being and happiness, and the world would not tolerate failure on her part. It was the Duchess who had to make the decisions, run the establishment, find friends and rebuild a new life from the ruin of her own and her husband's fortunes. If she failed she would be condemned. If she succeeded, the Duke would be praised. It was a battle which the Duchess could not win, but which she might avoid losing.

She set to work. Fortunately money was no object. The exact facts of the Windsors' varying financial fortunes are available only to their accountant, but this much is known. As Prince of Wales the Duke drew an income of $200,000 a year from the Duchy of Cornwall and $120,000 a year from the Duchy of Lancaster.

King George V left him no money whatever. The King's fortune was divided among Edward's three brothers, the Dukes of York, Gloucester and Kent. (This incidentally suggests that the Duchess of Kent is a much richer woman today than is widely believed, as presumably she inherited her husband's share when the Duke of Kent was killed during the war.) George V did, however, leave the palaces of Sandringham and Balmoral to Edward on a lease for life, together with various entailed treasures such as the royal heirlooms and the incomparable royal stamp collection. Edward, when he became King, also took charge of the $1,200,000 a year Civil List which Parliament granted the sovereign to look after royal expenses.

The Abdication created many legal puzzles. Edward could, if he had wished, have claimed to remain landlord of Sandringham and Balmoral even after he abdicated, but instead he sold his lease, and indeed everything to which he was entitled, to King George VI for a sum that has been estimated at between $3,000,000 and $4,000,000. This would not be subject to tax. He also received on Abdication a settlement from King George VI's personal funds, amounting to $100,000 a year. Altogether, from the moment of Abdication the Duke of Windsor could rely on an income, probably tax-free, of something like $280,000 to $360,000 a year.

On Abdication he automatically lost Fort Belvedere which was Crown property, and also the incomes from the Duchies of Cornwall and Lancaster. The Cornwall income normally belongs to the heir to the throne, or to the King when there is no direct heir (today Prince Charles gets it). However the Prince of Wales was always careful with his money, and the capital he piled up from the many years he spent drawing the income from the Duchy of Cornwall must have been large. After he married, he offered the Duchess a settlement of $2,000,000 but she declined this and accepted instead an income of $40,000 a year.

The Windsors' fortune, which was to be looked at rather enviously in later years by the hard-pressed British Royal Family, was their one major asset, and it helped considerably to ease their path. The Château de la Croe was an impressive home, and the Duchess had taken on a superlative chef. The water which flowed into the gold, swan-shaped bathtub was kept admirably hot, and the household comforts were many.

The Duchess's friends took a good look and began to re-emerge, and it was not long before she was once more the center of a thriving circle. Her new friends were not quite the same as those she had known in England, but they were rowdy and attractive, beautiful and witty, and all eager for invitations to Croe.

The Duchess had done a magnificent job on the Château's redecoration. In many of the rooms the Duchess played on the contrasting effect of blues and whites and in doing so made a lasting impact on Riviera fashion. The rooms had a blue and white motif. The cocktail bar at the top of the house was blue and white and cocktails were served in blue and white glasses. The breakfast trays which the servants brought to the guests' bedrooms would be white with blue cups or blue with white cups.

The Duchess invariably wore blue and white, and although she was much too good a hostess to try and influence her guests in their choice of dress they soon realized that it made her happy if they joined in the game, and soon her women friends were arriving at the Château in blue and white. The fashion persisted after the Windsors left, and even today there is a tendency among fashionable Riviera women to wear a standard daytime dress of white blouse and blue skirt or vice versa.

It was a typical inspiration of the Duchess's, the kind of idea which had always made her so stimulating a companion. There was no doubt whatever that the Duke was utterly happy in her company. He sloshed away energetically at golf balls, and began to putter conscientiously in his cutting garden in an attempt to build at Croe something as much like Fort Belvedere as possible. "I am a very happily married man," he told the Anglo-American Press Club gaily in Paris, "but my wife and I are neither content nor willing to lead a purely inactive life of pleasure." For their first Christmas together Herman Rogers let them have the Villa Lou Viei while Croe underwent decorations. The Duke had never before lived in such a small and intimate home and he reveled in it. He invited Winston Churchill to dinner and showed him with delight Rogers's new American furnace for the central heating, pressing the button so often to demonstrate its workings, that it was never quite the same afterwards.

Circumstances might now have improved had the Duchess's personality been different. But it seemed to many that with her elevation in society she left her American common sense behind her, and her attitude to life often seemed no closer to earth than her husband's.

The question of her title was unceasingly humiliating. The title of "Royal Highness," the right to a curtsy, were the tiny cankers of tragedy which ate into the soul. To the unsocial layman it seemed such a little thing for the Royal Family to withhold, and such a little thing for the Duke and Duchess to make such a big issue of, but the happiness of a married couple, living in a glasshouse under the eyes of the world, seemed to depend on it.

"The Duchess," the Duke was heard to say at the time, "is interested in courtesies, not curtsies." In fact the Duchess badly needed both. Officially protocol was satisfied by a curtsy to the Duke and a handshake to the Duchess, but this angered the Duke and has continued to anger him. Among the Windsors' friends there was total confusion. Grace Moore, the opera singer, was seen to drop the Duchess a curtsy at a party, and it started an international controversy.

Society became divided into those who did and those who did not. The Hon. Mrs. Helen Fitzgerald, a loyal friend of the Duchess's, did not. Lady Brownlow did not. Mrs. Colin Buist did not. These three had been in the old *Nahlin* party.

Mrs. Martin Scanlon, wife of the United States air attaché in Paris, did, Mrs. Euan Wallace (now Mrs. Herbert Agar) did, Lady Diana Cooper, wife of the late Duff Cooper (Viscount Norwich), did, and continued to do so even after her husband had become British Ambassador to France, thus starting a French tradition whereby Frenchwomen invariably curtsy to the Duchess. Lady Pembroke, one of the bluest bloods in English society did not—and went further. When she heard that Lady Diana and Mrs. Wallace had curtsied to the Duchess, she was annoyed and told them so in front of their husbands.

Many people have wondered if there were a particular enemy at Court who, by a mere formality, was preventing the Duke and Duchess from making a reasonable life together on their own standards in England. Queen Mary, until her death, was widely believed to be the person most unrelentingly opposed to the Duchess. Certainly there could be no point in minimizing the old Queen's hostility. She hated her American daughter-in-law and when one of her relatives asked why she did not relent for the sake of her son's happiness, she declared flatly that she would never tolerate seeing the Duchess of Windsor walking ahead of "my dear Duchess of Gloucester and my dear Duchess of Kent."

The opposition of King George VI to the Duchess was less clear-cut than that of his mother. He seemed to hate the whole subject, and avoided it as much as he could. Whenever the problem was presented to him, he met it either with silence or evasions. It was the weakness of this attitude which probably frustrated the Duke most, particularly as he had a solid suspicion that the King had no legal or historical justification for taking the attitude he did to the Duchess.

The Duke determined to do something about it. In January, 1938, eight months after the publication of the Letters Patent which denied the Duchess the right to the title of "Royal Highness," he invited Lord Jowitt (then Sir William Jowitt) to Paris to discuss it. Jowitt was one of the nation's leading lawyers with possibly the finest legal brain in the country. He had served in the Government as Attorney-General under

Ramsay MacDonald from 1929 to 1932. The Duke asked him what he thought were the legal aspects of recognition of the Duchess.

Jowitt took time to think it over, and in due course, delivered his opinion in writing. It was an opinion which illustrated the doubts and indefinables surrounding the whole matter.

First of all Jowitt considered it obvious, from the express terms of the Letters Patent of May, 1937, that the Duchess could base no claim to the title, style or attribute of "Her Royal Highness" on this document alone. But did that conclude the matter? What if the Duchess had a claim entirely independent of these Letters Patent?

In the course of his reflections Jowitt had traced at least one earlier issue of Letters Patent dealing with this very matter. It was dated Friday, February 5, 1864, and it said:

> The Queen (Victoria) has been pleased by Letters Patent under the Great Seal, to declare her Royal will and pleasure that besides the children of Sovereigns of these Realms, the children of the sons of any Sovereign of Great Britain and Ireland, *shall have and at all times hold and enjoy* the title, style and attribute of "Royal Highness," with their titular dignity of Prince or Princess prefixed to their respective Christian names, or with their titles of honour. . . . etc.

Here was a starting point. It was clearly laid down that the title of "His Royal Highness" was to attach to any son of the sovereign and to any grandson of the sovereign throughout the male line. Now nothing was more certain than that the Duke of Windsor was the son of George V and the grandson of Edward VII. He was therefore plainly entitled to the title of His Royal Highness under the Letters Patent of Queen Victoria, which contained no exceptions and no qualifications.

It was well known that if the son of the sovereign were to become a Roman Catholic he would consequently lose his right to accede to the throne—but there was no ground, it would seem, for asserting he would also lose his right to be styled "His Royal Highness." Similarly, in the event of abdication, he would lose his throne, but he remained his father's son. The Letters Patent of 1937 assumed that because he abdicated he also ceased to hold and enjoy the title, style or attribute of "His Royal Highness," for these Letters Patent purported to confer the title on him, and on him alone. In other words the Letters Patent were giving to him something that could not be taken away from him. Nothing in the Letters Patent of 1937 seemed to alter or cut down the provision of the earlier Letters Patent.

Was it possible that those responsible for the drafting of the Letters

Patent of 1937 were not aware of the Letters Patent of the Victorian age? Or if they knew of them why were they not referred to? Was it inadvisable to make it clear that the Letters Patent of 1937 were taking away from the Duke that which he already had? Were the Letters Patent of the Victorian days implicitly though not expressly repealed by the Letters Patent of 1937?

Jowitt was reluctant to accept the doctrine of implied repeal, and emphasized that the whole matter "cried aloud" for clarification. His argument so far helped to establish the position of the Duke. Now how was the Duchess affected by it?

It had to be borne in mind, Jowitt said, that when any one of the King's sons contracted a legal marriage his bride automatically became on marriage "Her Royal Highness." When, for example, the Lady Elizabeth Bowes-Lyon married His Royal Highness the Duke of York (later George VI), she became by the mere fact of marriage "Her Royal Highness the Duchess of York." She did *not* have this title conferred on her by any special order or decree. When therefore His Royal Highness the Duke of Windsor married, did not his wife by the mere fact of marriage become entitled to the style of "Royal Highness"?

It was one thing to say to the Duchess, you shall not have any claim to the title, style or attribute of "Royal Highness" under the Letters Patent of 1937. It would have been another more far-reaching thing to add that any claim to the title which derived from a wholly different source was to be invalidated.

Hence the uncertainty, the confusion, and hence the problem which confronted women who found themselves presented to the Duchess. Should they curtsy or not? All these doubts would have been so easily set at rest by an official pronouncement—but no such pronouncement was made. The only guidance was that given by the Letters Patent of 1937— and these seemed to have been based on the fallacious reasoning that by reason of the Abdication, the Duke of Windsor had ceased to be His Royal Highness. In reply it could only be said that the Sovereign, no doubt, is the fount of all honor, and in matters such as this his subjects would bow to the royal wish.

That summarized Jowitt's views. The Duke must certainly have pressed this opinion on his brother as vigorously as he could, but to no effect. Nothing was issued to alter, or make more rational, the Letters Patent of 1937, and the Duke, despite the best legal opinion in the world, was helpless.

So the Duchess was obliged to accept the position with as much dignity

The Duke and Duchess aboard their chartered yacht, Dipedon, in Nassau. U.P.
The fact that the luxurious yacht was fitted out with alligator-skin-covered bulkheads caused much comment in the American press.

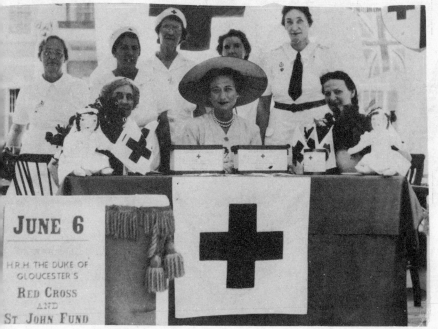

JUNE 6

H.R.H. THE DUKE OF
GLOUCESTER'S

RED CROSS
AND
ST JOHN FUND

DAILY EXPRESS

The Duchess officiating at a Red Cross benefit in Nassau during the Duke's term as Governor General. The date is D Day.

U.P.

*The Duchess hides a giggle after reading a note
someone sent her during a party in Biarritz recently.*

As part of the seemingly endless trek from resort to resort the Duke and
Duchess appear ready for a swim at Rapallo, Italy, in the summer of 1953.

U. P.

The Duchess, escorted by Prince Serge Obolensky, leads the fashion parade at the now famous "Duchess of Windsor Ball" in 1953.

as she could. The Royal Family had shown that it wanted no part of her, or of the Duke of Windsor either. Their wedding, which had been so ostentatiously boycotted, proved it. The King's refusal to give the Duchess the title they sought, confirmed it. His indifference to the publicity created established the fact beyond all doubt. Few wives have been so emphatically and publicly ignored by their husband's relatives.

Perhaps the Royal Family was right to resent a King who shook a shabby love affair like a saber in the face of history, the dynasty and the British Empire. Perhaps it was wrong to turn its back on the tradition of family charity; many a family in every class and period has taken to its heart a daughter-in-law or sister-in-law whose existence was repugnant to it. The problem is a matter for instinct and defies analysis.

What is beyond argument is the fact that the Royal Family's attitude made a frightful barrier in the way of the Duchess's efforts to make a contented life for herself and her husband. And this was not her only problem. She was being criticized, not altogether fairly, for her choice of acquaintances. Charles Bedaux was already being branded as a particularly unsavory specimen. Several others in the Duchess's circle at Croe were identified too closely for comfort with the extreme right-wing French appeasement group.

The Duchess of Windsor was bound by silence. She could not tell that she was forced to some extent into her present circle because her old friends had faded away. Two in particular had disappeared completely, and their absence was especially noteworthy and worth examination. They were "Dickie" and Edwina Mountbatten. Lord Louis had visited the Duke in Austria, but apart from that the Windsors saw almost nothing of them any more. They had been such a close foursome once upon a time that this drifting away was noticeable, one of the most interesting of the Windsors' many complex social relationships.

As young men the Prince of Wales and his cousin, Dickie, had been inseparable. They had much in common, including their star, the Prince having been born on June 23, in 1894, Lord Louis on June 25, in 1900. Both were good-looking, both were sailors, both loved the glitter of the world in which they lived, and both had strong social consciences. Both were unconventional and both were disliked by the more hidebound members of the aristocracy, even though their rebellion from accepted form had edged them in different directions, Mountbatten towards the Left, the Prince of Wales away from it.

Dickie and David were together in Japan, Australia, India and New Zealand, and they had been together at San Diego when the Duchess of Windsor was there with her first husband. In 1924, when Edwina

Mountbatten gave birth to her first daughter, Patricia Edwina Victoria, the Prince of Wales stood sponsor and provided one of the little girl's names.

Then when the Prince of Wales fell in love, Lord Louis and his wife had been the first to hear about it. Immediately they had taken Mrs. Simpson under their wing. They invited her to their famous penthouse in Mayfair with its super high-speed American elevator which Wallis cautiously declined to test. She in turn invited them to her parties in Bryanston Square.

The Prince of Wales, Mrs. Simpson, Lord Louis and Lady Louis became a foursome. They frolicked through the early thirties. Snapshots of the time show them hilariously sporting together at Biarritz, the Riviera, Paris, and from time to time even England. In 1935, Lord Louis was given command of the destroyer *Wishart,* and was ordered on a summer cruise through the Mediterranean. This was just the thing. When it put into port at Cannes, the first people to visit him were the Prince of Wales and Mrs. Simpson on holiday there with a group of friends. They visited the *Wishart* several times.

After King George V died, the new King appointed Mountbatten his personal A.D.C., and although in the Royal Navy service there was some disapproving talk about "favoritism," it must have seemed to many that Mountbatten's future was made. In the summer of 1936, King Edward VIII took the privileged members of his Court on the *Nahlin* cruise, and naturally the Mountbattens were there. Later, when he went to Balmoral, the Mountbattens were there, too. The King had to leave before the rest of the party, and Wallis returned to London with the Mountbattens and the Rogers. Finally Mountbatten, in his official capacity, accompanied the King on his visit to the Home Fleet shortly before the Abdication crisis broke. After that he faded into the background. He did not appear at all in the developments surrounding the Abdication.

Apparently Mountbatten did put himself at his cousin's service at the very end. In one recent Mountbatten biography, *Manifest Destiny,* the claim is made that Mountbatten offered to accompany the Duke of Windsor on his solitary voyage across the Channel. There seems to be no confirmation, however, for that statement among various men around the King at the time, and the biographer, Brian Connell, comes to the conclusion that "Whether by calculation or by chance Lord Louis never became so closely identified during these years with any group that its eclipse involved his own."

Although they did have one brief, dramatic reunion later in the story, the Windsors and the Mountbattens were from then on, apart. The

Windsors were not even present when the Mountbattens' daughter, Patricia, married Lord Brabourne in 1946.

The Duke of Windsor accepted to some extent the fact that in decline he could not command the friendships he did as Prince of Wales and as King, but in his memoirs, his cousin and bosom friend for almost half a lifetime was dismissed in half a dozen noncommittal references.

Yet in Britain, before the war, despite all the rumors, the conjectures and the half-conceived fears about the Windsors, a great fund of good will remained. A Gallup Poll was taken in Britain in January 1939, asking whether people would like the Duke and Duchess to come back and live in England. The result was:

Yes — 61%

No — 16%

Many people would have liked to see the Duke given a responsible job. The reasons were mixed: there were still remnants in England of his former popularity. There was curiosity to see what talents an ex-king is able to bring to civil life. There was a suspicion of abuse to the national sense of thrift that a man who had spent so many years training in public service at the taxpayers' expense, was now making a full-time career of getting a sun-tan on the Riviera.

But there was little chance of a job for the Duke. His activities had attracted too much criticism, and there was the ever-recurring obstacle of the Duchess's two former husbands which could not be kept down. A rumor circulated that the Duke sought the post of Governor-General to Canada, and another to the effect that the Canadian Government would have none of it. This may have been a pity. It was just the kind of job for which the Duke had been raised, and he might have made a great Governor-General and gone on to do other things, thus avoiding the sad drift of his later years. But the Windsors' stock with all the Dominions' governments was low, as Neville Chamberlain personally discovered.

In 1938, Chamberlain had replaced Stanley Baldwin as Prime Minister, a change that was of debatable benefit to Britain. Chamberlain had many friends in the country, and still has his defenders, but even his best friends do not give him the credit for having much understanding of personalities.

Chamberlain had been one of Baldwin's lieutenants during the Abdication crisis, but he had no strong personal feelings against the King. At first he was shown by his private papers to have been anxious at all costs to avert the Abdication and also to give Edward a chance of happiness. Later he deduced from discussions he had had at Buckingham Palace on the subject of housing in Britain that "the King was incapable of sustained purpose." It was after reaching the personal conviction that the King would use morganatic marriage as a stepping stone towards making Mrs. Simpson Queen that Chamberlain came out most solidly on Baldwin's side.

Chamberlain visited the Windsors in France in 1938. In the course of a pleasant chat he suggested that the Duke bring his wife to England on a visit, with semiofficial encouragement from the British Government. The Duke, as always eager to advance his cause in Britain, agreed enthusiastically. Chamberlain returned to London and mentioned the proposed visit in the course of official business to the Dominions. The reaction was such a loud and unanimous chorus of disapproval that Chamberlain was rocked. He realized for the first time that the Windsors were a problem to which there was no easy solution.

After pondering how to get out of the mess into which he had got himself, Chamberlain had a quite immoral idea. He sent for Beverley Baxter, the smoothest and most literate of all the journalist M.P.'s in the House. As indirectly as a Prime Minister must do to suggest anything so unethical, he gave Baxter the impression that he would not mind seeing an article in a London newspaper to the effect that it would be a very bad idea for the Windsors to come home at present. Baxter, just as evasive, hinted that such an article would be most interesting but that he was hardly in a position to write it himself. He gave several reasons but did not mention the fact that at that very moment the Windsors were suing him for libel.

In the end Chamberlain was obliged to do it the hard way and tell the Duke directly that the moment was ill-chosen, and that his idea had not been a good one. The Duke, rebuffed once more, retired into his cocoon on the Riviera.

XV

Bedaux, Bedaux, Bedaux

In the Labor magazine, *Forward,* at the end of 1937, Herbert Morrison, M.P., then leader of the London County Council, wrote, wonderingly, it seemed, rather than in anger: "The choice before ex-Kings is either to fade out of the public eye or to be a nuisance. Who are the Duke's advisers? I do not know, but either they are very bad ones or he will not take good advice."

Morrison said apologetically he was not criticizing because he wanted to. What stung him to such an attack was the Windsors' visit to Germany a few months after they were married, an ill-starred trip from the start, which did probably more than anything else to cost the Duke of Windsor the confidence of the British Government.

His plan was to tour first Germany and then the United States to study labor conditions. Every sane counsel urged on him the foolishness of an official Nazi-sponsored visit to Germany, including, it must be suspected, the secret, suppressed counsel of his own mind. The Germans had not troubled to mask their arrogance even to the Duke personally; the German press had insultingly ignored his wedding because of the presence of Jewish guests.

But the Duke was set on the trip, and Charles Bedaux was the man responsible. Bedaux was, of course, overjoyed at the windfall that had dropped people as eminent as the Windsors in his lap. It seemed to him that he was about to pull off, with their unwitting assistance, the biggest coup of his career. He did not imagine that the German trip would destroy him and almost destroy the Windsors, too.

Bedaux had made his millions with a scheme of industrial efficiency which estimated as closely as possible the ideal proportion between work and relaxation, so that the maximum productivity was achieved by all workers. The system worked from every angle except one: it made the worker feel as if he were an automaton and not a human being. Bedaux himself cared little about this, but in the depressed world of the early nineteen thirties the working man of the world was in a state of extreme sensitivity about his relationship to the machine. As a result Bedaux became the most hated man among all the classes of workers.

The Windsors might have discovered the fact that Bedaux was regarded by labor, and by much of management alike, as a scoundrel. Several friends had told them about him, and it was not difficult to see what he was up to concerning the trip to Germany.

Bedaux was eager above all at this time to ingratiate himself with the Nazis with whom he was negotiating for business concessions, his old German corporation having been closed down when the Nazis came to power. The Windsors, he knew, were both strongly attached to Germany, and during the evenings at the Château de Cande before the wedding he and the Duke had long discussions about labor conditions in general, discussions artfully channelled by Bedaux into the subject of labor conditions in Nazi Germany. Bedaux hoped that a tour of Germany by the Windsors would be regarded as heaven-sent publicity by the Nazis. In return, he hoped the Nazis would feel indebted to him and respond with business favors. (They did.)

Having caught the Duke of Windsor's enthusiasm, Bedaux left in early September for Berlin to tell his best friend in the German Government, Dr. Robert Ley, the labor leader. Ley, too, was enthusiastic. He had been drinking heavily and had to be supported by a military aide, but he put up what Bedaux called a "conversational struggle." Ley's idea for the tour was to put on a monster Nazi rally, with Swastikas and Hitler salutes everywhere. Bedaux cut him down, and pointed out that the Duke simply wanted to study labor conditions and see German workers living their normal lives. Ley, at an alcoholic disadvantage, agreed, and Bedaux's part in the incident was at an end. From this moment on he thought he would be clever to remain in the background.

It was obvious to anyone that the proposed tour had the most dangerous and explosive undercurrents, and when friends of the Windsors heard about it they were aghast. Yet the only person of repute that the Duke consulted was Lord Beaverbrook, and then possibly because he thought in advance that Beaverbrook might support him. Support, not criticism, was certainly what he sought.

Beaverbrook was contacted through their mutual friend Brigadier Michael Wardell, and it is Wardell who later recalled the lengths to which Beaverbrook went to try and talk the Duke out of the trip. At first it seemed that Beaverbrook, understanding at long last the obstinate character of the ex-King, tried to dissuade him by indirect methods, and advised him to consult Winston Churchill. "My private plane is here in Paris," he urged. "Let me send it back to pick up Churchill and bring him here." Beaverbrook was well aware that Churchill would be strenuously opposed to the trip, and that he, if anyone, would be able to dissuade the Duke from making it. Probably the Duke had the same idea and said that he did not want to bother Churchill.

Beaverbrook tried another oblique method of dissuasion. "Why don't you go to America first and to Germany afterwards?" he asked, obviously hoping that what could be delayed might then never happen. Again the Duke declined.

Finally, reluctantly, Beaverbrook spoke out plainly. First of all, he argued, the Duke was King no longer and consequently he could exert no influence on Hitler. Secondly he would be criticized by the British Government for interference in foreign affairs. Thirdly he would be censured by many for having truck with Hitler. Lastly, his reception by Hitler would be out of his control, and he would be putting himself in effect at Hitler's mercy.

The Duke would not be swayed, and every warning that Beaverbrook gave proved to be well founded. In Germany, the Windsors were treated with discourtesy from beginning to end.

On October eleventh they arrived at the Friedrichstrasse Station in Berlin where they were met by Dr. Robert Ley, looking, as usual, like a gangster. Neither Goebbels, the boss of Berlin, nor Ribbentrop, the Foreign Minister, who had once respectfully presented his credentials to the Duke, as King, could spare the time to greet them, but each considerately sent some minor functionary from their respective ministries to stand in for them.

The Duke and Duchess stayed at the slick Kaiserhof Hotel (now destroyed) opposite the Reich Chancellery. They saw many phases of Nazi endeavor: young Nazis bounding through some of their more spectacular physical training routines; factories; a coal mine—all overladen with lashings of "Strength Through Joy."

They saw Hermann Goering at his home in Karinhall. The Duke chatted to him in German while the Duchess was regaled with a running commentary by the interpreter. Goering showed the visitors his well-equipped gymnasium, most of the equipment being Swedish and designed (unsuccessfully) for the purpose of getting his weight down. He then took the Windsors to an attic where the Duke saw a superb model railway built for one of Goering's nephews, and the two men were soon absorbed in it.

They saw Robert Ley endlessly. This was the doctor's big show. They saw Goebbels being rather offhand in his Propaganda Ministry. Ribbentrop invited them to dinner at a smart restaurant, and Himmler entertained them. German officials were now boasting to British and American correspondents that the Duke was openly critical of British politics and had said that neither the British ministers of the day nor their possible successors were any match for the German and Italian dictators.

The Windsors saw an exhibition in Dusseldorf called "Creative Germany," and were hastily hustled past some anti-British slogans which had not been taken down in time. Finally they were insulted by Hitler.

Hitler and the Duke of Windsor fascinated each other, with a fascination that mingled curiosity with dislike. The Duke in his memoirs described Hitler as "a somewhat ridiculous figure with his theatrical posturings and his bombastic pretensions," but he felt strongly the force of Hitler's personality because he understood the German mind better than most other Englishmen. Hitler, for his part, openly despised the ex-King while at the same time seeing in him a person that might one day be of use to Germany, and combined with this was a sort of revolted fascination felt by a man to whom power was life and women were nothing, towards a man who had given up all power for one woman.

Hitler had followed the events of the Abdication eagerly, day by day, and had sent to London for further details. The German Embassy had obliged and sent him two short uncensored films which Hitler watched repeatedly. One showed Edward VIII looking over the preparations being made for his father's funeral. Mrs. Simpson was with him. The film appeared to have been taken secretly from a window opposite, and Hitler reportedly giggled throughout. The other film showed Edward and Wallis sporting in swim suits in the Adriatic during the *Nahlin* holiday. Hitler's only comment to this film was "Not a bad figure."

When the King abdicated, Hitler said, "If I could have had an hour's talk with him, it would never have happened." Hitler was probably overestimating his own powers again.

Hitler now made a point of impressing on the Duke the fact that he was a King no longer. It was just what Beaverbrook had forecast might happen. After a long drive through Southern Germany to Berchtesgaden, the Duke and Duchess were left for more than an hour kicking their heels at the foot of the mountain awaiting the Führer's pleasure. This was not the kind of reception they had expected when they were discussing their trip with Bedaux.

The interview when it finally happened, seemed to add up to very little. Hitler gave them the Nazi salute and was amiable in a casual way. Their talk was mostly in platitudes, the Duke expressing his admiration for the progress of social welfare under the Nazis. The Duchess spoke little, but Hitler seemed to be more impressed with her than he was with her husband. "She would have made a good Queen," Hitler said to Paul Schmidt, his interpreter, when they had gone.

Afterwards, the Windsors were entertained at dinner by Rudolf Hess. Hitler was not present. At the end of the trip, the Duke gave Ley a contribution, the amount of which was not disclosed. It was made to the German Winter Relief Fund and the Duke added a note which read: "You showed us every sphere of activity of the German Labour Front and we were deeply impressed by what is being done for the working population of Germany."

The Windsors then departed and Albion Ross, the Berlin correspondent of the New York *Times* cabled: "The Duke's decision to see for himself the Third Reich's industries and institutions and his gestures and remarks during the last two weeks have demonstrated adequately that the Abdication did rob Germany of a firm friend, if not indeed a devoted admirer, on the British Throne. He has lent himself, perhaps unconsciously, but easily, to National Socialist propaganda. There can be no doubt that the tour has strengthened the (Nazi) regime's hold on the working classes."

Everybody makes mistakes, and some of the greatest men make some of the worst ones. The Windsors' German visit was a bad mistake indeed. One would not labor on it or draw attention to it if it were an isolated mistake, but the Windsors neither profited by it nor appeared repentant of it. On the contrary they went on to make more.

As soon as they returned to France, they began to make plans, once more with the omnipresent Bedaux, for their first trip together to the United States. This they planned with the keenest of anticipation. The Duke adored America and the American achievement, and for the Duchess it meant her first real trip home in ten years. The trip was fiasco Number Two.

The rumblings started so early that they mingled in the storm of controversy over the Hitler trip, giving the impression of a prolonged, uninterrupted thunderclap. Most Americans wanted to welcome the Windsors, but the auspices were intolerable.

At first Bedaux convinced the Windsors that the criticisms were unimportant and they booked passage in the German liner *Bremen*. Bedaux, dreaming of this as his master stroke traveled ahead to complete the arrangements.

Janet Flanner wrote in *The New Yorker*:

> Bedaux spent nine devastating days in America. American labour and a large section of the American press had, when it became known that the proposed labour-studying trip of the Windsors was being sponsored by Bedaux, attacked him as a Fascist and an enemy of labour. The important men in the four American Bedaux management-consultant companies rebelled against the idea of the Windsor expedition, and he had to relinquish his control of these organizations.

> At the end of nine days he [Bedaux] fled the country . . . apparently being called a Fascist in forty-eight states had not sickened him, but failure had—failure for the first time in his career. He had lost . . . his pride; success was his natural element and vanity was essential to his state of well-being. . . . For three months he lay in a Munich sanatorium where his trouble was diagnosed as coronary thrombosis. An attempt at suicide was rumoured. For years he had been bothered with insomnia. He now developed a reliance on a German barbituric sleeping tablet called Medinal. From the beginning of 1938, sleeping drugs dominated his nocturnal existence, and six years later a fatal overdose ended it in Miami.

With the controversy raging all round him, Bedaux cabled the Duke frantically: "Sire, I am compelled in honesty and friendship to advise you that because of a mistaken attack upon me here, I am convinced that your proposed tour will be difficult under my guidance. I respectfully suggest . . . implore you to relieve me completely of all duties in connection with it."

The roars of protest against Bedaux and the Windsors' association became deafening, and two days before the *Bremen* was due to sail the Windsors canceled their reservations and called off their tour. The tormented then turned desperately on their tormentors with a communiqué which said:

> The Duke emphatically repeats that there is no shadow of justification for any suggestion that he is allied to any industrial system, or that he is for or against any particular political and racial doctrine.

The German affair had been inexcusable, and the still-born American tour showed shockingly bad judgment. Having offended both sense and discernment, the Windsors now committed, in 1939, a major error of taste, which almost resulted in a break between the Windsors and their most powerful ally, Lord Beaverbrook.

The war was very close in 1939, clearly and unmistakably close, the question "if" having dissolved after Hitler's recent annexation of Czechoslovakia into the question "when." The year was so exclusively stamped in history as the year the war began that the fact of King George's and Queen Elizabeth's visit to Canada and America in that year has been to a great extent forgotten. Yet this visit was a triumph of lasting importance to Anglo-American relations.

The Windsors were living in France, and had just taken a charming mansion at No. 24 Boulevard Suchet with marble floors, a delicate little *ascenseur* and back windows facing the Bois de Boulogne. In May, just as the King and the Queen were setting out for Canada, the Duke and Duchess visited Verdun, scene of some of the bloodiest fighting of World War I.

The thought of war was becoming an obsession with the Windsors. They had enthusiastically hailed Neville Chamberlain's visit to Munich of the year before, and remained voluble supporters of the Chamberlain appeasement policies and his sellout of Czechoslovakia even after second thoughts had set in with most of the other people who had cheered Chamberlain at the time. There were many criticisms to be made against the Windsors' support of the policy of appeasing Germany, but in justification it had to be said that it was no more extreme than that of Chamberlain himself, the Prime Minister of Britain, who was prepared to give Hitler almost anything in order to avoid war.

The Duke was profoundly and sincerely moved by his visit to Verdun, and he arrived at a plan to make a dramatic broadcast appeal for peace on the site of the old battleground. The appeal was to be directed principally to the United States as the country with the greatest potential power to prevent a new European war. In retrospect it is easy to see that the inspiration was futile, and that the last thing Hitler was listening for when he switched on his radio was an appeal for peace.

But there was nothing basically wrong with the idea except for the fact that the man who had replaced the Duke as King of England was at that moment on his way to America on a good-will mission requiring the utmost tact considering the sharp isolationism which then dominated American thinking.

Quite obviously no connection dawned on the Duke between his broadcast to America and his brother's visit to America. But in England a few old skeletons seemed to rattle in the cupboard. Was this a move of "the King across the water" trying to take over in the absence of the crowned King? Of course it was not, but there was an uncomfortable stirring of the fears that had arisen after the Abdication. There was a murmur of protest when the news of the Duke's proposed broadcast was announced. This was when Beaverbrook intervened to the anger of the Windsors. The press lord directed an editorial attacking the idea of a broadcast.

The *Daily Express* opinion column, on May 8, 1939, said:

> The decision of the Duke of Windsor to broadcast to the United States today is to be regretted. The moment is unhappily chosen. The King is on his way to America. Any word spoken on the United States at present should come from him. It would have been better for the Duke to wait. It is reported that the Duke will make an appeal for peace in his broadcast. Such an appeal would have been uttered more appropriately after the King's peace mission to the Dominion had been brought to a conclusion.

The whole incident became a mess. The B.B.C. refused to relay the Duke's speech, and Beaverbrook swung round on the B.B.C. with an even harder editorial fulminating against censorship. Within a matter of hours the Windsors were once more involved in a bitter and totally unnecessary controversy.

In a hotel bedroom in Verdun the Duke persisted doggedly with his broadcast. The Duchess sat by his side while he made it. His previous broadcast in December 1936 was something the world would never forget. This one flopped painfully. It was sincere, pious, indistinguishable from many other speeches that were being made by people appalled by the state of the world that Hitler menaced. The speeches were ineffectual. Hindsight shows that the cause of peace would have been better served had allied statesmen listened more closely to the warning growls of a man like Winston Churchill.

Both the Duke and the Duchess blamed Beaverbrook for the failure of the speech. In fact the Windsors could blame nobody, not even themselves. They had proved themselves to be two confused, ingenuous people dangerously prominent in a complicated world; obstinate only to be misled, well-read only to misinterpret what they read, well-informed by some of the world's best brains yet not understanding what they were told. The Duke needed the harness of royal duties, and the benefits of compulsory advice. Without them he was all at sea. However happy the Duchess made his private life, she was contributing nothing to his public stability. A fatal trait could now be seen in her character. She appeared to be claiming nobility as a birthright instead of an achievement. Instead of putting her invaluable background at her husband's service, she seemed anxious to forget it ever existed. The Windsors demonstrated the iceberg principle in exact reverse. Everything was on the surface. Underneath there was nothing. Four months after the Verdun incident Germany attacked, and the Windsors, along with the rest of humanity, went to war.

XVI

On the Run Again

The war brought the Windsors home. Major Edward Dudley Metcalfe was at Croe with them when it started and the three of them set out together by car, arriving at Cherbourg about teatime on September 12, 1939.

A destroyer, the *Kelly,* had been dispatched to France to pick them up and take them to England, and it was commanded by Lord Louis Mountbatten. A meeting that might once have been the subject for excited gossip throughout the length and breadth of café society was now almost casual. The war was so new and strange that by comparison other events had lost their capacity to surprise or impress, and they met as old friends.

They were, in fact, an unusually interlocked group. The Duke had been Mountbatten's best man, Mountbatten had been Metcalfe's best man, and Metcalfe had been the Duke's best man at their respective weddings.

The *Kelly* sailed at full speed for England and reached Portsmouth about nine o'clock that night. The Windsors' first view of England was the blackout, and they could only just see, as the *Kelly* slipped gingerly up to the wharf, a dim blue harbor light directed downward to a stretch of red carpet, and gleaming here and there on the brasses of the naval band assembled to welcome them.

The unaccustomed darkness and a strong ebb tide made docking a treacherous business, and the *Kelly* had to be edged in gently. But Mountbatten was a remarkable sailor and his directions were sure. The first to congratulate him as the ship was finally tied up was the Duke of Windsor.

Mountbatten and Metcalfe followed the Windsors ashore. "It's nice to be home again," the Duke said as he put his foot on English soil for the first time since the Abdication. Behind him the Duchess trod carefully down the gangplank with the assistance of a naval officer. The first person to greet them was Sir Walter Monckton. Lady Alexandra Metcalfe, wife of Major Metcalfe, and the Commander-in-Chief, Portsmouth, were also there. The sailors, lined up on the deck of the *Kelly*, gave the Windsors three cheers, and the band played a welcoming march.

They stayed that night at the Commander-in-Chief's house, and the following morning, after saying their good-bys to Mountbatten, set out for Coleman's Hatch in Sussex, home of the Metcalfes. Lord Louis then took the *Kelly* back to sea. It was sunk off Crete in 1941.

Britain had been at war nine days. In their own way the Duke and Duchess had done as much as any two people in their position could have done to prevent it. Now that it had started their fears were put behind them, and they were ready to make the best of it. And at least it had given the Duke a new opportunity for finding a job. Full of high hopes he unpacked at Coleman's Hatch, then drove to London to call on the Prime Minister, Neville Chamberlain. Though censorship had been imposed on Britain and no word was allowed to leak out about the movements of important people, a few Londoners recognized the Duke as he climbed out of his car at No. 10 Downing Street and cheered him.

Chamberlain greeted him cordially and passed him on to Hore-Belisha, the War Minister. The Duke emerged from the War Office with a brighter smile on his face than people could recall in a long time. A beaming Hore-Belisha saw him to the door and shook him warmly by the hand.

At long last the Duke had succeeded in getting an appointment from the British Government. To do so he had been obliged to make a sacrifice that does not seem much to the layman but must have been difficult for a man who had once been King. The official announcement read:

> In order that His Royal Highness might be able to take up an appointment the King has been pleased to permit him temporarily to relinquish the rank of field marshal in the British army and assume that of major general.

In other words the Duke had voluntarily dropped himself a couple of notches in the military scale, and from now on he would have to work as a small unit within the framework of an army he had once commanded. Censorship referred to "an appointment overseas," but did not

[169]

specify what it was. The Duke often wondered himself during the months that followed.

Officially he was to be attached under General Sir Richard Howard-Vyse to one of the two British military missions to the French Army. It sounded excellent. The Duke asked Metcalfe to join him as A.D.C. and Metcalfe agreed. Then the Duke sent for George Ladbrook. It was a typical act of loyalty on the Duke's part that his first thoughts were for his old chauffeur. "Would you like to work for me again?" he asked Ladbrook.

Eagerly Ladbrook said he would. Things had not been going too well for him since he had left the Duke's service in 1937. He had four sons—all godsons of the Duke—to bring up and he had found jobs difficult to get.

His Buckingham Palace pension was small. At first he had driven an American woman round Europe, but that job did not last long and he had been obliged to return to London and take a job as doorman of a West End night club for a few pounds a week. This was enough to keep him going but not enough to keep him out of adventures.

In the autumn of 1937 he was walking down Charing Cross Road, having had, as he philosophically admitted later, a couple of beers, and heard a soapbox orator declaiming under the statue of Sir Henry Irving. He caught the words "Duchess of Windsor" and stopped to listen. The speaker was delivering a tirade against Ladbrook's old employers. He felt compelled to interrupt.

"Lies," he shouted.

The speaker paused, surprised, then resumed.

"Lies," shouted Ladbrook again.

In the end they hauled him off to Bow Street and charged him with being drunk and disorderly, but when a sympathetic magistrate heard the case he dismissed the charge and cleared Ladbrook completely.

"I couldn't help myself when I heard that fellow's slanders," Ladbrook said afterwards. "But the Duke will be annoyed when he hears about it. 'Ignore them' he would have said to me."

His new job was a private one, the Duke explained, and he would wear civilian clothes not uniform. It would consist chiefly of driving the Duchess as the Duke would often have to travel in official cars.

The Windsors returned to France in the destroyer *Express* (later mined off Holland). With her husband working for the first time in their two and a half years of marriage, the Duchess now gave the impression of wanting to do something herself but not knowing quite what. She discussed the idea of turning the Château de la Croe into a convalescent home for wounded officers, and talked about it to Herman Rogers. As a neutral American opportunities for Rogers to help in the war effort were limited, but he had joined the Red Cross and was agreeable to the Duchess's suggestion that he should supervise the convalescent home once it was established. Nothing came of it.

The Duchess herself joined the French Red Cross and emerged in a smart uniform. She called on Lady Mendl, wife of Sir Charles Mendl, the British press attaché in Paris. Lady Mendl was the former Elsie de Wolfe, renowned interior decorator and hostess, whose several claims to fame included an ability to stand on her head at the age of seventy. Together they issued an appeal as two American women, to the United States to send woollen garments for the soldiers in the Maginot Line. The Red Cross office in Paris was promptly buried under with gifts from all over America. It was probably the most constructive thing the Duchess did in this period.

All the time she maintained the house in the Boulevard Suchet and the Château de la Croe for the comfort of the Duke whose brief delight had disappeared abruptly. The last time he had held a job he had been King of England and the comparison with his work then and his work now was a depressing one. He was attached to the French GHQ in Paris. He had an office and a desk. What he was called on to do he did efficiently, but he wanted to be something more useful. It was a relief for him to get away from his Paris office and visit the various French army commands in the Maginot Line. Here some of the old Prince of Wales sparkle returned. He would spend four or five days in the front line talking to the generals and inspecting the defenses, and although there was no fighting going on, it reminded him to some extent of his exciting young days in the trenches in World War I. Back in Paris from these trips, the work would close in on him like a blanket. He would draft long reports on his visits and send them to the War Office in London, but suspected that the reports contributed very little to the conduct of the war.

The battle fronts were silent. The great German offensive had not yet begun, but already the Windsors' contribution had dwindled to nothing. So this storm-tossed couple, both in uniform, sat out the twilight war in Paris, eager to help but with nothing to do, all dressed up, as it were, but with nowhere to go.

The Duchess's attempts to be useful were completely ignored by the British authorities. Her efforts for the Red Cross were met with silence. Women's memories are longer than men's, and the Duchess was paying the penalty for too many witty sayings made in the past, too many good jokes casually thrown out but relayed from dinner table to dinner table. Wit is a treacherous dart. It is perhaps the only weapon with which it is possible to stab oneself in one's own back. The Duchess's sense of discouragement was probably deeper even than the Duke's.

The Duchess, however, was always there to keep his social life in Paris agreeable. On Christmas Eve she gave a large party in their blacked-out house. The war was forgotten for the moment. Noel Coward was there. He played the piano and sang "Tropical Heat Wave." The Duke, wearing the kilt, walked downstairs playing the bagpipes, a difficult feat and a standard test for the expert player. He did it very well.

About a month afterwards the Duchess of Windsor appeared at another party alone. It was noticed that she was called to the telephone several times in the course of the evening. Though little was said at the party, it was learned that the Duke had made a quick trip to London to try and get himself a more active job. On January 23, 1940, he called on General Sir Edmund Ironside, Chief of Imperial General Staff. It got him nowhere, and he returned, frustrated, to Paris.

The Duke began to spend more and more time at home, and more and more afternoons at the St. Cloud golf course. Long furloughs were spent at the Château de la Croe and at Biarritz. But he kept at his job, doing what little was necessary. Once or twice he took his wife with him on his official visits but this did not prove popular with the other officers.

The German invasion of France changed everything. The Duke sent the Duchess to Biarritz out of harm's way, and every morning at four o'clock he went north with Metcalfe to visit the collapsing French front which was grinding closer to Paris every day. The organization of the British Military mission began to crack up together with the rest of the Allied effort. From Biarritz the Duchess called repeatedly, urging the Duke to escape south before the Germans captured him. One night, after a visit to the front, the Duke decided to go. He left the deserted house in the Boulevard Suchet, climbed into his car and traveled south to the Château de la Croe. Metcalfe managed to get back to London alone. A few days later the Germans were in Paris.

It was all over so quickly, and confusion on the Riviera was utter. No real news was coming through from Paris or the battle fronts, and the wildest rumors were believed. All round the Windsors the British colony was packing up and hastily departing by whatever means it could. One large group—Somerset Maugham was in it—boarded a Polish coal boat which had put into Cannes and ultimately reached safety after a nightmare voyage.

The Duchess had arrived at Croe from Biarritz, and with the Duke wondered what to do next. They were informed that Paris had fallen and that France had surrendered, and it was clear that they could not stay on the Riviera as the Germans might turn up at Antibes within a matter of hours.

But the Duke refused to be panicked. He remained calm and assured anxious friends that there was nothing to worry about. "There is no reason for alarm," he said on several occasions. "If we were in any danger the British Government would send a warship for me."

They had been at Croe together for a few days when Captain George Wood, a big, humorous, but harassed army officer joined them with his Austrian wife Rosa. The Windsors had known the Woods in Austria, and Wood was shortly to take an appointment as the Duke's aide. Wood had been in Vienna when the Nazis had swept through, and his daughter, who was married to Prince Hohenberg, second son of the murdered Archduke Franz Ferdinand of Austria, had just disappeared somewhere under the holocaust of the blitzkrieg (they were both discovered undernourished but safe in Austria when the war ended).

Major Grey Phillips, the Duke's comptroller, followed the Woods to Croe on the evening of June eighteenth, and a long conference was held to decide the next move. The Duke himself was in favor of staying put, feeling that to leave would look like running away. Phillips agreed. Wood, who had seen the Nazis enter Vienna and was touched more closely than the other two by the Nazi menace, was for getting out. In the end the Duke decided he could not rely on the British Government for help, and that he had better leave. His liaison job to the French Army had disappeared along with the French Army, and there was nothing to keep him on the Riviera except the physical difficulty of getting away from it with the Germans closing in from the north and Mussolini's Italians holding the east only a few miles away. The whole thing must have seemed quite unreal to all the characters caught in the trap of this sun-drenched paradise, the luxury hotels and millionaires' villas disgorging wealthy refugees of all nations, panic, anxiety everywhere, only the blue sea unruffled, the Germans, for all anyone knew for certain, on the other side of the superb mountain coastline.

The Windsors began to pack and by June nineteenth, several days after the French surrender, the Croe party was ready to move. The Duke had contacted the British Embassy, which had been evacuated from Paris and was trying to maintain some kind of fugitive organization at Bordeaux. In spite of all their other problems the British officials were relieved to hear the Duke's voice, and more relieved still to hear that he was about to make a bid for safety. Already the Foreign Office had been anxious about the possibility of the Windsors being taken prisoner by the Nazis. The Bordeaux officials asked him to keep in touch and promised to try and help him to get into Spain.

A high wind was blowing as the Windsors, now changed out of uniform into civilian clothes, prepared to say good-by to Croe, a home that had been a very happy one for them. One obstacle, however, had still to be overcome before they could finally leave. The large entrance hall was crammed from ceiling to floor and from wall to wall with trunks, crates, bags, boxes. The Duke had hired a truck to carry the stuff, but it looked at first as if it would be too much for half a dozen trucks. Somehow it was all squeezed aboard in the end and the party was almost ready to go.

The Windsor Buick was the first in line with George Ladbrook at the wheel and the Duchess's maid beside him. Behind sat the Windsors and Phillips. Then came Wood's Citroen with Wood at the wheel, Mrs. Wood and her personal maid. A luggage trailer bumped along behind. In the rear was the truck driven by a hired man. That completed the human roster. There were also four dogs. Mrs. Wood's Sealyham was already curled up in the car. All that remained was to catch the Windsors' three Cairn terriers—"my three little princes" the Duke used to call them—which was not so easy. The terriers thought the whole thing a fine frolic and disappeared into the brush, yapping in amusement and the party was delayed fifteen minutes while they were collared one by one.

For the second time in her life the Duchess of Windsor was setting out in flight. First it had been from the British, and now it was from the Germans, a combination of enemies that would have daunted a weaker woman. Progress was fairly good along the roads that afternoon, although it was inevitably slowed because of the difficulty the heavily laden truck had in keeping up with the two cars. The war had not yet reached the Riviera (the Germans did not, in fact, appear for another two years), and though there were quite a lot of refugees, there were not enough to bother the Windsor party seriously.

It was not until they reached Arles that evening that the full impact of the French disaster really struck them. Here was a city literally shuddering with war, with tanks and gun carriers clattering through the streets, soldiers everywhere, airplanes flying constantly overhead. With difficulty the party managed to get accommodation for the night, the Windsors in a large, old-fashioned bedroom with a double bed.

The electricity supply at Arles had been cut off two days before, and the town was in total darkness. The royal party ate a dismal meal that night by the light of two smoky yellow candles. This was war, a harsh, flickering war commentary which may have reminded the Duchess ironically of one of her most sparkling peacetime maxims that at dinner "a woman over forty looks her best by candlelight."

Next day on the road from Arles to Perpignan the little convoy ran into hordes of refugees, most of them soldiers of several nations, who had lost both officers and organization and were wandering helplessly not knowing where to go or what to do next. In spite of frequent hold-ups the Windsors showed no impatience and were unflaggingly cheerful, almost as if they were on an outing in the country. After several delays in traffic-choked villages, the Duke developed a simple but apparently effective way of breaking through. Whenever the convoy was forced to stop, he would get out of his car, wave his arms and say in his abominable French, "*Moi, je suis le Duc de Windsor.*" His popularity had survived even the French defeat for invariably there would be a feeble cheer, and cries of "*Vive le Duc de Windsor!*" occasionally "*Vive le Roi!*" and the road would open to let the party pass.

They arrived at lunchtime at Perpignan, a French city on the border of Spain, crammed with British refugees trying to escape into neutral territory. By that time the royal party had been joined by two jittery British consular officials also fleeing from the Germans.

The Spanish frontier was closed tight and held by troop reinforcements, and rumors, started probably by Fifth Columnists, kept rippling through the bursting town: the Germans were only twenty miles away; Perpignan had been picked out for devastation by the Luftwaffe. Bordeaux, however, on the phone to the Duke, was reassuring. Visas had been obtained for the Windsors and were waiting for them at the Spanish Consulate.

So they were—two of them, one for the Duke, one for the Duchess. The Duke looked at them blankly, and demanded, "How about the rest, Major Phillips, Captain and Mrs. Wood, the two consuls and the servants?"

The Spanish Consul, a big-built impassive man, just shrugged. The Duke argued, but the Consul was immovable. Only two visas had been granted. After getting nowhere the Duke refused to accept them and pushed his way back to the hotel to ring the British authorities in Bordeaux. The official with whom he spoke promised to do what he could and advised the Duke to return to the Consulate. The Duke did so, but there were still no visas. He went back to the hotel to call Bordeaux yet again. Now one member of the party had suddenly discovered that his British passport was marked "not valid for Spain." On the Duke's recommendation he climbed into a car and streaked to the nearest British Consulate. There he found one French assistant remaining alone, burning papers and rubber stamps. A stamp marked "Valid for Spain" was salvaged, impressed on to his passport, and he returned as fast as he could to Perpignan.

He need not have hurried. The Duke had made no progress. The Spanish authorities refused to grant him further visas. The Duke refused to desert his friends. Three times he had traveled back and forth between the Consulate and the hotel.

Only once did the Spanish Consul appear to soften in any way. As the Duke was leaving after another fruitless argument, the Consul said awkwardly, "Excuse me, Your Highness. My little daughter collects autographs. Would you give me yours?" He took an autograph book from a drawer and held it out.

The Duke, in his ebullient way, grinned. "I tell you what," he said. "Let's swop signatures. I'll sign your daughter's book if you put your signature on the visas for my party." The Consul's face instantly hardened, and the proffered book was withdrawn.

The Duke may have felt he had done himself no good with his little attempt to be pleasant. "Oh, come on," he said. "I was only joking. Give me the book and I'll sign it."

It was almost certainly a coincidence, but on the Duke's next trip back to the Consulate, he found the Spaniard's manner had changed completely. He was smiling broadly and held out visas for the entire party, including the member whose passport mark "not valid for Spain" had been only unconvincingly obliterated. Watched by hundreds of envious British refugees, the convoy rolled over the border towards Port Bou on June twentieth at five thirty P.M. after which the gates dividing safety from danger snapped shut behind them. The party sighed with relief at the abrupt cessation of tension.

There was a long delay while they unpacked the truck which was not allowed to travel through Spain. They hired a Spanish truck and headed for Barcelona. It was a long and rough drive, and the party was tired, but there were no stops except for a picnic dinner of tea and sandwiches by the roadside.

Barcelona was reached very late that night, and accommodation was found at the Ritz Hotel. For the first time in several weeks the refugees were able to sleep with a feeling of security without wondering whether the Germans would be at their front door by the time they woke up. The Windsors rested for three days in Barcelona, leaving finally on the morning of June twenty-fourth. Their saga was not yet over. All day they traveled through the killing heat of a Spanish summer day, and arrived at Saragossa that night, running right into a big Spanish fiesta, the fiesta of the Virgin of la Pillar. While the Windsors slept that night in the Gran Hotel, there was dancing in the streets outside until the festivities were stopped by a rainstorm.

Next morning the Duke and Duchess visited the cathedral at Saragossa and it was not until twelve thirty, with the rain still falling heavily, that they got on the move again with Madrid next stop.

They reached the capital seven hours later, and moved into rooms the British Embassy found for them at the Ritz Hotel.

They celebrated with a quiet dinner party in the hotel garden restaurant. The food was as good as anything one could find at the time in Spain so quickly after the Civil War was over, but one thing spoiled their appetites. At the other end of the restaurant, a man in evening clothes, his head close-cropped, stared at them unblinkingly and with an almost frightening malevolence. Who, they wanted to know, was that?

That, a waiter told them, was Doktor Eberhard von Stohrer, Hitler's Ambassador in Madrid.

Von Stohrer maintained a regular table at the Ritz, and every evening the two parties, British and German dined at the same time in the same room, neither acknowledging the existence of the other, although sometimes a mutual friend would stop first at one table and then at the other, which produced a feeling of shock as though two electric currents had been suddenly joined.

Sir Samuel Hoare, now Lord Templewood, had just become British Ambassador in Madrid, and the Duke saw him several times. War throws the most unlikely people together, and it must have been a reunion with the most dramatic undertones, as Templewood had been one of Stanley Baldwin's chief lieutenants during the Abdication crisis. Yet in the midst of collapsing alliances and dreadful menace, how far away the Abdication and even the world in which it happened must have seemed at that moment in battered, hostile Madrid.

As in his reunion with Mountbatten at the beginning of the war, so now with Templewood, the Duke of Windsor showed no rancor for past differences, and his sessions with the Ambassador were very friendly.

The Windsors were in Madrid for a little over a week and seemed quite content to stay there until the government decided on a job for the Duke. In London, however, there was anxiety over the aggressive German activities existing in Spain, especially in Madrid, and instructions were sent to the Duke to move westward into the friendlier atmosphere of Portugal. Bags were packed and the little party set off for Lisbon, heading, though they did not know it then, for a month of adventure as strange as any they had ever encountered in their strange lives to that date.

XVII

Quest for the
Soul of a Prince

The Windsors made their way across the Iberian Peninsula under the fascinated eyes of the Nazis. They were watched out of Spain by the agents of Dr. Eberhard von Stohrer, German Ambassador in Madrid, and they were watched into Portugal by agents of Baron Oswald von Hoyningen-Huehne, the German Minister in Lisbon.

At the border the Germans might even have seen the Duke lose his temper for the first time on this eventful journey. With the Duchess he had taken cheerfully in his stride every previous development. Now, on arriving at Merida near the Portuguese border with rooms booked for him at a government resthouse, he discovered that the truck had taken a different route via Badajoz, and was temporarily lost somewhere along with the Duke's pajamas and shaving kit. The Duke hit the roof but had to be content to borrow the necessary accessories from his aides.

On the morning of July 3, 1940, the Windsors crossed into Portugal and, accompanied by a British Embassy official named Hogg, they drove into Lisbon, making the last stretch of the journey by ferryboat. They were then escorted out of the city to a mansion in the romantic little village of Cascais just outside Estoril, the home of their host, Dr. Ricardo de Espirito-Santo Silva, a Portuguese banker and connoisseur. Esperito-Santo means "Holy Ghost," and he named his house "Boca do Inferno," which means in Portuguese, "The Mouth of Hell," the name being taken from a cavernous rock formation in the vicinity.

The man responsible for this arrangement was Sir Walford Selby, the British Ambassador in Lisbon. Selby, as British Ambassador to Austria, had greeted the Duke in Vienna immediately after the Abdication. An old-school Englishman, Selby was a wise and experienced Ambassador, and he and the Duke were close friends. When Selby heard that the Windsors were on their way he asked Espirito-Santo if the Duke might stay at his house "for a night or two," and the banker had willingly agreed. The Windsor party was expected to arrive by teatime, but there were various delays and it did not turn up at Cascais until shortly before dinner. In the conference that followed Selby was able to tell the Duke that an airplane would be ready to take him and the Duchess to England the following day, but the Duke would have none of this. The notice was far too short, he said, and he would not be ready to leave.

So it was agreed that the Windsors would stay a week in Espirito-Santo's treasure-crammed house in Cascais, while Espirito-Santo and his wife moved to another house which they owned in Lisbon itself. The Duke would then wait for his next assignment. It arrived in due course by telegram. He was offered the job of Governor of the Bahamas, a post so insignificant that he was appalled. As a result, instead of staying only a few days, he stayed a month at Boca do Inferno, aptly named for a place where the Duke was forced to wrestle with his conscience, his aspirations, and the German devil.

It would be pointless to deny that the Windsors had little enthusiasm for the war. The diaries of Ernest von Weizsäecker, a permanent head of the German Foreign Office, quote General Halder, Chief of General Staff, that in July 1940, the month the Windsors spent in Portugal, the Duke had written to the King suggesting that peace be negotiated.* This letter and one from Lloyd George, expressing similar sentiments caused Weizsäecker to assume that there was a latent peace party in Britain.

Now Hoyningen-Huehne, the German Minister in Lisbon, was brought in. The German Foreign Office wanted to know the prospects for the Duke of Windsor remaining in Lisbon "inside the German circle of communications." The Germans had hit on the fantastic idea of keeping the Duke around, and if it seemed politically advantageous to them, of trying to return him to the throne of Britain as "Friedenskoenig" or "peace king" once the country was occupied. A subsidiary part of this idea was to install Lloyd George as a puppet Prime Minister. There was even some softening-up propaganda on the Axis radio, the Italians send-

* *The German General Staff,* by Walter Goerlitz.

ing out a broadcast that Churchill had ordered the Duke's arrest if he should ever land on British soil.

The plot fitted Hitler's general policy in occupied Europe. He liked to hang on to Europe's kings, to keep them on the throne and issue orders through them, thus giving his control some semblance of legality. He did his best to catch King Haakon when the German Army invaded Norway, and only narrowly failed. He was furious when Queen Wilhelmina escaped from Holland. So far as he could foresee developments in the forthcoming battle for Britain, he guessed he would never get his hands on the British Royal Family, who would be whisked off to Canada rather than risk capture. Almost inevitably he turned his attention towards the Duke of Windsor, exiled and accessible.

Around the Duke there emerged two important men—important because their particular personalities were largely responsible for deciding the course of the story. Had their characters been different the Duke might never have reached the Bahamas. One was Ricardo Espirito-Santo, a handsome cosmopolitan who spoke many tongues and knew many people. He was a personal friend to one degree or other of all the four sons of King George V, most intimately of all, however, of the Duke of Kent. In fact Kent had been in Lisbon only a few days before on an official mission, and had spent some time at Espirito-Santo's house, returning to England hardly more than twenty-four hours before the Windsors arrived.

Besides his British sympathies (he was once or twice rumored as a likely Portuguese ambassador in London) Espirito-Santo, through his bank, had commercial relations in Berlin, and his bank held large Portuguese deposits of the Reichsbank. Dr. Salazar, Portugal's Prime Minister, relied heavily on him for information both from Britain and from Germany. Salazar was pro-British and though he quailed before the German might, he wanted to do what he could to help his traditional ally. Espirito-Santo reflected entirely Salazar's attitude.

Espirito-Santo was a close personal friend of the second character involved in the affair of the Duke, namely Baron Oswald von Hoyningen-Huehne, who now had before him Ribbentrop's message about the Windsors and was digesting it without a great deal of enthusiasm.

Hoyningen-Huehne had been in Lisbon for many years and had already decided to make it his home on retirement. He was an able, humorous, popular diplomat, a typically lazy anti-Nazi in that he disliked Hitler but not enough to do anything about it. His mother was an Englishwoman. A cousin, George Hoyningen-Huehne, was and is one of

New York's best-known photographers. A nephew married Nancy Oakes de Marigny in 1952.

So far as Hoyningen-Huehne was concerned it was at least as important to remain in Salazar's good books as it was to remain in Ribbentrop's. He was not at all happy about the legion of German agents slipping unobtrusively from Spain into Lisbon, and he kept as remote from them as he could, particularly as he knew that British agents were also around keeping him under careful watch. Salazar, he realized, was not going to like the idea of the German Minister interfering with a member of the British Royal Family on Portuguese soil.

However orders were orders and something had to be done. Hoyningen-Huehne approached Espirito-Santo as a friend and asked him for his co-operation. What happened next is rather obscure, but it seems that the Germans communicated their point of view that the Duke should remain "inside the German circle of communications"—that phrase seemed to be the key to the German idea. The Duke replied to the effect that his one aim was to be of service to his country. He was prepared to serve that country as best he could.

That was all. But intrigue could be felt everywhere. The Foreign Office in London feared for the Duke's safety. At the Espirito-Santo mansion the Duchess, feeling that she and her husband were trespassing too long on their friend's hospitality, sent an aide to try and get some accommodation at the fashionable Hotel Aviz. A British Embassy official heard about it and was startled. "For Heaven's sake stay put and don't move into a hotel," he told the aide. "This city is swarming with German spies, and there are rumors that they are going to try and kidnap the Duke."

All the time the Duke, probably unaware of the tension he was creating in both London and Berlin, carried on, playing golf with Espirito-Santo in the afternoon, turning up once or twice at the Estorial Casino, and once at a bullfight, at which the Portuguese crowd, recognizing him, rose to give him an ovation.

Boca do Inferno, and its large staff of silent servants, were at his disposal, and the servants were sometimes disconcerted by his simple ways. ("Madam," the chef once said despairingly over the telephone to Senhora Espirito-Santo, "I wish to prepare His Highness some of my finest dishes, but all he keeps asking for are sardines and salad.")

The world is always small for famous people and the coincidence is sometimes more the rule than the exception. Among the small group of people to whom the Windsors were introduced in Portugal was a beautiful young Frenchwoman, Mrs. Lucy Fury Wann, wife of a senior officer of the R.A.F. Mrs. Wann had escaped from France and was now waiting for a chance to return to England and rejoin her husband. (Some years later her husband died, and in 1949 the Windsors were witnesses when she married Herman Rogers, whose wife had also died.)

The international developments revolving round the Duke went on quite unknown to him, and a word should be said about people whose tradition stems from two countries rather than one. Many men, particularly Englishmen—the eternal expatriates—have a second country which they cherish almost as dearly as their own. To many Englishmen that country is France. To others it is the United States. To some it is even the Argentine.

Germany is a less usual choice, but some Englishmen love Germany, too. This second loyalty, however, has only in cases on the lunatic fringe —like that of William "Lord Haw Haw" Joyce—conflicted with their basic patriotism. Such men have always taken pride in being regarded as a "bridge" between their own country and the country they love. They fight to the end to defend their own soil, sometimes with even greater fanaticism than those with easier minds in order to quell the doubts persisting in their own consciousness. The Duke never tried to hide his attachment for Germany. He frequently spoke with pride of his German blood, and although he did not say this in his memoirs there is reason to believe that, thanks to his tutors, he spoke German as a child before he spoke English. Once Britain declared war on Germany, there might have been regret in the Duke's mind, but there was no thought of disloyalty to his native land. In fact his chief objection to the Bahamas appointment was that it would take him so far away from the fighting.

All the same, the British Government in London was frankly worried at the Duke's continued stay in Lisbon, and his resistance to the appointment to the Bahamas. Despite the pious quotation of Queen Victoria ("There is no doubt in this house . . . the possibility of defeat does not exist," etc.) that was appearing on the walls of offices and public houses all over Britain, the possibility of occupation was always present in the minds of the Government, and had even been given official voice by Churchill in one of his greatest speeches ("and even if . . . this island were subjugated and starving . . . we will never surrender"). Even Prime Ministers come and go, but goodness knows what would happen to British traditions if war and defeat meant chopping and changing British kings. The Duke of Windsor became, in British eyes, the one Englishman the Germans absolutely must not capture.

The situation was complicated yet further by a quarrel between Winston Churchill and the Duke, who had finally and grudgingly agreed to go to the Bahamas. The Duke felt that he should be taken in a warship. Churchill replied that he must go in a neutral ship because warships were stretched to the limit on convoy duty. The Duke insisted.

In the end the situation became so serious that Churchill flew Walter Monckton out to Lisbon to settle the differences. Monckton arrived about the twenty-eighth of July and was also put up at the home of Dr. Espirito-Santo. With all his lawyer's powers of persuasion he urged the Duke to accept the position. Espirito-Santo also added his voice and pointed out how potentially important the Bahamas were. For one thing he said the islands were close to the still-neutral United States to which the Duke was so closely drawn. For another thing they were important strategically. For another they were a focal point of Allied censorship (Espirito-Santo was wrong here; the central point was Bermuda). Reluctantly the Duke yielded on all points, and it was with great relief that the Colonial office in London was able to announce:

> His Majesty the King has been pleased to appoint His Royal Highness, the Duke of Windsor, K.G., to be Governor and commander in chief of the Bahama Islands.

The next few days were spent in a frenzy of shopping for clothes and equipment. Reservations were made on the American liner *Excalibur*, sailing to Bermuda with a cargo-load of American ex-Ambassadors and wealthy American refugees. The Windsors reserved a veranda suite with six two-bed cabins. Eighty-five pieces of baggage accompanied them on their journey. No attempt at secrecy was made. It would have been futile since Portugal was a neutral country and the *Excalibur* was a neutral ship. So the Duke and Duchess gave a noisy party the night before the sailing for Lisbon newspapermen.

George Ladbrook was invited to travel with the party, but his part in the story had finally come to an end. The bombs were beginning to tumble down on London, and Ladbrook felt his place was there beside his family. (Later one of his sons was killed in the R.A.F.) Farewell was also made to the Buick which had played such a big part in their adventures. Today it belongs to a London car dealer.

Even then there was a slight holdup. On the morning the *Excalibur* was due to sail, the Duke asked Espirito-Santo if he could see Dr. Salazar and thank him for his hospitality. The Duke and Salazar met in the President's house behind Lisbon's Houses of Parliament and chatted for an hour. This meant a last dash through Lisbon to get to the ship. The Windsors were the last people aboard. The gangplank was pulled up after them and the ship sailed half an hour late.

The German incident was over, and Hoyningen-Huehne cabled Berlin that the birds had flown. The Duke was able to leave Portugal unharmed, partly because of the influence of Ricardo Espirito-Santo, partly by Monckton's intervention, partly because of Hoyningen-Huehne's inert attitude.

When Salazar handed Britain bases in the Azores, Hoyningen-Huehne was almost the only diplomat in Portugal taken by surprise. Ribbentrop was so furious that he called him home and then arrested him. In his place he tried to send a hundred-per-cent Nazi. Salazar, shocked, refused to accept him and personally protested at the treatment of the popular Hoyningen-Huehne. Nevertheless, Hoyningen-Huehne remained under guard for the rest of the war in Germany. Today he lives contentedly in retirement in Estoril.

Had Hoyningen-Huehne been a different type of man, had he been an ardent Nazi, the result might have been different. The war was still young at the time but already something had been seen of what determined cloak-and-dagger agents could do. Best and Stevens, two Britons, operating secretly in neutral Holland, were captured by German agents and spirited across the frontier. Later in the war when systems had been perfected, alert agents moved backwards and forwards across battle lines with ease, and the culminating point came when Mussolini was rescued from captivity behind the Allied lines by German paratroopers.

Under circumstances only slightly different, it would have been a comparatively minor coup for specially picked Nazis to descend one night on Boca do Inferno and snatch the Windsors into Germany.

Fortunately it did not happen that way. England was braced for the shock of the German invasion across the Straits of Dover. The original copy of Magna Carta had been transferred across the Atlantic to the United States for the duration, and the Windsors were on their way to the faraway Bahamas. With both safely out of harm's way, the British felt easier in spirit as they set about their task.

XVIII

Troubles in
a Tropical Paradise

In Bermuda the Duke did manage to get his warship. He had transferred from the neutral *Excalibur* to a small Canadian passenger ship, *Lady Somers,* and a destroyer was detached to escort him on the last step of his journey to the Bahamas.

The whole town turned out with pomp and regalia to welcome the new Governor, and apart from the killing heat of the day, the reception went without a fault.

The period of the Windsors' reign in the Bahamas was marked by many big and unexpected events. The Americans were given bases there. Controversial good-will visits were made to the United States. There was a riot and a fire. On the night of July 8, 1943, the Windsors' circle of friends decreased violently by one. The Windsors still attracted criticism, but for a change they also received some well-merited praise.

The Duchess of Windsor spent in the Bahamas probably the greatest years of performance and achievement in her life. Some local politicians rate her among the greatest Governors' wives in the history of the colony.

She made no secret, however, of her dislike for the Bahamas. She complained in private and she complained in public, and about nearly everything. This offended many residents, but it increased in a way their respect and admiration for a strong-minded woman who could work so hard in the interests of a country to which she wanted only to say good-by.

Even before she arrived the famous wit of steel had been turned on her husband's appointment. "St. Helena, 1940 fashion," she commented to a friend in Lisbon. Later on she varied her place of exile. In letters to friends she sometimes crossed out the words "Government House" at the top of her stationery and wrote in *Elba*. This fact was drawn to the attention of King George VI, who totally failed to be amused.

One of her first remarks on landing was a complaint about the heat and the mosquitoes. In 1940, shortly after arriving, she exploded so succinctly to an American woman reporter, Adela Rogers St. Johns, that a question was asked about it in the House of Commons. "How can one expect the Duke to live here?" she reportedly demanded. "I, too, wish to do our duty. But is there scope here for his great gifts, his inspiration, his long training? I'm only a woman, but I'm his wife, and I don't believe that in Nassau he's serving the Empire as importantly as he might."

But it has always been the Duchess's habit to say what she thinks, and it does not take a long experience of Nassau to sympathize, in some degree, with her position. Nassau is a village community with a compelling capacity for inspiring dislike. The climate is the least pleasant in the Bahamas. The prevailing wind is the trade wind which sometimes blows from the northeast, sometimes from southeast. Most of the Bahamas get this wind off the water, and it comes in cool and refreshing in the appropriate manner of the tropical paradise. But New Providence Island on which the town of Nassau stands is an "in-island" (distinguishing it from most of the other islands which are called "out-islands"). The waters which surround it, while superb for yachting, are warm shoal waters, and the humidity becomes intense. In Nassau, the water supply is low and it comes up dank. Nassau flowers in consequence have relatively little smell. Mosquitoes are only a minor problem, but the islands breed a virile sand fly which penetrates mosquito nettings with ease and laughs in the face of DDT. There are few singing birds, and the whole atmosphere is like that of a painted postcard. Count Alfred de Marigny, the man who was acquitted of the murder of Sir Harry Oakes, gives a short bitter picture of the Bahamas in his skilful and plausible autobiography, *More Devil than Saint*:

> Mediocrity is the word for the Bahamas. The country is mediocre in everything. There are no rivers, fresh water lakes, mountains. Even from the earliest days the people were mediocre. After the American revolution when the British Government became tired of their demands for "compensation for the losses they had suffered on account of their loyalty to His Majesty during the late trouble in America" they developed a mentality which exists to this day—"The Nassau Pirate Mentality." They were not

bold, daring pirates of song and story. They lived on the wrecks that were thrown up on the coral reefs.

The town of Nassau itself can be traversed comfortably in a ten-minute stroll. The Government House is a chocolate-box affair, tiny, rather comic, with a heroic statue of Christopher Columbus at the entrance gazing down George Street towards Bay Street, which is the Nassau shopping center and a street which visitors suddenly transplanted from London might forgivably mistake for a somewhat commercialized mews in Margate.

But its smallness, meanness and tourist-chiselling are only the surface irritants of Nassau. As a seat of Government it presented problems which the Duke of Windsor was never trained to handle easily. Unlike most of the other outposts of the British Empire where the Governor, as the personal representative of the King, is expected to be above politics, the Governor of the Bahamas, like the Governors of neighboring Bermuda and the Barbados, contributes actively to local political policy.

The Bahamas Legislature itself has three parts, the House of Assembly, the Legislative Council and the Governor. The House of Assembly is equivalent to the House of Commons, and it is guided in debate by Mays Parliamentary Procedure which is the textbook of the House of Commons.

The Legislative Council is appointed by the Governor representing the King. This body of eight or nine members is presided over by a President, also picked by the Governor. It is equivalent to the British House of Lords, though it has more power. The Governor convenes Parliament, signs bills. He has veto powers over legislation and often uses it. He can dissolve the Legislature and sometimes does. He presides over an Executive Council and acts in a way like a British Prime Minister. In effect his function is more like that of a President of the United States than a representative of the King, in that he is both the head of the state and the initiator of policy.

In other words, of all the appointments far from home that the British Government could have handed to the Duke of Windsor, they handed him one in which his opportunities to utilize his impartial training as a Prince were at a minimum. He now had to embroil himself in the party politics of a particularly inert community, comprising seventy thousand people, eighty per cent of them colored, twenty-nine islands, most of them uninhabited, and a few thousand cays, coral reefs and sandspits. On the one hand his job was made easier by the fact that there was little extremist urge in the islands—few Communists, fewer secessionists, and a population lethargically content with its position in the Empire—but on the other hand it was made complicated by the population's sloth, its selfishness, narrow outlook, reluctance to pay taxes or to compromise in any way with its own comfort.

All Governors get criticized steadily in the Bahamas, and the Duke did not care for this either. He protested mildly to a Bahamas editor at one attack on some political proposal he had made. "In Britain the newspapers do not usually criticize the Royal Family," he said.

"Sir," replied the editor, "I would not dream of criticizing you as a member of the Royal Family. I am criticizing you as Governor of the Bahamas." The Duke took the reproof in good part, and laughed.

The Duke depressed the community no little in his first, excellent speech when he warned darkly that it was not only in Britain that blood, sweat and tears must be shed. "My wife and I will work as a team here," he added. "That is how I want all of us to work." Happily for the Bahamians the Duke's bark proved to be worse than his bite. In the Bahamas community there was little blood or toil, infrequent tears though plenty of sweat.

On arrival in August, 1940, the Duke and Duchess took adjoining offices in Government House and set to work. The first thing the Duchess did was redecorate Government House, a cracked and flaking edifice which in the past had survived with about as much warmth and atmosphere as Wellington Barracks.

While she was still in Lisbon the House of Assembly had granted $6,000 to the Board of Works for the reconditioning of the Governor's residence "so that it will be put in a befitting state" for the Windsors' arrival. The Duchess then cabled Nassau that nothing was to be done until she arrived. Once she was installed, she imported a New York decorator and detailed her ideas. Unable on one occasion to express herself adequately, she was reported to have smeared her face powder on a wall and said, "I want it this color." She ordered softer lighting, and arranged for candlelight in the dining room. She had fun. Three years in France had given her the craze that reaches its greatest frenzy among sophisticated French people, the craze for interior decoration, and with it a passion for moving furniture around. Bespecked with paint and plaster, she would emerge weary from a day of consultations with designers and workmen, and in reply to people who urged her to rest she would say, "I must make a home for the Duke." At the end of it all the Board of Works added up the bills and found that expenditure had exceeded the authorized grant by $15,000. Instead of spending $6,000 the Windsors had spent $21,000, but the House passed the excess without comment, and the Governor's House was now so charming that the Duchess of Windsor has since been blessed by every succeeding Governor's wife.

The Windsors then set about once more depressing their well-wishers by making still more injudicious acquaintances. Their most important new acquaintance was a blue-eyed Swedish giant named Axel Wenner-Gren, a multimillionaire, with an industrial empire ranging from Sweden to the United States and Mexico. He owned valuable real estate in Nassau, including the glorious Paradise Beach.

Wenner-Gren entertained the Windsors royally in his yacht the *Southern Cross,* and continued to do so until America entered the war. Thereupon the British and American governments blacklisted him. Wenner-Gren had been a close friend of Hermann Goering and had acted as a go-between in settling a truce to the Russo-Finnish war of 1940. The Allies felt at the time that he was excessively friendly to the Nazis.

The sense of doubt that troubled the Duke in Portugal followed him to Nassau. Both of the Windsors were appalled when Russia was grabbed by the scruff of the neck by Hitler and chucked into the Allied camp, but even before this happened with Britain alone in the war, there was a note of anxiety in some of the Duke's statements. In March, 1941, in an interview with Fulton Oursler, then editor of *Liberty,* he said:

> When this war is over, many strange things are going to happen. There will be a new order in Europe whether it is imposed by Germany or by Great Britain. Labour is going to get a more equitable distribution of the world's good things in this new order. The new peace will have to be as just a settlement as the human spirit can provide . . . there will have to be a world league with everybody in it, but this time it will be buttressed by police power. When this peace comes there is going to be a new order of social justice and when that time comes what is your country going to do about its gold?

In a free world everybody is entitled to his opinion, and in the Bahamas the Windsors made up for most things by the excellence of their performance. They were given a flying start when they were able, at the beginning of their reign, to turn a particularly unfortunate faux pas to their own advantage.

The story was revealed by *Life* Magazine in 1940. It was at the Windsors' first social appearance in the Bahamas, at a ceremonial dinner. Sir Frederick Williams-Taylor, an elderly Canadian millionaire, formerly head of the Bank of Montreal, whose wife was the leader of what social set then existed in Nassau, presided and made a speech of welcome—

to the Duke only. Somehow the name of the Duchess was left out. Williams-Taylor was a kind man and an old man and it must be that this was unintentional.

According to *Life:*

> . . . the Duke, with the practised anger he, as a husband, reserved for any slur on the lady who is his wife, rose, stated that in Sir Frederick's prepared speech as originally submitted to him, the Duchess had been included and that he, the Duke, wondered if the light were so dim that on reading his speech Sir Frederick had inadvertently made the oversight which he, the Duke, could not overlook. The Duke went on to give his own speech which included the correct gracious references to Sir Frederick's spouse, known as "Lady Jane," who was social leader of Nassau until the Duchess arrived. Emerald Beach guests said that this was the most magnificently embarrassing moment of their lives. . . . Later the Duchess started to rise with the rest of the guests. "You don't have to stand up for me, darling," the Duke domestically advised her. "It's a pleasure to stand up for you, darling," she countered with double meaning.

Once installed the Duchess assumed her duties energetically. She lent her name and her time to the Red Cross. She more or less took over the United Services canteen, and did hard work for the YWCA, and the IODE (Independent Order of Daughters of the Empire). She discovered that many native children were suffering from deficiencies in their milk diets and had been for years. She organized an office to distribute milk to the children. She opened clinics. One, built with donated funds at the Duke of Windsor's disposal, was given her name.

Decisions were not always easy, nor were the problems concerned solely with the war effort. During the course of one Red Cross drive the fashionable ladies of Nassau were covered in confusion when Miss Sally Rand, the American burlesque queen, turned up and offered her services. Miss Rand was appearing in Nassau, and was eager to perform at the gala charity concert to be held that night. The Duchess was with other Red Cross committee women when the request came through. She laughed and commented, "I am playing no part in this. You must decide," and left. Sally Rand duly appeared and did her bubble dance. At the tables Nassau society, including the Windsors, watched stonily. At the end the Duke said, "Come on. I'm not having my staff hang around here," and the party left. Next day the Duchess asked a friend in delight, "What are they saying in Nassau this morning?" Incidents like this tended to break the stuffiness of Bahamian life.

In the worst period of the year of war in which England stood alone, many torpedoed seamen were being unloaded destitute from rescue ships.

Responsibility for their welfare was assumed by the Duchess, who supervised their accommodation and equipped them with clothes and toilet articles. She and the Duke were the first to visit the celebrated Tapscott and Widdicombe, those two iron sailors who had established a record of two and a half months in an open boat, and who were later landed by rescuers at Nassau.

The U-Boats were so audacious that they brought the Bahamas close to the front line, and the Duke became concerned about the Colony's defenses, which were pretty much limited to some good rifles and old pirate cannon. He convinced the War Office that his uneasiness was justified, and a company of Camerons was transferred to Nassau from Curaçao where it had been guarding Dutch refineries.

The services canteen in Bay Street was the Duchess's pride. She would drop in at all hours of the day and evening to see how things were going, and, when necessary, help out herself. One night three tired American sailors, newly arrived in the Bahamas, came into the deserted canteen and asked for food. It was ten P.M. "Sorry," said the girl behind the counter, "we are closing."

"We don't want much. Just give us some eggs," one of the sailors said politely.

"Sorry," said the girl with the unbudging deference to convention which is one of the most depressing characteristics the Bahamians have inherited from the British, "we are closing."

The sailors became less polite. "Eggs," said one loudly. "We'll pay extra," said another.

"No," said the girl.

"Listen," said one of the sailors exasperated. "This is the Duchess of Windsor's canteen, isn't it? Well, the Duchess is an American girl, and if she were here she'd kick you so fast into that kitchen to get us some eggs, you would——"

At this moment the Duchess came into the canteen from the street, and paused, startled by the noise. "Hey, Duchess," the sailor yelled, "this dame won't give us any food. All we want are some eggs."

The Duchess reached for an apron. "How," she asked, "do you want them?" Without more ado she went into the kitchen, took a pan, and personally served the eggs to the delighted sailors.

Nassau, of course, was too small for much standing on ceremony and the Duchess became a familiar—though always formidable—figure in her light, gay frocks, driving round in a rather dilapidated station wagon. "It's cooler than the Governor's car," she would say cheerfully in answer to the raised eyebrows.

In 1942, a big fire broke out in Nassau. Both the Windsors helped to fight it and returned to Government House covered with soot.

Meanwhile the Duke was also going about his own business. He urged a minimum wage of eighty-five cents a day for laborers, twenty-eight cents more than they were getting at the time. The Legislature resisted the move and after an acid debate rejected it. In 1942, laborers rioted over the wage the United States Government was paying them at the American naval base under construction. They marched through Nassau shouting and breaking shop windows, though there was little personal violence. The Duke, who was in Washington at the time, personally intervened with the American authorities and managed better there than he had done with his own Legislature. The laborers' wages went up—by twenty-eight cents a day.

The Duke then tried to create an office to distribute jobs on government projects in the out-islands, and once more the Legislature, in its wisdom, booted the measure out. The Duke did manage, after a struggle, to get tariffs reduced on war-essential imports. But an attempt to draw the teeth of the "Bay-Street-pirate" merchants then sucking tourists dry got nowhere.

By and large the Duke was proving active enough, but he did not satisfy the Bahamas. Few Governors ever do. The Legislature found him too liberally inclined for their own tastes. The colored population, recalling his statement to the Welsh miners—"Something must be done"—did not find him liberal enough, and criticized his apparent lethargy and the modesty of such reforms as he tried to put forward.

The Duke frequently turned to his wife for guidance and sometimes his naïveté in this respect was all too revealing. Local officials, presenting the Duke with an issue, would be told, "I will consult the Duchess about this." He would return after the consultation and say, "The Duchess thinks your suggestion is inadvisable at the present time and"—apparently unaware of the conclusions to be drawn from the afterthought—"I do too."

Happily for the Bahamians the arduous wartime life which the Duke promised them did not materialize. It was too hot, for one thing. The Duke settled down after a very short while to an easier-going routine, which included golf and swimming most afternoons of the week. The Windsors continued to dress for dinner at night, the Duke often in the kilt, though evening dress had been socially barred in England for the duration.

Their problem was a delicate one. On the one hand they represented a colony at war, demanding austerity in the local economy and sacrifices from the population. On the other hand the Bahamas remained a favorite American holiday resort, and a certain amount of display and color was needed to keep the dollars coming in.

The Duke could have done more than he did, but the fact had to be faced that there was simply not a great deal of work to do in the Bahamas. There was justice in one of the Duchess's outbursts when she bewailed life in Nassau. "I wish to do whatever is loyal and right," she said. "I will do everything I can as Governor's wife. But would any American wife be happy or satisfied if her husband were put in a position where there was little chance for him to do the big things of which she knew him to be capable?"

The Windsors continued to live to a large degree in the manner to which they had been accustomed before the war. The Duchess had her clothes supplied by Mainbocher in New York. They made use of a large Criscraft-class yacht put at their disposal by an American friend, Arthur Davis.

Public opinion in the United States was shocked when it was rumored that the Duchess had sent to New York to have a hairdresser flown down to her. In the middle of a war, such luxuries seemed utterly beyond excuse, but the Duchess defended herself against the criticisms which the story aroused, and explained to a reporter what happened.

Harold Christie, a big Nassau real-estate man, told the Duchess that every year he brought down a hairdresser to Nassau to work through the season at one or other of his big hotels. The Duchess had been having hairdresser trouble as her hair is very fine and soft and not easy to dress.

"Since you have no trained maid," Christie reportedly said, "I'll be quite happy to get the New York hairdresser down a little earlier to attend your hair. Is there any hairdresser you prefer?"

"Antoine used to do my hair in Paris," the Duchess said, "and he has a place in New York. He is probably the best."

So at Christie's request, Antoine's sent down one of the firm's star hairdressers, Wayne Forrest, who now has a salon of his own on Fifty-seventh Street in New York.

Once a week while he was in Nassau, Forrest attended to the Duchess's hair, and in between times trained a Bahamian girl to do the job so that she could take his place when he returned to New York. However, the incident caused such a storm that the Duchess did not venture to repeat it.

In 1944, the Windsors were criticized over a matter which must have taken them by surprise. It involved a sum of $1,494. The table in the dining room had been riddled by termites, and the Duke asked for $1,494 to buy a new table and some new chairs to go with it. Four years earlier the House of Assembly had approved an excess expenditure of $15,000 by the Windsors without a word of comment. Now, presented with a request for $1,494 some of the Legislators blew up. They said that the colony could not afford it, that sacrifices were demanded from everyone, *everyone,* and was the Governor aware of the fact that there was a war on? They scrutinized the request. They demanded to know whether the furniture was to be locally made or imported from the United States. In the end, grudgingly, the request was allowed. The Duke got his furniture and with it a new illustration of the limits of his powers.

In spite of such incidents as these the Duke's performance was, in the final count, above average. He made some good nonpolitical speeches, and with his extraordinary adding-machine mind in which names were as automatic as sums, he never forgot anyone he met, however briefly, and this made a gratifying impression on everybody with whom he came in contact.

As a tourist attraction alone he was worth his twelve thousand dollars a year salary. The year he arrived Nassau's luxury hotels were packed to the maids' rooms for weeks beyond the normal tourist season, accommodating the hordes of American tourists pouring into the island for a glimpse of the fabulous Duke and his equally fabulous American wife. The local statistics office recorded in delight that the tourist influx was nearly fifty per cent up on the previous year.

The tourists were not disappointed. The Duke really was incredibly attractive with his serious boy's face and sad quizzical eyes, going about his tasks with the perfection of appearance that the world expected of him, in his tropical general's uniform. The Duchess was always smiling, always totally in command of herself. Or nearly always.

One American tourist was rewarded, according to a reliable account, with an incident that made her one-thousand-mile trip worth while. She was strolling around the island when she saw the Government car whizzing past, the Duke with his bagpipes, serenading the Duchess in the back seat, the Duchess clapping her hands to her ears and protesting through hysterical laughter.

At home, the Duchess, as always, put the Duke's personal comfort above all other considerations. They read the papers from England and America. They worked out jigsaws, and played patience and poker, the Duchess more ably than the Duke.

In December, 1940, Lord Lothian, Britain's clever ambassador to the United States, died. President Roosevelt had left America on December second, in the United States cruiser *Tuscaloosa* for a Caribbean cruise.

The Duke went out to see him and met him on the ship just off the Eleuthera Islands. It was a well-known fact that the Duke would have dearly liked Lord Lothian's job, and it was assumed that he was asking the President to put in a good word, although all he would say to reporters when he boarded the ship was "No comment." He did not get very far, and Roosevelt seemed to be in one of his most elusive moods for when aides broke into their private conversation, the President was giving the Governor some sage advice on the administration of the Bahamas.

The Duke did not get the job. It went instead to Lord Halifax, an appointment that must have been a stroke of pure genius on Winston Churchill's part, for the man who had been one of Britain's less effective Foreign Secretaries quickly established himself as one of the greatest ambassadors England ever sent to the United States.

XIX

America—and Murder

The Windsors finally succeeded in visiting America in October, 1941, and this time there was no Charles E. Bedaux, and no hitches.

Ten thousand people lined the streets of Baltimore to greet them. In Washington, while the Duke called on Cordell Hull, the Secretary of State, the Duchess was mobbed by thousands of screaming girls, and it was only after a quarter of an hour of strenuous effort that the police were able to cleave a way through the crowd to rescue her. The Duchess emerged slightly shaken, but intact and smiling dutifully.

They traveled to Calgary in Alberta to see the Duke's ranch, a wild barn of a place. By early October the winds which sported around its wooden buildings already contained the first warning chills of the Canadian winter. However pleased the Duke was to be back after so many years, the ranch obviously did not appeal to them as a place in which to make any sort of a home after the war was over.

After Canada they visited New York and were smothered in a ticker-tape welcome in the good New York tradition. The Waldorf-Astoria played host to them and gave them an entire floor on the twenty-ninth story of the Waldorf Towers. This was more to the Windsors' taste than the Canadian farm, and in later years they were to make the Waldorf the most permanent home they had.

Everywhere there were invitations to parties, banquets, balls. The Windsors, however, showed good taste, and politely declined, punctiliously reminding well-wishers that there was a war on in England even if it had not yet extended to the United States. Instead they decorously visited the Bundles-for-Britain societies and the seamen's canteens.

Altogether it was a spectacular visit. Wherever they went they ran into walls of cheering crowds. There were receptions and speeches. The comparison between the tumultuous American welcome for the Windsors and the icy British refusal to have anything to do with them was so great it almost seemed self-conscious. The crowds seemed to say: See how much we love you in America, come back to us, and shouted a moral that seemed to prove that in America at any rate the American woman was welcome with her royal husband to make a new home whenever she wanted.

That is what it seemed, but there were also indications that approval for the Windsors, though vociferous, was not universal. On September ninth, the British Embassy had announced that the Duke and Duchess would visit Washington on September twenty-fifth, and be received by President Roosevelt and Mrs. Roosevelt. The reception never happened. At first it was postponed for causes beyond anyone's control. Mrs. Roosevelt's brother died, so the luncheon to be given in their honor was held over for two weeks, the President receiving them alone and informally.

It was not until October twenty-eighth that the Windsors dined at the White House in the manner originally planned, but once again the President was alone. Mrs. Roosevelt was "unavoidably absent," away on a lecture engagement in Chicago. She had left only that morning, rather abruptly it seemed to certain American newspapers, rather unfortunately it seemed to many people.

Mrs. Cornelius Vanderbilt, Queen Mary's closest American friend, received the Windsors only after an inner struggle, and reportedly commented, "I knew him at the zenith of his glory. There is no reason why I should shun him now."

As the Windsors began to make more frequent trips to the United States, enthusiasm tended to subside and newspapers began to lace their editorials of welcome with increasing criticisms. Some newspapers were particularly disapproving of the Windsors' standard of living and of the large quantities of luggage they always brought with them. So long as America remained neutral, this disapproval was academic—or at least detached. Once Americans themselves had joined the war, they started to get rather peeved.

Nor were the Windsors too lucky in defending themselves. Once an American reporter commented on the load of luggage that accompanied her everywhere. "No one," the Duchess complained in reply, "pointed out how much luggage Mr. Churchill had when he was in the United States." The reporter was so dazed at the comparison between Winston Churchill, on a visit of historical importance to Washington, and the

Duchess of Windsor on a social and shopping expedition, that he faded into the background without asking a follow-up question. The Duchess, of course, intended no such comparison.

In June, 1944, Helen Worden, the sob-sister-in-chief for the Scripps Howard newspapers wrote for the *American Mercury* Magazine an article on the Duchess the repercussions of which have still not disappeared. It told all the old stories of her attention to her wardrobe and her purchases, her influence with her husband, and her isolation from high society.

The article became a big talking point in America, and in Nassau it had the impact of an earthquake. The Duke was so furious, that, against the advice of some of his assistants, he sat down to write a letter in reply, an unusual course for royalty. It was the first answer he had ever made to the many attacks on his wife. The letter duly appeared in the *American Mercury*. The Duke wrote:

Sir,

I have just read with considerable astonishment and some disquiet the article in your June issue entitled "The Duchess of Windsor." The writer, Miss Helen Worden, claims to have "observed the Duchess since 1936 and has talked with her on her recent visits to America." The fact is that the Duchess met Miss Worden once—at a formal press tea in New York—but beyond shaking hands with her on introduction had no conversation with her on that occasion and has never seen her since.

Apart from the utterly fantastic and completely untrue stories of the Duchess's expenditure on clothes, jewels and furs, two references in Miss Worden's story are criminally libellous fabrications and call for categorical denial. These are statements that:

(1) "The State Department foots the Windsors' bills on Lend-Lease arrangement."

(2) "An autographed photograph of von Ribbentrop once hung over her toilet table at Nassau."

A telephone call to the Department of State will immediately disprove the first allegation. I can only give you my personal assurance that the second is equally untrue, but both the Duchess and myself would be interested to know whether you or Miss Worden can name the "friend" who is supposed to have seen the picture.

I have used the words "criminally libellous" to describe these two statements because the first accuses my wife of being a kind of black marketeer evading currency control regulations and the second depicts her as a sympathiser with the enemy. These are extremely dangerous accusations to make against anybody in wartime let alone the wife of a Governor of a British colony.

I can well appreciate Miss Worden's dilemma in wartime, when, like all gossip-writers, she must find it difficult to unearth items of news that are readily discoverable in peacetime, but not so easy to come by now-a-days because most people's lives are grim rather than glamorous. But unnaturally, therefore, she falls back on her imagination. The surprising thing to me is that a magazine with the honourable traditions of the *American Mercury* should dignify these malicious flights of fancy by publishing them.

Edward Duke of Windsor

The Windsors did not allow the criticisms to curtail their American visits, and they became familiar wartime guests in the United States. They paid visits every year from 1940 to 1945, sometimes for British propaganda, sometimes on shopping expeditions, sometimes to take care of the medical needs of the Duchess. She had a tooth attended to in Florida in 1941, and was also treated for a stomach ulcer, caused possibly by excessive dieting. Whatever the purpose of the visits, they must always have been a welcome escape for the Windsors from the tedium of the Bahamas, a tedium that, however, came to an end suddenly after three years of their reign.

One night in July, 1943—appropriately enough on a night in which Nassau was whipped with rain and storms—there occurred one of the great classics in the history of crime. The murder of Sir Harry Oakes will not be told in detail here because it touches on the Windsors only in part, but even today when one thinks of the Oakes murder, one almost instantly thinks of the Windsors whose rule in the Bahamas was highlighted by the crime.

Oakes was a crude, tough, able, generous, gold-mining tycoon of an almost legendary ferocity. He had been born in Vermont, traveled the world in search of gold, and found it at the age of thirty-eight when a train guard kicked him off a freight train onto some of the greatest undiscovered gold deposits in Ontario.

Oakes became a British citizen and a baronet. He married an Australian girl who had waited twenty years for him to make his strike. Before World War II he had withdrawn from England to Nassau to avoid paying taxes, and at the time of his death was eying Peru as a possible home with the advantage of being further away from the Chancellor of the Exchequer. Oakes laughed at the veneer of civilization and hated wearing ties or formal clothes. His venom and his generosity were equally violent.

One of his chief delights was knocking down trees with a bulldozer. No tree was safe from his leveling mania. This charming habit did, however, produce one beneficial result for the Nassau community. He built Oakes airport on one spot after knocking down enough trees, and the airport was later taken over by the Government.

The Duke of Windsor has always been attracted to men who pioneered in the wilderness of the Empire. It was one of the characteristics which had made him so popular as a Prince of Wales. He and Oakes became friends, and the Windsors visited Oakes's home, Westbourne, frequently while Government House was being redecorated. The Duke even managed to persuade the roughneck baronet to wear morning dress on suitable occasions.

Oakes was sixty-eight when he died. He had given a small party for friends that evening. When everybody had gone home the murderer slipped into Oakes's bedroom, bashed his head in, turned a blow-torch on him and sprinkled the body with feathers. He then left, without trace to this day.

As soon as Oakes was found, the Duke was informed at Government House. The Duchess was overwhelmed by the news, and her first breathless comment was, "Well, never a dull moment in the Bahamas!" In deciding what to do, the Duke took a step which he subsequently admitted was a mistake. Excusably he decided this was something too big for the Nassau police. The logical result of this conclusion would have been to call either Scotland Yard in London, or the F.B.I. in Washington. The Duke did neither. He called Miami, and got in touch with a Captain Edward Melchen, a man who had been the Duke's bodyguard on one of his American trips and who had impressed the Duke with his efficiency.

The Duke reported that something terrible had happened, then added, "It might be suicide." Melchen and an assistant, named James Barker, flew over to Nassau with the comparatively simple equipment needed to determine suicide.

In taking statements, the detectives' suspicions fell on Count Alfred de Marigny, a professional playboy, a native of Mauritius, and husband of Oakes's eighteen-year-old daughter, Nancy. Oakes and de Marigny had some deadly quarrels, and once Melchen and Barker became convinced that de Marigny had committed the murder (he could not adequately account for his movements on the night of the crime, and his hands were burned, according to him, because he had lit storm lanterns when the storm became violent), they went all out to convict him.

Meanwhile Nancy Oakes de Marigny had gone to New York and returned with Raymond Schindler, one of the best private detectives in the world. Although the trail had gone cold, and Schindler was finding evidence mysteriously disappearing, not to mention letters addressed to him from New York and Washington mysteriously not arriving, he dug up enough to explode the case against de Marigny, who was acquitted, and deported as "undesirable." No new arrest has been made since. A few years afterwards, a woman who went to Nassau to try and discover the murderer was found dead in a ditch.

Barker was later dismissed from the Miami Police Force for manufacturing evidence. He was ultimately shot and killed in Miami by his son, and the coroner's jury returned a verdict of justifiable homicide. Schindler insisted that he knew the identity of the murderer.

The inescapable inference of the Oakes crime is that an unconvicted murderer, of a particularly savage type, lives and works today in the tiny community of Nassau. Yet three succeeding Governors have made no attempt to reopen the case, although the stain of evil it has left behind remains a pervading and ominous force in the island, hampering its development, and causing a deep degeneration in its communal character.

The Duke went on to do good work in the Bahamas and was praised by a Parliamentary mission which visited the islands in 1944. Unexpectedly in March, 1945—three and a half months before completing his five-year tenure of office—the Duke resigned his post as Governor. He broadcast a farewell message to the people of the islands referring to "an interesting and happy chapter in our lives." The Duke was presented with an address of appreciation by the House of Assembly.

Both the Duke and the Duchess had lost weight and suffered in health during their stay in the Bahamas. The Duchess had declined from one hundred and ten pounds to ninety-five. Faults had been found but one could count in their favor—and particularly in the Duchess's favor—solid and lasting achievements for which they are still remembered. Many women in the British Empire received high decorations for doing much less for the war effort. The Duchess of Windsor received nothing, not even a note of thanks.

The one fact that emerged most clearly as the Windsors said good-by to the Bahamas and sailed for newly liberated France was that after five years of war service they had made no progress whatever in winning their way into official favor. In Buckingham Palace and Downing Street, not to mention Ottawa, Capetown and Canberra, the backs were still towards them.

Her Friends and
Her Enemies

A last flicker of optimism could be observed in the Windsors' outlook in the summer of 1945. They were in France, and it had been announced that a general election would be held in Britain. The Duchess began to express herself enthusiastically and volubly in favor of the Labour Party. This was hardly surprising. She had suffered a lot from the Conservatives. A few months earlier, when the Duke was nearing the end of his tenure in the Bahamas, he had applied to Churchill for another job. He hoped to be either British Ambassador in Washington, or Governor-General of Canada. Instead he was offered the Governorship of Bermuda, a position which offered no advancement whatever on the Bahamas. The Duchess was heard to comment that she had had enough of the islands, and the Duke said "No."

An election opened entirely new prospects, and it is certain that she felt the Duke would be given a better reception by the Socialists than he had ever been given by the Tories. The Labour Party did win, by a landslide, and in October, 1945, while the Duchess stayed in Paris, the Duke visited London for the first time since 1940. Wherever he went crowds gathered to give him a cheer. He called on his mother, whom he had not seen for some years, toured some of the blitz-devastated areas of the East End, and on October eighth, saw Ernest Bevin, the new Foreign Secretary in the Attlee Government.

The Duke's hopes were quickly dashed. Bevin made no suggestions and had nothing whatever to offer. The Labour Party dream was quickly over. The Socialists were clearly no more sympathetic to the Duke's aspirations than the Conservatives had been. But the Duke had one last card to play, a card he had been holding for seven years.

The Lord Chancellor in the new Labour Government was Lord Jowitt, the man who, in 1938, had given his legal opinion to the Duke that recognition of the Duchess as "Her Royal Highness" came automatically with marriage. By now the problem of recognition had become a dominating issue with the Duke. He invited Jowitt to Claridge's and reminded him of his opinion.

This was a difficult problem dropped in Jowitt's lap from his days of private practice. He told the Duke he would investigate the matter and make what inquiries he could. Presumably he did so. But once again no enlightenment came from the King. Neither war nor the unexpected triumph of Socialist philosophy in Britain had caused any unbending of the Court's attitude to the Windsors. The Duke accepted the inference of the King's silence and returned to Paris to report to the Duchess that his mission had been a failure, both politically and socially.

The Duchess, despite the best legal opinion in the world, was helpless. Her position with regard to the question of recognition was literally agonizing. She was like a prisoner holding the key to a door which could be opened only from the other side. All reason, all legal argument, all precedent, all that and Christian compassion too urged that she should be styled "Her Royal Highness." But the British Court would not be moved.

So yet again the Duchess was to hear from her husband the words that had been pounding on her brain ever since the Abdication, "No recognition. No job. No success. No anything."

In October the following year the Duchess accompanied the Duke to England. They stayed together at Ednam Lodge, home of the Earl of Dudley in Sunningdale, near Ascot, a fine house on the southern rim of Windsor Great Park, not far from Fort Belvedere. This time the Duke's idea was to tackle the King rather than the politicians, and probably he hoped to persuade his brother to receive the Duchess—the two had not met since the long-ago holiday at Balmoral in September, 1936, when the Yorks and Wallis Simpson were fellow guests. The Windsors received a jarring welcome.

On the night of the sixteenth, while the Windsors were away, a nimble burglar climbed the drainpipe, forced his way into the Duchess's bedroom and made off with her jewel box. The box itself was recovered by detectives in the Lodge grounds where it had been jettisoned by the thief. One or two important pieces of jewelry were also found. But the burglar got away with jewels worth $60,000. Valuable necklaces, bracelets, rings, earrings, clips and brooches were in the haul, and no trace was ever found.

It was a bold, spectacular robbery, one of many that were being carried out in southern England at the time. Robbery is an occupational hazard of the wealthy, but once more circumstances counted against the Windsors more than they would have counted against most other people. Only one month before, the British newspapers had been enlarged from their wartime ration of four pages a day to six. Not much, but enough for Fleet Street to start flexing its muscles a little. With the joy of youth renewed the newspapers hurled themselves on the story. For six years there had been nothing but war news in the papers, and this was a first-class prewar vintage robbery, arriving just at the moment when the press was able to do it something like justice. The newspapers made the most of it. Reports of the value of the jewel haul soared, one newspaper estimating it at a solid three hundred thousand dollars. In the approaching winter of 1946, a year steeped to the depths in postwar austerity, the revelations, however inaccurate, of so many jewels made a profoundly painful impact on an austerely rationed people. King George ignored the incident.

The following year the Windsors returned yet again to Britain to celebrate their tenth wedding anniversary. It was spent quietly at Sunningdale. No members of the Royal Family were present. Later that year Princess Elizabeth was married to Prince Philip of Greece. The Windsors were not invited.

It was finally dawning on the Duke and the Duchess that their cause in England was close to hopeless, that they were viewed without favor by the Royal Family, and aroused no interest in the statesmen of either party. Still the Windsors remained members of royalty, and had to be treated as such. Whenever the Windsors stayed, for example, at the Palm Beach home of their friends, the Robert R. Youngs, all the other guests would be briefed in advance as to the correct form of behavior and address (this according to Cleveland Amory, the writer). The guests must be assembled before the Duke and Duchess arrive. They must curtsy to the Duke and call him "Sir." They must not curtsy to the Duchess, and they address her as "Your Grace." The Duke and Duchess would then be placed at the head of the table which is the traditional position for the King and Queen at all times, even when they are guests.

The anomalous nature of the Duke's position finally drove him to a decision he would never have dreamed of making before. He decided to break the silence that traditionally binds all members of the Royal Family and publish his memoirs. He hired a secretary and a ghost writer and got to work.

His material was the phenomenal memory he could apply to his past life as prince and king, a past that had appeared to become very dear to him. In fact some of his friends were glad he was writing the book simply because they thought it might release him from an increasing devotion to his youth. They had noticed that he seemed to turn constantly in his mind to the early carefree days when he was Prince of Wales and first in love. Flowers, his favorite hobby for many years, became part of this attachment to the past. He would look at flowers and see them not as they were but only as he remembered them growing once upon a time at Fort Belvedere.

His preoccupation with the past was illustrated a few years ago to a cosmopolitan American woman, a slight acquaintance of the Windsors, whose hobby it was to collect pencils. In 1936 she had been in London and had bought a gross of pencils, adorned by portraits of King Edward VIII whose forthcoming Coronation was just beginning to plaster itself on the shoddier brands of British and Japanese trinketry. In 1948 she was carrying the last stub of the last pencil in her handbag when, quite unexpectedly, she found herself in the same room as the Duke and Duchess, in New York.

"Sir," said the woman, "believe me this is a complete coincidence, but I have a pencil marking your Coronation."

The Duke took the pencil and stared at it in fascination. "It's me," he said in ungrammatical amazement. "Wallis, it's me." He continued to stare at it for a long time. Then an expression of melancholy spread over his face. "But look," he said sadly, "I'm almost whittled away."

"To be as happily married as I am, I call that a good life," he told a reporter in 1950. "I don't miss being King, but I do miss my country and not being able to work for it."

In 1950, one of the secondary characters out of the earlier part of the Windsor story re-emerged into the picture by dying. He was the Reverend Robert Anderson Jardine, the man who had married them. In the years since the ceremony Jardine had been heavily shadowed by a misfortune which he had not foreseen. Cheering crowds had greeted him at Darlington Station after he returned from performing the ceremony, and after years of poverty a glorious future seemed to be opening for him as "the man who married the Windsors." The bishops and Jardine's fellow-clergymen were furious, but he did not care.

He went to America to capitalize on his adventure, and signed up for a lecture tour. It was not a success. He did not make the fortune he hoped for. He wrote a book about the wedding. It failed. He settled down in Los Angeles, the place where preachers with a "gimmick" or a new angle have, traditionally, become rich. Jardine did not. He found that Episcopalian clergymen in America were little friendlier than they had been in England. Jardine became a bitter man. In 1950, he was offered a good appointment in South Africa and accepted. He stopped off in Bedfordshire, England, to visit relatives, and there, in May, he died. Jardine had been a mistake on the part of the Windsors, and it must have seemed to them like a long time ago.

The Duchess had now become the Duke's entire world. Whenever they were together his hand would seek hers. The Royal Family's persistent refusal to grant her the rank of Royal Highness had become almost an obsession to her husband, and he brought the matter up at every opportunity. He insisted that his servants accord to the Duchess the privilege that the Royal Family denied her, and ordered them to refer to her as "Her Royal Highness."

The Duchess, too, was hurt by the Royal Family's attitude, and more than once displayed her resentment in conversation. She clearly felt the strain of all the pressures that had been put on her marriage, pressures that were directed against her rather than against the Duke. But she continued to behave with ostentatious correctness, traveling on a British passport, and more than once she took American acquaintances by surprise with her polite references to "your country."

Her husband with his memories, his sensitivity about rank, his inexperience in the ways of the world, was not an easy man to live with. A typical example of the Duchess's hard work occurred in 1953 when a reporter asked the Duke what he thought of Princess Margaret's rumored romance with Peter Townsend.

The Duke expanded agreeably. "If Margaret wants . . ." he began. The Duchess swept in. "*Rien,*" she said quickly, "*rien*" being French for "nothing." "*Rien,*" the Duke said to the reporter and ambled away without concern.

The Duke would not have cared if his remark made big news, but the Duchess could imagine the consequences. The obstinacy which had helped to lose him his throne was as strong as ever. When a friend offered them tickets to a fashionable Broadway première, the Duchess, thinking of the sight-seers and autograph hunters, said, "It will be all right if we can get in by the back door."

"No, Wallis," the Duke said reprovingly. "If we cannot go in by the front entrance, we will not go in at all."

It was hard not to admire her capacity to rise above her problems and her personal difficulties. Her sense of humor, and her flair for taut, monosyllabic phrases was unimpaired.

Example: "I don't make plans any more. I see the plans the newspapers make for me, and I choose the one I like best."

"Much as I hate youth (this after she was almost knocked sprawling by a deb party at the Stork Club), I must say I admire it."

"I love shopping for something simple at Christian Dior's. It's like looking for a needle in a haystack."

But both the Windsors began to welcome outside diversion. It arrived first in the person of a young man of charm named Russell Nype, who for his part in the Broadway production of "Call Me Madam" assumed a crew cut and horn-rimmed spectacles and became a new kind of matinee idol. Later the diversion was supplied by the rollicking iconoclast, Jimmy Donahue. Donahue was always funny, with a gift for sustained nonsense. He was too rich to have to work, too jolly to want it. In his own way he was good for the Windsors. He introduced into their lives something that, with very good reason, had been noticeably absent—laughter. Donahue made them—and still makes them—laugh.

After several years of endeavor, the Duke's Memoirs came out, and the Duke buried himself on the Riviera "for a long rest." The book proved to be absorbing, sensitive and sometimes beautiful and moving. It made close to a million dollars.

Once it was finished, a mental barrier was removed from the Windsors' lives. There were reports that the Royal Family did not care for the book, but the Windsors decided to go ahead and do more as they wished instead of always behaving in a way to win the favor of Buckingham Palace. This new approach became more determined after the death of King George VI, when the seventy-five-thousand-dollars-a-year annuity which had been paid the Duke came to an end.

The Duchess announced her intention of writing her own memoirs, and the Duke pondered on other subjects to write about.

By now the Windsors had settled into a way of living that showed every sign of permanency. Both complain a good deal about money, but large amounts of it are spent in order to maintain the Duke's position. The spending sometimes seems more spectacular than it would be if the Duke had responsibilities more in accordance with his rank as a member of the British Royal Family. But being without homes or estates, the money must go for clothes and rented houses. Not having children to leave their fortunes to, the Windsors spend their money on themselves, the Duchess determined always that the Duke's comfort and enjoyment of life be put above all other considerations. In an analysis of the Windsors' spending practices published in a British newspaper in 1953 it was estimated that they spend one hundred and twenty thousand dollars a year on pleasure alone. On their French country house which they have taken on lease they have spent an estimated one hundred thousand dollars on redecorations. Thousands of dollars are spent on flowers. The Duchess has been known to spend close to thirty thousand a year on clothes, and much of her day passes under the attentions of her hairdresser, manicurist, masseuse, beautician. Her appearance is almost a full-time job, not only for her but for her maids, although most people agree that the result at the end of all these ministrations justifies the labor involved.

The Duchess of Windsor literally dazzles. She dazzles with jewels. She dazzles with sartorial and physical perfection. Not a hair is out of place, not a blemish on the cultured mask of beauty. She is also considered by some the world's greatest hostess. Even Elsa Maxwell declares that the Duchess can decorate a house more tastefully than the late, renowned Elsie de Wolfe. Many of those who disagree do so only because they are made uneasy by the very perfection of it all, a perfection which makes it hard for some guests to relax.

Her candlelight dinner is always superb, and begins invariably with soup, followed by a fish course, meat, dessert and a savory, with the soup, sherry; with the fish, white wine; with the meat, a red Bordeaux ("a good conversational wine," says the Duchess) and with the dessert, champagne.

The party will be organized into two tables, the Duke, often wearing the kilt, at the head of one, the Duchess at the head of the other. Music will be supplied by a French woman pianist whose playing pleases the Duchess. The decoration of the dining room, as of the rest of the house, is tasteful without being too original, the most notable items being two large gold flasks adorned with the Royal coat of arms, presented to the Duke by the City of London when he was Prince of Wales.

Conversation, taking its cue from the Duchess, is quick and jumbled in the New York manner, without the rounded monologues enjoyed so much by English dinner conversationalists. Officially politics are barred "because my husband as a member of the Royal Family, must eschew politics," but nobody takes much notice of that, and the conversation often rattles off on to politics, usually American politics.

After dinner the Duke keeps the English habit, which Frenchmen so deplore, of the men staying behind at the dinner table. When the party forms again, the Duchess keeps it moving, making sure nobody is bored.

Sometimes the guests sing, the Duke himself obliging from time to time with a song in his pleasant baritone voice.

In spite of the excellence of her food and wine, neither the Duchess nor the Duke eat or drink much, and they keep a careful eye on their weight. A whisky and water at six P.M. is their first drink of the day and almost their last. Most people who visit the Windsors comment on the good spirits of the Duke. Inevitably for a man who has been through so much, he is capable of deep depressions, but the Duchess is always able to restore his spirits with the peculiar champagne-like atmosphere she generates.

There is no doubt that the Duke is a changed man, a more cautious man. As Prince of Wales and as King, he was quite fearless. His habit of falling off horses was notorious. He liked flying, and altogether his pranks endangered the blood pressure of countless numbers of his loyal admirers throughout the Empire. The old insouciant attitude to life has gone. He has repeated checkups with his doctors. He will never climb inside an airplane.

The Coronation of Queen Elizabeth II, far from depressing him with the thoughts of what his own might have been, gave him a new zest for life. He wrote a series of articles on his own thoughts about the Coronation, picking up approximately one hundred thousand dollars for the job. He was in France when the Coronation took place, and French friends prepared to move gently and leave him alone with his reflections.

They misinterpreted his feelings. The Duke was fascinated and delighted with the celebrations surrounding his niece's crowning. He accepted an offer to be guest of honor at a spectacular Coronation party to be given in Paris by Mrs. Margaret Biddle, and even made an agreement with the United Press giving them the sole right to photograph him watching the ceremony on television. During the course of the Coronation he sat in front of the TV camera explaining the ceremony to the Duchess and to other guests, delighted when he spotted his friends on the screen, occasionally joining in the singing of the hymns.

July, 1953, found the Duchess of Windsor at the Carlton Hotel in Cannes, completing arrangements for a Mediterranean cruise. The Duke was in Biarritz alone playing golf. Shades of his grandfather here—Edward VII had loved Biarritz, and the Duke, as he revealed in his Coronation articles, often felt that his own reign would have acquired something of the personality of Edward VII's had it run its course. The Duke's golf form was great and he was in high spirits.

He joined his wife a few days before the cruise was about to begin.

The Duchess, who never forgets such things, reminded him that Herman Rogers and his pretty wife, the former Mrs. Lucy Fury Wann, were about to celebrate their fourth wedding anniversary. Rocklike, reliable Herman Rogers had watched the Duchess of Windsor story from its early days, and he almost alone of the old friends continued to see her from time to time. He still lived in the mountains behind Cannes. The Villa Lou Viei still belongs to him, but he has moved to a smaller and more modern house a mile or so away.

The Windsors invited the Rogers to an anniversary dinner, and the two couples had a delightful evening at the Carlton. The Duke was at his most ebullient, gay and full of amusing anecdotes. The Duchess, slender as a rail from a close-to-starvation diet, was more inclined to be sentimental. She pointed out to the guests how good a friend Rogers had been to her for so many years. "Not once but many times," she said seriously, " 'home' to me has been where the Rogers were."

She talked with Rogers about old times, and they both managed to dig up from the recesses of their minds a few phrases of Chinese. Rogers permitted himself to say that he preferred her when she was less thin. The Duchess let that one pass and thanked him for doing so much for her.

Next morning the boat, a small, rented yacht, the *Hidalgo*, prepared to put to sea, first stop Monte Carlo. Friends arrived in the morning. The Windsors came on board at midday, and the *Hidalgo* weighed anchor. Eighteen years had passed since that other Mediterranean cruise of King Edward VIII, Mrs. Simpson, and their celebrated "court" in the yacht *Nahlin*, a cruise that carried in its wake so many incredible adventures.

On the *Hidalgo's* deck the passengers waved good-by to friends—the Duchess wearing sunglasses, her hair parted, as always, in the middle; the Duke in yellow trousers, and a maroon and yellow shirt, smoking a pipe, looking tanned and contented. Donahue was saying something funny to one of the passengers, Charles Blackwell, an American millionaire, who was laughing heartily. From their mountain home the Rogers watched them go.

Has it all been worth while? Would the Duke not rather be on the throne?

The trouble with royalty, even fallen royalty, is that it is too remote for such questions to be asked. One of the few men who has been in a position to take the Duke to task, a European friend of the Royal Family's, did so in these words:

"Forgive my frankness, Sir, but I am a monarchist, and I feel very strongly about your Abdication. What I cannot forgive is the fact that, by abdicating, you jeopardized the institution of monarchy."

"But I could not help it," the Duke replied simply. "Without her life would not have been worth living." He paused for a moment then added sincerely, "And I can say this, that only since I have been married to her have I known what real happiness is."

So much for the Duke. But how about the Duchess? Is she happy or does she sigh for the day when the British Crown was within her grasp? One can do nothing but guess, but an interesting change appeared to come over her in the course of the year 1953, the year that opened so riotously with the Duchess of Windsor Ball. She seemed to settle down. The voyage of the *Hidalgo*, in spite of the discomfort of the boat, was made in an atmosphere of serenity. In December, 1953, after Queen Elizabeth II and the Duke of Edinburgh had left on their trip round the world, she returned to England with her husband, and made a charming impression on the crowds who gathered everywhere to give her a cheer. They stayed at Claridge's, went shopping, and called on old friends like Helen Fitzgerald who had been unswervingly loyal ever since the days of the *Nahlin*. There was not a single discordant note. When they were able to escape from their social duties, they wandered alone over the scenes of their courtship. It may well be that the Windsors, after all the storms and troubles, are at last finding peace.

So the old reign has given place to the new: winters in America, summers in France. Much has happened to the Duchess since the days when only an old and wily statesman stood between her and the throne. The clamor of that conflict has still not been silenced, even though life itself seems to have died in many of the places where it touched. Fort Belvedere stands empty, the gardens overgrown; No. 16 Cumberland Terrace was blitzed in World War II and is now a Government office; No. 7 Grosvenor Square, the mansion of Emerald Cunard where Wallis met the Prince of Wales so often is unoccupied; the Villa Lou Viei where she found refuge, uninhabited and up for sale.

Still the Duchess of Windsor remains in the center of world attention. Every move she makes is reported in detail. Denied royal recognition, royal acceptance and royal responsibility, she enjoys only royal pleasures, and lives to please her husband and herself. The very rigidity of Buckingham Palace opposition seems to drive her more and more into the gossip-ridden, vendetta-ridden jungle of international café society where enemies prowl waiting to wing her with wounding epigrams, but where at least she can wing right back at them, and also find friends and company.

All this would matter less if the rest of the world did not worry so much about it. But the world does worry. The Abdication remains on its conscience, a problem that is made worse because the Duchess of Windsor story, in spite of the tremendous gesture of the Abdication, does not come out as a pretty story; and today neither Queen Elizabeth's aloofness from her once-favorite uncle and his wife, nor the Duchess's night-club way of life commend themselves to the favor of a world which wants above all a happy quiet ending in some form or other.

It is this lack of any quality of grace or mercy which spoils the story and makes it something less than romance and less than tragedy. Not only the Windsors themselves are exposed by the crisis they created. Most of the leading characters involved in the Abdication look smaller and meaner in the eyes of history than they would have done had there been no Abdication. It is certainly true that nobody, then or since, has been elevated by it. It has made Christians act without Christianity, great men like mediocrities, wise men without wisdom, kind men without charity. Friends have sometimes appeared to act like traitors. Gentlemen have behaved like scoundrels, ladies like fishwives. How abysmally London society emerged from it all. Dukes surrounded Mrs. Simpson once, and earls and barons, all waiting eagerly on a smile or a friendly word from her. As hard as those actors fought then for her favor, so later did they stampede to get out of the line of fire. As the Abdication artillery crashed, the doors of town houses and country mansions banged shut behind beating hearts and heaving breasts while Mrs. Simpson suffered the crisis out deserted in a Cannes villa. "Mrs. Simpson? Oh, her we hardly knew . . ." With her at the end were three friends, one Englishman, two Americans, the loyal remains of a once fabulous court.

Yet she might have been Queen of England today. It has been seen earlier in the story how close she and the King came to winning the battle. Now she suffers the fate of an active woman condemned to a life of inaction, an intelligent woman with nothing except trivia on which to apply her wit, a kindhearted woman who has turned herself to steel in order to survive.

What kind of a Queen would she have made? Compassion, intelligence, experience, exuberance are formidable qualities for any woman, and the Duchess has them all. Judgment, wisdom: here the qualifications are not so strong, but a Queen does not have to act alone. She does not have to make all the decisions as the Duchess of Windsor has done since her marriage. There is no doubt that as Queen she would have had enemies everywhere. The Church of England would have remained hostile. The fact of two husbands still living would have continued to goad her existence even on the throne. But a Queen has friends as well, and a study of what has happened to the men who took sides during the Abdication touches the Duchess of Windsor story with a curious irony.

There is a verse to the British National Anthem that damns the Queen's enemies with the lines:

> *Frustrate their knavish tricks,*
> *Confound their politics,*
> *God Save the Queen.*

Had the Duchess been Queen, these words would have been apt indeed. Even for the Duchess of Windsor, they have remarkable point and application.

Stanley Baldwin, Mrs. Simpson's nemesis, died in misery, his last days and nights surpassing one another in apprehension and wretchedness. The hero of the Abdication, the imperturbable personification of John Bull, the man who received the greatest ovation of all at the Coronation of King George VI in 1937, was broken and ruined three years later. "Admiration," wrote G. M. Young, his authorized biographer, "turned to the bitterest hatred. . . . Baldwin knew that far and wide throughout his own England men and women under the rain of death were cursing him as the politician who . . . had lied to the people and left them defenceless against their enemies." For a while in World War II he was frightened even to come to London because "they hate me so," and throughout the war he cowered as silently as a mouse in his West Country home. Once when he emerged to unveil a memorial to Thomas Hardy in Dorchester "he seemed to have death in his face—leaning on a stick, trembling." He died in his sleep in December, 1947.

The Archbishop of Canterbury, Dr. Cosmo Lang, was surely among the most unpopular men ever to hold the highest office in the Church of England.

He suffered his greatest wave of unpopularity as a result of the Abdication, and this is curious because the Abdication was itself popular, yet the public reviled him for the part he played in it and for the venomous broadcast he made after it. He died in 1942 and time has not mellowed his memory. He is remembered, despite his erudition and culture, as a strangely un-Christian kind of man. He was at one time the subject of a popular London street ballad the words of which ran:

> *My Lord Archbishop what a scold you are!*
> *And when your man is down how bold you are!*
> *Of Christian charity how scant you are!*
> *And auld Lang swine, how full of cant you are!*

Geoffrey Dawson, autocratic editor of the *Times* through the 'thirties, molder of public opinion in favor of Munich and the Abdication, was ignominiously sacked in 1941. He knew some time before that dismissal was coming, and tried everything he could think of to hold on to his job, even offering at one time to split his salary with his appointed successor, Barrington Ward, on condition that he, Dawson, could keep the title. But the blow fell all the same, and Dawson was actually told, while he was washing his hands in the *Times* editorial toilet, that his editorship was not to be extended. He died in 1944, a complex figure of this century, and, like his friends Baldwin and Lang, not popular, not well remembered.

Major Alexander Hardinge, King Edward VIII's private secretary, who went over to Baldwin's side, is the only member of the team still living. He continued as Private Secretary to King George VI until 1943, but during all that time Sir Alan Lascelles, seven years Hardinge's senior, continued as Assistant Private Secretary, a post he had held under George since 1935. In 1943, Hardinge retired, although he was not yet fifty, and Lascelles took his place. Today, Hardinge, who has succeeded to his father's title of Baron Hardinge of Penshurst, still lives in retirement, and must be about the only ex-Private Secretary in many years to hold no directorships. Usually Private Secretaries are given directorships as soon as they retire. Lascelles, when he retired, was made a director of the Midland Bank and the Midland Executor and Trustee Company. Not long ago Hardinge's wife wrote a book in the course of which she appealed to the Duke of Windsor to admit that Hardinge had acted correctly during the Abdication. The Duke did not reply.

So much for Mrs. Simpson's enemies. Now for her Abdication friends, Churchill, Beaverbrook, Monckton, Allen, Brownlow, men who for different reasons, moved by varying emotions and ideals, served and fought for King Edward VIII during the crisis. The comparison is striking.

First and above all, of course, is Sir Winston Churchill, who rose from the apparent ruin he had brought down on himself for his advocacy of the King's cause, to achieve a glory that sets him among the great heroes of British history. Beaverbrook, the inimitable, twice a Minister of the Crown, received praise second only to that of Churchill himself in 1940, when as Minister of Aircraft Production, and against all odds, he turned out the fighter planes which won the Battle of Britain. Today he stands unique, the most gigantic and the most colorful of the world's newspaper barons.

Faithful Walter Monckton—one senses the Duke of Windsor in his memoirs softening every time the name is mentioned—was King's Counsel in the true and literal rather than the conventional meaning of the phrase.

All the time he was advising, helping, obeying the King, he must have been aware that he was risking his whole career. But Churchill called on him during the war and made him resident Minister in Egypt during some of the most complicated days of the campaign in the Middle East. He was given a knighthood. Today Monckton is Minister of Labour, one of the most able and popular members of the Conservative Government. There is only one thing likely to prevent him from rising even higher —divorce. He has been divorced by his wife, and he has married again. And the new Lady Monckton, a woman of understanding and charm, with a genuine flair for politics, was herself divorced by her former husband.

George Allen never wavered in his devotion to the interests of the Duke and Duchess of Windsor, and through all the troubled years the royal refugees have been together he has remained their solicitor. His integrity has been so clear-cut that this has never slowed the advance of his career, and in 1952 Queen Elizabeth conferred on him the K.C.V.O., a royal, not a political, order, and one of the highest in the land. Today Sir George Allen is one of Britain's most eminent and wealthy solicitors.

Lord Brownlow remained Lord Lieutenant of Lincolnshire until 1950 in spite of criticisms of his steadfast friendship for the Duke of Windsor. During the war he was Private Parliamentary Secretary in Beaverbrook's Ministry of Aircraft Production.

So Mrs. Simpson, although she herself went down to defeat, has lived to see her enemies perish and her friends exalted. This is a fact, an item of academic interest without moral or poetic justice, because today the Duchess of Windsor is as remote from the misfortunes of the one as she is from the fortunes of the other. The irony of it is overwhelmed by the last and strangest irony of all.

For the existence the Duchess has now created to please her husband is nothing more than an imitation of the existence he once disliked so much. Edward VIII used to be impatient of courts, and the restrictions of court etiquette. He was contemptuous of courtiers, and he escaped from the formalities whenever he could—usually in the direction of Mrs. Simpson. But he has escaped from one court only to find himself in another. It is now playboys and millionaires who act as courtiers.

There is no exaggeration in the description of the Windsors' present circle as a court. A court it is. The court procedure is meticulously observed. All the old trimmings which the Duke used to despise so much are there—the sycophants, the protocol, the rule of precedence by which a king, and presumably also an ex-king, enjoys the right to go first and sit at the head of the table even when he is a guest. These are the mere tatters of royalty, but the Windsors cling to them tenaciously. The throne room is mobile—here a restaurant, there a night club, now a rented house in Paris, next a hotel suite in New York—but the rules are rigid.

So the story ends in a mirage. The throne, the crown, the adulation of the people, the proud palaces, the carriages, the confidences of statesmen, all of which might have been the Duchess's, have faded away. All that remains is the café-society court—that and a persistent feeling, defying all slander and beyond all reason, that had Mrs. Simpson managed to become Queen, she would have been a good Queen.

Bibliography

"A King's Story," *H.R.H. the Duke of Windsor.*
History of the Times, Volume IV, Part 2.
"Stanley Baldwin," *G. M. Young.*
"Her Name Was Wallis Warfield," *Laura Lou Brookman.*
B.B.C. Broadcast, *Lord Beaverbrook.*
"The Last Resorts," *Cleveland Amory.*
Profile of Charles Bedaux and other New Yorker pieces, *Janet Flanner.*
"Time" Magazine on the Abdication.
"Neville Chamberlain," *Keith Fieling.*
"Into the Wind," *Lord Reith.*
Articles in Sunday Dispatch, Daily Mail, Sunday Pictorial, *Lord Temple-wood, Viscount Norwich, Thelma Lady Furness.*
"The Little Princesses," *Marion Crawford.*
"Manifest Destiny," *Brian Connell.*
"The German General Staff," *Walter Goerlitz.*
"Zwischen London und Moskau," *Joachim von Ribbentrop.*
"Cosmo Gordon Lang," *J. G. Lockhart.*
"His Was the Kingdom," *Frank Owen & R. J. Thompson.*
"This Man Ribbentrop," *Paul Schwarz.*